My Christian Quest

FROM JEHOVAH'S WITNESS TO SON OF GOD

by
Ronald E. Frye

Published by
Christian Respondent, Inc.
42851 260th Lane
Aitkin, MN 56431

Bible translations used and their abbreviations:

American Standard Version (*ASV*)
New American Bible (*NAB*)
New International Version (*NIV*)
New Jerusalem Bible (*NJB*)
Revised Standard Version (*RSV*)
New Revised Standard Version (*NRSV*)
New World Translation (*NWT*)
Revised English Bible (*REB*)
Phillips Modern English (*PME*)
Today's English Version (*TEV*)
New English Bible (*NEB*)
New Living Bible (*NLB*)

CONTENTS

Author's Forward

Author's Forward

The journey of the spiritual life can never be easy. All Christians are faced with choices. The cumulative effect of those choices determines what he or she becomes as a person and as a servant of the Lord Jesus Christ. Making right choices requires personal character and a heartfelt desire and willingness to follow the path of truth and righteousness wherever it leads; whatever the cost. This is what I would define as the Christian quest.

My own Christian quest was hindered and made difficult by two primary factors: my flawed character and flawed religious mentoring. To work through and overcome these obstacles has required the painful discipline of self-discovery and the irresistible attraction of the godly life in Christ. Both of which could only have been made possible by the corrective guidance of Scripture and the transforming power of God's Holy Spirit. It has been said that the Christian faith is grace and its doctrine is gratitude. While oversimplified, it contains an essential truth.

Surrendering to God's benevolent grace is always costly. Cherished beliefs, religious loyalties, family ties, friends, social structure and the tenacious pull of self-interest tests our determination to remain on that "narrow path" of which Jesus speaks. Those who come to religious faith do so with a certain mindset that has been influenced and formed by many things: genetic makeup, family background, religious training, culture, education and their experiences. It is only when one has grown sufficiently in a spiritual way that he or she can begin to objectively reevaluate themselves and their belief system to determine if changes are needed to more fully obey the Master's commands.

On the eve of his death Jesus said: "Now this is eternal life: that they may know you, the only true God, and Jesus Christ, whom you have sent." (John 17: 3) To please God we must "bend the knee" in servitude to Jesus Christ as Lord. (Phil 2: 10,11) No human relationship or love can be allowed to equal our devotion to him. (Matt.10: 37-39) To take up one's cross and follow him requires a complete faith and confidence that he will shepherd us faithfully through this life and prepare us for the life to come.

Hopefully, telling my story will give encouragement to others who find themselves struggling with issues of faith and facing difficult choices. It is my hope that such ones will find the moral courage to make the right choices; those that lead to a more enlightened and complete surrender to the one who gave his life for them.

— Ronald E. Frye, April 2, 2006

iv

Those who have been captured by the love of God
find themselves between two shores.
They can never go back to where they once were,
but they are not yet where they will be.

Chapter 1

My
Mother's
Memorial

THE large meeting room was filling with people warmly greeting one another and filling the air with the pleasant sound of their voices. Trying not to appear obvious, I glanced about in search of a recognizable face. I knew my three grandchildren were here, and I was hoping I might be able to recognize them. It would not be easy. They were mere children when I last saw them and now, fifteen years later, they would be young adults. A young man who appeared to be in his late teens caught my eye. Could that be Matthew, I wondered? I couldn't be sure. Matthew, my youngest grandson, was only three when I last saw him. Our eyes met for a brief moment, and I caught a hint of curiosity in his gaze. Separated by some distance I spoke a word of greeting, and he responded but with no show of friendliness. Neither of us moved to close the space between us, and after a few more seconds I looked away, still uncertain that it was Matthew.

A moment later my only child, my daughter Jamie, approached and directed me toward the front of the room where a row of chairs had been reserved for our family. As I moved forward, an attractive young woman with a small child in tow came toward me, smiling warmly. This had to be Francesca, my only granddaughter, and the oldest of the grandchildren. She was thirteen the last time I saw her, passing through that magical transormation from child to young lady. Now she was an attractive young woman, wife and mother. I always had a special affection for her.

She extended her arms, inviting an embrace. I held her tightly for a long moment, unable to speak and resisting the tears my emotions wanted so desperately to release. In that precious moment the many years of separation melted away to a reaffirmation of familial love and affection. I would relive that moment many times in the weeks and months that followed. As we separated, she said, "I remember you as being much taller." And I said, "I remember you being much shorter," We laughed. She introduced me to her three-year-old daughter, Mesha, who was blonde and blue-eyed. I knelt down to look into that lovely little face and heard her mother ask, "Can you give Papa a kiss?" She shyly hung back and looked away, not prepared to kiss this strange old man. Then her mother asked, "Can you blow Papa a kiss?" This she was able to do. I stood up, and the two of them moved away. I would not see them again that evening or in the season of years that would follow.

It was now time for us to assemble together for the evening's service. I took my seat at the left end of the row of chairs reserved for our family: Jamie, sat to my right, followed by her husband, Frank, then Francesca, her husband and daughter; the two grandsons, Andrew and Matthew; and finally my mother's sister, Lucretia. My aunt Lucretia, was the youngest of my mother's five sisters and now with mother's death she was the lone survivor. She never had children and had been a widow for many years. She and my mother had moved with Frank and Jamie to Tucson, Arizona several years earlier and shared an apartment together. They had been very close – almost inseparable, most of their lives. You seldom saw one without the other. In my youth she had been like a second mother to me. I knew that of all the people there, her loss was the greatest. I felt a special sadness for her. I wanted to hold her and tell her I understood how difficult mom's death was for her, but she had informed me through Jamie that I was not to approach her under any circumstances. I tried to catch her eye a few times in an effort to at least smile her way but she would have none of it—pretending not to see me. Her steely resolve seemed a strange companion to her deep sorrow. Her hardness towards me deepened the sadness I felt for her.

A pleasant looking middle-aged man mounted the low stage, and the assembly grew quiet. Jamie told me that he was an elder in the congregation and the father of Francesca's husband, Thomas. He would lead the memorial service for my mother who had died several days earlier on Friday, January 19, 1996. Since she had been cremated, there was no viewing of her body. Earlier, I had passed a table that displayed a picture of her taken many years earlier. I was reminded of how attractive she once was. Born February 26, 1906, she had lived to within one month of her ninetieth birthday. Like the other members of the family who were present, I hadn't seen her for the last fifteen years of her life. Her mother had died when she was a little girl, and when I was small she told me of what a terrible loss that was for her and her sisters and brother. Their father was unable to care for them after his wife's death, and the children were parceled out among relatives. Their lives would never be the same. As a child I was terrified by the thought that my mother might die. What would I ever do without my mother? As matters turned out, both my father and my mother lived a long time. Dad died back in 1980 just a short time before his eightieth birthday. I have always been grateful that our little family of three survived premature deaths.

As I listened to the speaker, the whole occasion seemed surreal to me. Several days prior to this evening my daughter had phoned to inform her mother and me that mother was in a hospice in Tucson and near death. She said that if I wanted to speak to her before it was too late, I should do so soon because she was drifting in and out of consciousness. Because it had been years since I had spoken to her, I suggested that they tell her I would call so she could have time to prepare herself for that. But before I made that call our daughter phoned again to say I had best speak to her immediately before it was too late. I heard Jamie say in a loud voice: "It's daddy." This was followed by a pause and then she said, "It's Ronald." She told me she would hold the phone to my mother's ear. I said, "Hello Mom." She made a sound that was unintelligible followed by silence. I remained silent for a moment and then all I could think to say was, "Go to sleep Mom, I will see you in the resurrection." Whether she heard or comprehended what I said, I do not know. It was an awkward and very sad ending. Jamie broke the silence, and I told her what I had said to mom. She thought it was good to say what I did because it gave her permission to let go. After a moment she hung up, promising to let us know when mother died.

The next day my son-in-law, Frank, phoned to say that mom had died. He explained that they would be making arrangements for her memorial service. The matter of my coming to that service was discussed. He said he realized that I had a right to come if I so decided. How strange, I thought, for a son to be told he had the *right* to attend his mother's memorial service. Yet, under the circumstances, it was not strange at all. I told him I would give it some thought and get back to him. I discussed the matter with my wife, Mavis, who, knowing what I would be subjected to, argued against it. She knew I would be exposing myself to considerable humiliation and, in the end, what good would it do? After all, mom was dead and would not be aware of my presence. I knew she was right, of course, yet something in me demanded that I be there. After all, she was my mother, and I loved her very much. I wanted to honor that love even if other members of the family did not want me there. I phoned my son-in-law and informed him that I had decided to come. He said that someone would meet me at the airport and help me find a motel, as I would not be welcome in their home. He also informed me that the family had a meeting and it was "unanimously decided that there should be no socializing with me either before or after the service."

I had arrived in Tucson about noon on the day my mother's memorial was to be held. At the gate I looked around to see if my daughter or son-in-law were there to meet me. Instead, I saw two men standing apart from the rest, and I recognized one of them as being my oldest grandson, Andrew. There was just enough of the boy of eleven remaining in the face of the 26-year-old man for me to recognize him. I must have been something of a shock to him. I had been in my mid-fifties when he last saw me. I was now a grey-haired man of seventy. I don't recall if we shook hands. I learned that the other man was Francesca's husband, Thomas, whom we had never met. When he and our granddaughter were married in Minnesota about ten years earlier, we were informed of the coming marriage and told that it would be best if we did not attend. We didn't. We never received a wedding picture.

Andrew was polite but cooly reserved. He asked how grammy was. I told him she was well. Thomas offered to carry my luggage, and we made our way to his car. They drove me to a motel and waited until I registered and paid for one night's lodging. Andrew said that his mother and dad would stop by to see me later that afternoon. A couple of hours later I got a call from the desk telling me that they were coming up to my room. I braced myself for our meeting. I hadn't seen Frank in 15 years and had only seen Jamie on two brief occasions in that same space of time. I decided that I would not initiate any show of affection. The reason for this was that about ten years earlier we had had a chance meeting, and I had impulsively hugged her. Later she wrote to say that my doing so had made her feel "unclean." I decided I wouldn't make that mistake again. When they knocked, I opened the door and the first thing Jamie said was, "Daddy, you're looking old." Then she gave me a hug. I felt I had been given permission to hug her back, which I did.

After a few minutes of small talk, they explained what the evening would be like. Thomas would pick me up and bring me to the Kingdom Hall and after the service they would bring me back to the motel. Jamie had brought along a basket of fruit and other treats for me. She also gave me a small cardboard box which contained a few of my mother's momentos: photographs, a pair of baby shoes and several other trinkets. She said I was welcome to anything I wanted from the box. This little box would be the only tangible glimpse I would have into my mother's things. I would not see where she had lived for the last few years of her life, look at her things or touch her clothing to experience something of the presence of her person. I had to be content with the contents of that little cardboard box. Their visit lasted about a half hour, and they left. It was dark when Thomas and I arrived at the Kingdom Hall. Frank had explained earlier that the building was shared by three different congregations of Jehovah's Witnesses—two Spanish-speaking, and one English-speaking. They had a rotating schedule which allowed each congregation specific times to use the building. Frank said that one of the Spanish-speaking congregations had a meeting scheduled that evening so things would have to move along at a goodly pace. I did not look at my watch, but I would judge that from the time I arrived at the Kingdom Hall until I left was less than an hour. In that space of that time I spent only a few minutes with Jamie, Frank and Francesca in any meaningful interaction. Neither of my grandsons approached me.

The minister began his discourse by speaking about my mother's faithfulness and what a fine example she had set for other Jehovah's Witnesses. I reflected on that as he continued to talk. My mother had been a woman who had the courage of her convictions. I hadn't the slightest doubt that she was the sort who would have died for her faith. There was nothing artificial or pretentious about her. She was incapable of superficiality. She personified the saying, "What you see is what you get." As a boy I witnessed how she was transformed by her newly-found faith as one of Jehovah's Witness. Once she committed herself to what she believed to be the truth, she never looked back. The last fifty-five years of her life had been lived in dedication to what she believed with all her heart to be God's truth revealed through his early organization under the direction of the Watchtower Bible and Tract Society.

The speaker made a point of mentioning that "Nanny," as she had come to be called, had never missed "reporting some time every month," in all of the fifty-five years she lived as a Witness. The Witnesses are required to keep a record of the hours they spend going from door-to-door presenting their *Watchtower* and *Awake!* magazines, conducting home Bible studies or simply talking to non-Witnesses about their faith. Each person's activity is carefully compiled, recorded and kept on file under their name at the Kingdom Hall. Those who regularly report such monthly activity are spoken of as "regular publishers." Those who miss a month now and then are called "irregular publishers." Those who fail to report such activity for six consecutive months are called "inactive publishers," and that is also recorded and kept on file. So, for my mother to have *never* failed to report time each month during all those fifty-five years was viewed as a badge of honor. In fact during her final days in the hospice, Jamie said she had "witnessed" to a fellow patient and given her one of the Watchtower Society's recent books. That came as no surprise to me.

My mother was a compassionate woman, having a special affinity for those who appeared disadvantaged in one way or another. This fact was illustrated by the speaker in his recounting of an experience she had while living in Minnesota. During one of her days going from house-to-house she spotted a badly deformed young man scooting along the sidewalk on some sort of homemade contraption. Moved by what she saw, she tried to get his attention, but he scooted away too fast. On another day she saw him again, and this time she managed to get his attention and speak to him about Jehovah God and his promised kingdom. He led her to where he lived, and she spoke again of these things to his mother. As a result she was able to start a Bible study with them and eventually he was baptized into her faith. This sort of sympathetic compassion was typical of her. As the minister recounted this experience in his portrait of "Nanny," I relived it, as I had met that young man and his mother and had visited them with my mother in their home.

"She had hoped," the minister continued, "to live until Armageddon. But that was not to be." What was meant by this remark was that my mother expected that God's war of Armageddon would come within her lifetime and she would survive that war which would destroy all the earthly wicked (everyone except Jehovah's Witnesses), and she could continue living forever on earth without ever having to die. That expectation had been carefully taught by her religious leaders, who set forth a timetable that assured her of this possibility. That was why the minister said she had hoped to live until Armageddon. Regarding that expectation, he went on to say, "We will have to prove faithful so we can tell her what it [Armageddon] was like." In saying this, he revealed his own personal expectation and that of his fellow Witnesses. Like my mother, they too believed that the war of Armageddon would come within *their* lifetime. As I listened I thought of the several generations past in which I often heard the same expectation expressed. Indeed, there had been a time when I, too, entertained that hope. The Watchtower's many date-setting errors and failed expectations for the end of the world were of no consequence to these people. I understood their conditioned thinking as I had shared that thinking for many years. I felt a certain sadness for these devoted people.

The memorial service ended with a song and prayer. During that closing prayer, Jamie took my hand in hers. That gesture meant a great deal to me and told me there was love in her heart for her father. The Witness elder had done a good job in summing up the essence of my mother's life. I shook his hand and thanked him for that. As a few people came by to offer condolences to the family, I stood aside, assuming that I would not be included in that ritual. However, Jamie told me to stay by her and she introduced me to a number of those who spoke to her. "This is my father, Ronald Frye," she would say. Everyone was smiling and pleasant as they offered me their hand. I was pleasantly surprised at this display of common courtesy. By now, members of the Spanish-speaking congregation were filtering into the Kingdom Hall. It was time to leave. We made our way toward the exit. On the way we passed a table that displayed an opened guest book. Jamie asked if I had signed it? I said, no. She suggested I sign it, so I took the time to do that. We exited the Kingdom Hall without any of the grandchildren approaching to say goodbye. Jamie and Frank drove me back to my motel and we said our brief goodbyes. I gave each of them a hug and then they were gone.

Back in my room I reflected on the events of the day. Did this really happen or did I only dream that it happened? It was that strange. For an instant a door long closed and tightly bolted had been opened and I was treated with a measure of human dignity and kindness. Now that door was firmly closed and bolted again, perhaps never to be reopened. I felt somewhere between reality and unreality. I turned my attention to that little box of my mother's things that Jamie had left. Among the pictures my mother had saved was one of Francesca and Thomas' wedding. I looked at it a long time. Another picture was of Mavis, Jamie and myself taken many years ago when we were serving in full time ministry. On the back of that picture my mother had written, "Servants of Jehovah." I took those two pictures and the baby shoes, which I understood were mine. Early the next morning ,Thomas picked me up and drove me to the airport. Within a few hours I would be back in Minnesota.

I had been in Tucson less than twenty-four hours and had seen members of my family for only a fraction of that time. So much had happened in that compressed, emotionally-charged moment, I was having difficulty putting it in perspective. Years of separation and silence had ended, but only for a breath of time. Now it was back to reality. It had been important to me to control my emotions and maintain my composure. I did not want them to think that I was a broken man, nor did I want to appear hardened in any way. Above all else I wanted to honor my Lord and not bring reproach upon him by anything I might feel, say or do. Yet, I was able to convey my affection for them within the perimeters they allowed. I was not sorry for having exposed myself to their guarded attitude towards me. There were now new facial images to replace the out-dated ones filed away many years ago. There never has been a day like it before or since. It left me emotionally drained and profoundly sad. However, I knew it had been difficult for them as well, especially Jamie. There was pain on both sides. On one level I knew they loved me but on another level I repelled them. To have welcomed me into their home or taken a meal with me would have compromised their religious faith.

Why? What had I done to deserve this extreme degree of rejection? What outrage had I committed that was so villainous—so unforgivable, that no amount of time could ever assuage their rejection of me? The offense for which I was truly guilty was that I had walked away from being a Jehovah's Witness. In 1981, after more than thirty years as such, I wrote a brief note to my congregational elders, informing them that I no longer wanted to be identified with a religious organization that called me an apostate because I questioned some of its teachings. By this act (in their minds), I had turned my back on Jehovah God and his earthly organization—the one and only true Christian religion on earth—apart from which there is no salvation. For one to have been a Jehovah's Witness—to have been "in the truth,"and then to thrust it aside, was unforgivable. *That* was my crime.

In what follows I will explain the reasons for my becoming a devoted Jehovah's Witness in the first place and how, after many years of devoted ministry, a series of events led to my disenchantment with it. More importantly, I will share with the reader the spiritually fulfilling and fruitful life I have had since leaving the Watchtower movement.

Chapter 2

My
Formative
Years

My introduction to Jehovah's Witnesses took place more than 65 years ago, when I was a boy of 12 living on the East Side in St. Paul, Minnesota on Maria Avenue. Up to that moment my youth was only lightly seasoned by an awareness of God. My mother had taught me a simple prayer to say before going to sleep: "Now I lay me down to sleep; I pray the Lord my soul to keep. If I should die before I wake; I pray the Lord my soul to take." Sometimes she would sit on my bed and repeat the prayer with me. But as far as the daily flow of life was concerned, religion played no role in our family. My parents were focused on paying the rent and putting food on the table. They were earthy, honest, hardworking people who struggled along with millions of other Americans through those hard, lean years of the great depression. Both parents were employed at meat packing plants situated on opposite sides of the Mississippi River south of St. Paul. Even with two incomes it was a struggle to provide for the three of us. Their chosen escape from life's hard realities was often found in local taverns. And while their Saturday night drinking provided a brief respite of medicated pleasure, it did nothing to resolve the deep personal issues that undermined their relationship. In fact, it exacerbated those issues. At this tender age of life I knew nothing of the root causes of those conflicts, but witnessed and listened to the often violent outbursts they created. Usually, but not always, those violent episodes took place following a night of drinking. Many years later my mother told me that when she looked in on me late one night after one of their bitter outbursts, she found me asleep with my fingers in my ears.

There were happy moments in our lives and times when we functioned reasonably well as a family. We had vacations and nearly every year we would travel to Iowa where we had many relatives on both sides of the family. I was well provided for and given the times in which I grew up, I had more in a material way than most of my friends and school-mates. Moreover, I was never abused or mistreated in any way. While my dad could be violent towards my mother when he was intoxicated, he never ever struck me. What I didn't know early on was that he was not my biological father. Before she married my dad, my mother had an affair with another man, and I was a product of that affair. She married my dad before I was born, even though he knew the child she carried was not his own. I think this fact prevented him from taking more of a fatherly initiative in raising me. His own upbringing did not prepare him well for fatherhood. He never did those things that fathers do in a healthy, loving father-son relationship that nurtures young life and prepares a boy for adulthood. Unfortunately, I was told, I looked like my biological father, whom my dad had known, and I don't think this helped matters. I also learned later in life that my mother continued to have feelings for my biological parent and I believe dad knew it. Whatever feelings of resentment he may have had he never took them out on me. He had been abused by his father and he swore that he would never be that way should he have a child. But the abuse was not one-sided: my mother could also be verbally abusive and throw a punch or a pan which she sometimes did. I make mention of these negative factors in our family to help the reader understand why my early impressions of Jehovah's Witnesses were positive ones.

My mother's early childhood was such that she grew up with a personal aversion to churches. She often spoke in loving terms of her mother who had been a devout, Bible-reading, church-going person, but who was sometimes critical of things her minister would preach. She told her children that the minister was not telling people the truth from the Bible. My grandmother's evaluation of matters made a deep impression on my mother. I have no doubt that this predisposition against traditional prot-estant religion and preachers made her more receptive to the unorthodox message Jehovah's Witnesses would later bring her. Interestingly, at that time (1930s-1940s), the Witnesses categorically condemned *all* religion. The Witnesses told my mother that Christianity was not a religion at all—it was the Truth! Religion, on the other hand, was a product of the devil. This way of putting matters resonated with my mother. It was as if her suspicions were being validated.

It would sound strange to Jehovah's Witnesses today, but back then the word "religion" was a pejorative one. At a convention of Witnesses held at Royal Albert Hall in London, England in 1938, nearly a thousand

Witnesses walked through London's business district carrying placards that read: "RELIGION IS A SNARE AND A RACKET." It wasn't until 1951, that the Watch Tower Bible & Tract Society (WBTS) officially changed its view and acknowledged that Christianity was, in fact, a form of religion. This new view of matters was presented in the book, *What Has Religion Done For Mankind?* (1951) where it was argued that religion simply identifies "a form of worship," and covers both good and bad forms of such worship. No explanation was given as to why the word religion had been freely used to identify Christianity in the writings of Watchtower founder, Charles T. Russell, but later rejected by his successor, Joseph F. Rutherford.

My mother's initial contact with the Witnesses came about through the efforts of one of her sisters, my aunt Ethel, who lived in Bloomington, Indiana. She was the first of the six McLaughlin sisters to get caught up in the Watchtower movement. Sometime during the mid-1930s she began sending Watchtower books, booklets and magazines to her sisters living in Iowa and Minnesota. In this way seeds were planted that would change our lives dramatically. Symbolic of the changes that began to take place in our family was that 1938 would be the last year we celebrated Christmas—a holiday the Witnesses roundly condemn. I remember being embarrassed about not being able to tell my friends what I got for Christmas, but I did accept my mother's explanation for our not celebrating it. She said the date of Jesus' birth was not accurate, and the exchanging of gifts and the symbols used to observe the holiday were all of pagan origin. Her explanation satisfied me.

As my mother became more and more influenced by the Witness teachings and her reading of the Bible, she underwent a moral reformation. She would no longer accompany my dad to taverns, and she became less confrontational and mean-spirited when he was drinking. This resulted in a more peaceful atmosphere in the home. I was very grateful for that change. My father didn't share my mother's new-found enthusiasm for the Witnesses and resented her getting more and more involved. This resentment contributed to a few discouraging moments for her. I don't remember the incident, but years later she told me that one night when she was tucking me into bed she said that maybe she should stop studying with the Witnesses. I said, "Oh, you don't want to give that up." I realized that those desirable changes I saw in her were due to the good influences she was getting through the Witnesses, and I didn't want her to let go of that.

Despite moments of discouragement, no one could have dissuaded her once she fully embraced the Witnesses' message. I believe she was baptized in 1940 and she never deviated from that moment on as a loyal and devoted Witness. The McLaughlin sisters were by temperament a strong-willed lot and my mother was no exception. This feisty, sometimes combative nature, served her well as she gradually became active in the public ministry of this quarrelsome and radical movement. I was 13-years-old when she began taking me to their meetings in downtown St. Paul. They rented an upstairs hall in one of the office buildings on Robert Street. We also attended some mid-week meetings in private homes. I would guess that there were fewer than 50 Witnesses in the whole of St. Paul at the time. In 1940 there were less than 100,000 Witnesses worldwide. The meetings were not the least bit interesting to me. *The Watchtower* magazine was studied in a question and answer format every Sunday, and sometimes they would listen to recordings of Joseph F. Rutherford's talks. The rented hall was drab and the chairs uncomfortable. The content of the study material was theologically deep and revolved around the unique belief system that had evolved since the days of Pastor Russell. There was no program for children. "Sunday School" was viewed as a product of "Christendom" and not acceptable to those who had the "Truth." As a result there was never anything for me to look forward to in those meetings except for them to get over. I was sometimes taken from house-to-house by one of the men in their public witnessing campaign and it was not uncommon for them to be cursed or accused of being a communist by those we contacted. I believe that the public leveled the charge of "communists" at the Witnesses, at least in part, because the Witnesses insisted that they were not a religion. By the time I was 15-year-old I was openly resisting going with my mother and she did not force me to go.

So it was that my early impressions of the movement were truly mixed. On the one hand I welcomed the changes in behavior I saw in my mother, but there was nothing other than that to attract my youthful interests or personality. My mother left booklets published by the Watchtower Society lying around the house which depicted the global anarchy and violence that was about to burst upon the world to be followed by God's war of Armageddon. There were frightful drawings of people fleeing the coming judgments of God with wild-eyed terror. Mixed into such scenes were religious clergy and judges depicted as hating the innocent Witnesses and conspiring to illegally curtail their public witnessing. The Watchtower publications depicted the embattled Witnesses as standing faithfully and courageously alone against a Satan-controlled world bent on killing them all. I found that scary. Of course, there was a positive side to their message regarding the promise of a cleansed and peaceful new world order following Armageddon (which only the Witnesses would survive), but this futuristic promise brought me little comfort. The here-and-now of their worship focused on battling the forces of evil with their verbal attacks on their definition of "Christendom" and all churches.

The clergy of Christendom were viewed as the chief protagonists of truth and the devil's primary agents in stirring up trouble for the Witnesses. They were in league with the governments of the world intent upon destroying God's people. The Witnesses world view was that they were in GOD'S ORGANIZATION, while everyone else was in SATAN'S ORGANIZATION; there was no middle ground. We were told that there would be increased persecution in the short time remaining before the great battle of Armageddon. Those convictions became my mother's convictions and she frequently expressed them to me. While I had no reason to disbelieve her, those convictions did nothing to instill in me a basic love for God or a personal relationship with him through Jesus Christ. I was not emotionally prepared nor spiritually fortified to enter into the warfare carried out by the Witnesses under the direction of the WBTS. In addition to their public declaration that "RELIGION IS A SNARE AND A RACKET," they organized campaigns in which cars were equipped with public address systems. They would park near a church and blare out Rutherford's fiery diatribes against the clergy and "Christendom," to unappreciative audiences. Later they went from door-to-door with portable phonograph machines that played his lectures— sometimes starting such records without the approval of the householder. All of these things stirred up considerable resentment and antagonism, not only from the religious clergy who were the special targets of Rutherford's condemnation, but also among people who might other-wise have been neutral religiously. Certain zoning laws and restrictions on canvassing were applied against such tactics and their enforcement against the Witnesses would be fought in local and state courts.

This militant, clergy-baiting rhetoric of the Watchtower Society's president, was viewed as the example to emulate. He was a tall, impos-ing figure of a man with a stern countenance and a lawyer's forceful style of speaking. He was referred to by the Witnesses as "Judge" Ruth-erford, having practiced law in Missouri before getting involved in the Watch Tower movement. He served on occasion as a special judge in the Eight Judicial Circuit Court of Missouri, and this was used as justifica-tion for his taking that title to himself—a title he used to modify his name in the books he wrote. His animosity toward the churches–especially the Roman Catholic Church, was often intemperate and caustic. An example of this style of rhetoric was recorded in relation to an assembly in Columbus, Ohio in 1937, when his latest book titled *Enemies,* was released to the assembled Witnesses. Commenting on the intent of that book the WBTS offered the following:

> On Saturday, September 18, following his morning discourse, Brother Rutherford released the tan-colored book *Enemies*. It denounced false religion as a "great enemy, always working injury to mankind." False religionists were identified as "agents of the Devil, whether they are aware of that fact or not." When presenting the book to the audience, Brother Rutherford said: "You will notice that its cover is tan, and we will tan the old lady's hide with it." To this the audience gave loud and enthusiastic approval.— Jehovah's Witnesses Proclaimers of God's Kingdom, 1993, page 84.

The "old lady" whose hide was to be "tanned" by the book alluded to the "woman" identified in Revelation 17 as, "Babylon the Great, the mother of harlots." This "woman" represented to the Witnesses the world's religious system of which the Roman Catholic Church was viewed as foremost, and was often reviled in Watchtower literature. And while I do not believe the Witnesses should have been mobbed or otherwise persecuted for their exercise of free speech, it is understandable that such *public* declarations aroused the bitter animosity of the clergy and their congregants. Many years later I questioned this combative and intemperate language used by Rutherford, and my mother said, "Oh, he *had* to speak like that." In her mind, his harsh, condemnatory language was justified because the Witnesses were under attack and he was exposing the religious clergy who instigated that attack. It was as though the Christian principle of not returning evil for evil did not apply to him.

This aggressive rhetorical warfare spearheaded by the Society's president was being waged against the backdrop of World War II. After the bombing of Pearl Harbor on December 7, 1941 the United States declared war on Japan and was soon followed by declaring war on Germany. These events gave birth to a new wave of patriotic fervor that washed over the nation. As Witnesses would not serve in the military nor salute the American flag, they were seen as unpatriotic. Such things were simply unthinkable to most people, who had no understanding of why the Witnesses took these positions.

The flag salute issue was fought in local courts as school districts across the country began expelling Witness children for refusing to perform this patriotic ritual. In June of 1940 the United States Supreme Court ruled that such saluting by children in school was mandatory. These children had to endure the ridicule and oftentimes abuse of their class-mates and teachers. These were very difficult times for the children of Jehovah's Witnesses. It reminds me to some extent of the trials that later faced black children when public schools were desegregated in the 1960s. As for the flag salute issue, regardless of how one may feel about the matter, it took considerable courage for these young people to stand up for what they had been taught as right. By the time the flag salute matter became a public issue, I had completed elementary school and was at-tending Harding High School where that ritual was not in place at the start of each school day. They did sing the national anthem and do flag saluting at some school assemblies but it was easy to absent myself dur-ing those times. I never had the courage to openly refuse the salute.

The refusal to salute the American flag was another of those sym-bolic gestures which separated Witnesses from the "world." That they were the subject of persecution over the matter was just another evi-dence to them that they were God's chosen people and everyone hated them just as Jesus said they would by hated. In June of 1943 the United States Supreme Court reversed its earlier decision and ruled that flag saluting was an individual matter and not compulsory. This was hailed as a victory and a vindication by the Witnesses who had fought the mat-ter through the courts. I didn't think about it at the time, but in later years I came to appreciate our American judicial system more because of this decision. The United States was embroiled in a life-or-death struggle for the survival of democratic rule around the globe and its Su-preme Court was courageous enough to reverse the previous ruling by a 6-3 margin. I found that quite remarkable.

Much of the groundwork for civil liberties that would later be tested during the Civil Rights Movement in the 1960s was laid by court victo-ries secured by Jehovah's Witnesses in the 1935-1945 period. Many lo-cal peddling ordinances were wrongly enforced to prevent the Witnesses from using public streets and parks for open-air meetings or the distribu-tion of their publications from door-to-door. Such rulings were chal-lenged by the Witnesses in the courts throughout the United States and a significant number of them were ultimately decided in their favor by the United States Supreme Court. In this way the Witnesses won significant victories in the domain of religious liberty and civil rights. This pro-tracted legal battle and the beneficial effects for all Americans that re-sulted from that battle did not go unnoticed:

> It is plain that present constitutional guarantees of personal liberty, as
> authoritatively interpreted by the Unites States Supreme Court, are far

broader than they were before the spring of 1938; and that most of this enlargement is to be found in the thirty-one Jehovah's Witnesses cases (sixteen deciding opinions) of which *Lovell v. City of Griffin* was the first. If "the blood of the martyrs is the seed of the church," what is the debt of Constitutional Law to the militant persistency–or perhaps I should say devotion—of this strange group.–*Minnesota Law Review*, Vol. 28, No. 4, March 1944, page 246.

There is no denying that the Witness community definitely stood fast for what they perceived the will of God to be during those difficult years during World War II. Their "neutrality" in relation to the world conflict, as they called their position, cost them dearly. Besides prison terms for many young men who refused military service—here in America and around the world, many others became victims of mob violence in America. Matters were much worse in Europe where the brutal German war machine dominated. The English historian, Paul Johnson, presents a strong contrast between the conduct of the major churches in Germany as Adolf Hitler rose to power, compared to minority groups like the Jehovah's Witnesses.

He [Hitler] hated Christianity and showed a justified contempt for its German practitioners. Shortly after assuming power, he told Hermann Rauschnig that he intended to stamp out Christianity in Germany "root and branch. One is either a Christian or a German. You can't be both." He thought the method might be to "leave it to rot like a gangrenous limb." Again: "Do you really believe the masses will ever be Christian again? Nonsense. Never again. The tale is finished . . . but we can hasten matters. The parsons will be made to dig their own graves. They will betray their God to us. They will betray anything for the sake of their miserable little jobs and incomes." This harsh judgment comes close to the truth. Neither the Evangelical nor the Catholic Church ever condemned the Nazi regime.

Only the free sects stuck to their principles enough to merit outright persecution. The bravest were the Jehovah's Witnesses, who proclaimed their outright doctrinal opposition from the beginning and suffered accordingly. They refused any cooperation with the Nazi state which they denounced as totally evil. The Nazis believed they were part of the international Jewish-Marxist conspiracy. Many were sentenced to death for refusing military service and inciting others to do likewise; or they ended in Dachau or lunatic asylums. A third were actually killed; ninety-seven percent suffered persecution in one form or another. They were the only Christian group which aroused Himmler's admiration: in September 1944 he suggested to Kaltenbrunner that, after victory, they should be resettled in the conquered plains of Russia.—*A History of Christianity,* Paul Johnson,1976, (pages 485, 486, 489.)

It would be a mistake, I believe, to minimize or discount the commendable courage shown by the Witnesses during those terrible war years. Most of them had the courage to act in a manner consistent with their convictions, often at great costs to themselves. They truly believed that God's final war of Armageddon was just ahead and the peaceful kingdom of God on earth was just beyond the horizon. Remaining faithful and not compromising themselves at this most critical juncture in world history was of the greatest essence. They were convinced that Jehovah God was directing them through the Watchtower Society, and failure to faithfully respond to its direction would have been tantamount to rebelling against Jesus Christ himself. Their faith in that organization was (and is) inseparably bound up with their faith in God and Christ. There was no doubt in their mind that through Jehovah's earthly organization they had been given the message of the hour. Their confidence in *this truth* was complete and unshakable.

However, the outworking of history proved that they were not where they thought they were in the outworking of God's purposes and timetable. They were not delivering Christ's final message to the world. They were delivering a gospel and a timetable created by the genius of men who claimed that God was directing them by his Spirit and speaking through them. End times Bible prophesies were being explained as undergoing fulfillment at that very moment in time. They thought they knew exactly where they were in relation to these prophetic events and saw themselves in the maelstrom of never-to-be-repeated events.

Those convictions infused them with a zeal seldom matched by a collective body of believers. While they were mistaken in many ways, their convictions produced a zeal that was genuine. It reminds me of something the apostle Paul had to say about his fellow Jews who were still laboring to please God under the law covenant. "For I bear them witness that they have a zeal for God; but not according to accurate knowledge." (Romans 10:2 *NWT*) Paul knew what he was talking about because had once shared that same zeal as a Pharisee. That is how I feel about Jehovah's Witnesses. I grant that they do have a zeal for God but it is not according to accurate knowledge. Notwithstanding, their collective stand to resist being caught up in the horrific slaughter that took the lives of tens of millions of people was commendable, in my opinion.

I was 16-years-old when our country entered the war in 1941. I was not committed to my mother's religious convictions, nor did I fully understand them. I was unnerved by the hostility that I perceived existed against Jehovah's Witnesses. By nature I deplored acrimony and violence. I was also morally weak and gravitated toward self-interest and pleasure. I had dropped out of high school after the ninth grade and spent much of my time in a local bowling alley and pool hall on Payne Avenue on St. Paul's east side. I was not preparing for the future or the life-altering decisions that I would soon be forced to make. Personally conflicted by my half-hearted involvement with the Witness, I drifted along following the line of least resistance.

Chapter 3

"Due Now Any Day"

In August of 1941, about a month before my sixteenth birthday, my mother took me to an international convention of Jehovah's Witnesses in St. Louis, Missouri. We rode with another family in their car. During the long hot drive from Minnesota, the adult conversation included speculation about the prospect of seeing the "Princes" at the assembly. The Princes were understood to be the many Hebrew prophets like Abraham, Isaac, Jacob, Moses, David and others who were expected to be resurrected back to life on earth just *before* the great battle of Armageddon. Those resurrected "Princes" would then serve as the earthly administrators of the new Theocratic Government that would rule the earth under Jehovah's appointed king, Jesus Christ. The speculation advanced by the adults was that the "Princes" might appear at the convention, and if that should happen, maybe Armageddon would begin right then and there while most of Jehovah's people were assembled in St. Louis! That would be wonderful, they agreed. I thought about that during the remainder of the drive to Missouri.

After arriving in St. Louis, we made our way to the huge complex called The Arena, where the week-long assembly was to be held. I remember standing in a large open area that fronted the huge building and feeling terribly sad because my dad wasn't a Witness and if Armageddon came while we were there, he would be destroyed forever because he was not a Jehovah's Witness. I couldn't hold back the tears. The thought of my dad being destroyed ruined any enthusiasm I might have had about the "Princes" showing up. For the record, they didn't.

On the last day of the convention, Sunday, August 10, Joseph F. Rutherford, had all the young people between the ages of 5 and 18 seated in a special section in The Arena. Official Watchtower records say that about

15,000 children were present, either in The Arena or assembled at a tent/trailer city just outside of St. Louis and connected to the convention by a direct transmission line. I was one of those sitting before him in The Arena. Rutherford addressed us as, "potential children of the King," the King being Jesus Christ. He stressed how close the battle of Armageddon was and that the "Princes" were "due now, any day." In view of that and the immediacy of Armageddon and the end of the world, he admonished us not to be thinking of a future in this world. Thoughts of marriage were discouraged. His advice to us was to wait until after Armageddon, when the "Princes" would guide us in the proper choice of a marriage mate. This advice was coming from Jehovah God's chief spokesman to God's people. That was how he thought of himself and that was how he was viewed by the Witnesses. At one point in his admonition especially addressed to the young men present, he said:

> Ask yourself now. Why should a man, at this time, vigorous and strong and has the prospect of hope of being of the great multitude [scheduled to survive Armageddon], tie himself up now to a sack of bones and a hank of hair?

This demeaning reference to women as a "sack of bones and a hank of hair," was received with a spontaneous burst of applause. I didn't comprehend how distasteful and insulting that remark was at the time, even though it included my mother. It was years later as an adult that I realized how degrading of God's creation the remark truly was. I have a recording of this speech on audio cassette which I made from an 78-rpm phonograph recording made during the convention. I found a copy of it years later in a Kingdom Hall. I have listened to that recording a number of times to refresh my memory of the occasion and the exact words Rutherford used as recorded above. At the end of this session each child was presented with a gift copy of a new book the WBTS was releasing for future study and public distribution. The title of the book was, *Children*, and was heralded as the instrument now being provided by Jehovah God for the Witnesses to use in their door-to-door ministry during the short time remaining before Armageddon. The occasion and significance of this book was addressed the following month in *The Watchtower* magazine:

> Receiving the gift [a copy of the *Children* book], the marching children clasped it to them, not a toy or a plaything for idle pleasure, but the Lord's provided instrument for most effective work in the remaining *months* before Armageddon.—*The Watchtower*, September 15, 1941, page 288. (Italics not in the original)

The sense of urgency that charged the activities of the Witnesses at that time in 1941, is captured in the phrase, "in the remaining months before Armageddon." It explains the speculation that my mother and the others engaged in while we traveled to St. Louis. For many years it had been taught that Jesus Christ returned *invisibly* in October of 1914 and began a judgment work of separating people either for life or destruction. This judgment work was to be completed within the span of one generation and the WBTS was being used by Jesus as his earthly channel to proclaim his invisible presence and the end of the world. What was being preached by the Witnesses was directed by God's Spirit and those who would be saved through the coming war of Armageddon needed to put faith in that message. Those who rejected that message would be destroyed at Armageddon. The *Children* book was the "Lord's provided instrument" to be used in completing that dividing work.

The book, written by Rutherford himself, featured a fictional couple: John Alden and Eunice Rogers. John was 20 and Eunice was 18. They were in love, and wanted to marry and raise a family. They also had a love of truth and the Bible, so they decide to study it together. This maudlin literary device was used to draw the reader into the esoteric doctrines taught by the Witnesses regarding the invisible presence of Jesus Christ in his capacity as judge and the imminent end of the world. The book explains that God installed Jesus Christ as King in A.D.1914, marking the beginning of a generation of increased world calamity to be climaxed by the war of Armageddon. About these things the book said:

> The "end of the world" means the end of Satan's uninterrupted rule. For centuries Satan has exercised ruling power over the world without hindrance. In 1914 Christ Jesus was enthroned by Jehovah. That marks the end of the uninterrupted rule of Satan, which is to be followed soon by Armageddon."—*Children*, page 85.

> All the facts show that the woes beginning in 1914 have continued to increase upon the earth, and at the present time the distress and woes are greater than ever before known, and this indicates that Armageddon is very near.—*Ibid,* page 151.

Just as Rutherford's discourse to the children in St. Louis had done, this book stressed the urgency of the times and the need to set aside personal desires and interests to devote oneself to getting the message to the world that Armageddon was at hand. John and Eunice discussed their future against that backdrop. Not surprisingly, by the end of the book they had made their decision to postpone marriage until after Armageddon and devote their lives now to exclusively serving the King, Jesus

Christ, by working full time distributing Watchtower literature and teaching others what they had come to believe. Their noble sacrifice was presented as follows:

> Now we see by faith the great THEOCRACY, and we are wholly and unreservedly committed to that righteous government. From now on we shall have our heart devotion fixed on THE THEOCRACY, knowing that soon we shall journey for ever together in the earth. Our hope is that within a few years our marriage may be consummated and, by the Lord's grace, we shall have sweet children that will be an honor to the Lord. We can well defer our marriage until lasting peace comes to the earth. Now we must add nothing to our burdens, but be free and equipped to serve the Lord.—*Children,* page 366. (Emphasis in original)

Had "John" and "Eunice" been a real couple, they would now (in 2006) be 85 and 83 respectively—still deferring marriage and raising a family, still waiting for Armageddon. Many young Witnesses took Rutherford's advice to heart and determined to remain single until after Armageddon which, according to the WBTS was only a matter of months away. Some went so far as to take a vow of celibacy. I personally knew two sisters, Irene and Margaret Keipper, whom I met years later in the Owatonna, Minnesota congregation of Jehovah's Witnesses in the 1970s. They had been mere youths in the 1940s and on the basis of what they were being taught at that time they each vowed to remain single until after Armageddon. And even though Rutherford's advice was premised on error, they felt honor-bound to live out their vow to remain single, which both of them did. They were very devoted Witnesses and spent their lives advancing the Watchtower's world view. I respected their decision to live out their vows, but I also felt a certain sadness of them. There is no doubt that Rutherford's counsel in the *Children* book, played a significant role in their decision.

The *Children* book also addressed the propriety of Witnesses already married having children. It was argued that it was not a good time to be doing so. Jesus' words, addressed to his generation destined to experience the extreme difficulties that would attend the destruction of Jerusalem in A.D. 70, were taken out of context and applied to the present generation to back up this advice. Jesus had said, "Woe to the pregnant women and the ones suckling a baby in those days! For there will be great necessity upon the land and wrath on this people." (Luke 21:23, *NWT*) The book also pointed out that Noah's sons and their wives did not have children until after the Flood. This, too, was seen as a "prophetic picture" indicating the impropriety of having children now:

Should men and women, both of whom are Jonadabs or "other sheep" [terms used to identify those said to have an earthy hope of life] now marry before Armageddon and bring forth children? They may choose to do so, but the admonition or advice of the Scriptures appears to be against it . . . The prophetic picture seems to set forth the correct rule, to wit: The three sons of Noah and their wives were in the ark and were saved from the flood. They did not have any children, however, until after the flood. They began to have children two years after the flood . . . that would appear to indicate it would be proper that those who will form the "great multitude" [the same group identified above] should wait until after Armageddon to bring children into the world.

It is *only a few years* from the time the "other sheep" are gathered to the Lord until Armageddon. That entire period is a time of much tribulation, concluding with the greatest tribulation the world will ever have known. Speaking of that very time, Jesus says: "Woe unto them that are with child, and to them that give suck in those days!" —*Ibid*, pages 312, 313. (Italics not in original)

Again, it needs to be emphasized here that this advice was not viewed by the Witnesses as coming from any man—not even the man who wrote the book, Joseph F. Rutherford. No, these admonitions were coming from Christ Jesus himself through his appointed spokesman on earth! The book was, *"the Lord's provided instrument!"* To disregard it was to disregard what the Lord himself was providing. Not to believe it was to question the Lord's wisdom and truthfulness. In other words, accepting the WBTS perception of matters determined whether you were a lover of truth or not. To reject the "advice" presented in the *Children* book was to reject Christ's advice. This was the air the Witnesses breathed—it was their world—their reality.

A decade later, even though the "Princes" had not made an appearance and Armageddon was still future, the Witnesses continued to frown on those who chose to have babies. In the early 1950s in St. Paul, a young married woman who was married to a non-Witness, became pregnant with her second child, and I recall how critical my mother was of her. Another young Witness mother, whose husband was also a Witness, told me she hesitated to let her fellow Witnesses know she was pregnant with her second child out of fear of their disapproval. She waited as long as she possibly could before doing so. This extreme attitude about marriage and childbearing no longer exists among the Witnesses today, and would seem radical to them now, but back then it was the right attitude, as revealed through *"the Lord's provided instrument."* It was "the truth."

.Truth, according to their theology, is whatever the WBTS teaches at any given moment in time. If a new teaching replaces a former teaching, then it becomes "the truth."

At the time the *Children* book was published there were about 100,000 Witnesses in the world, yet the first printing of it ran to 3,000,000 copies. It was designed to be taken to the public in the door-to-door ministry to provide people with the truth they needed to know and act upon if they were to survive the rapidly approaching battle of Armageddon. People were viewed as being divided, not by the Witnesses, but by the King Jesus Christ, through the message the Witnesses were preaching. People were either for or against THEOCRACY as that term was defined in the book. Accepting the message or rejecting it was the dividing issue. This arbitrary reasoning justified their putting people into one of two categories: "sheep" or "goats." (Matthew 25) Those who responded favorably were viewed as "sheep." Those who rejected the message were thought of as "goats," and heading for destruction. It was not uncommon to hear those terms bandied about by the Witnesses when discussing their witnessing experiences. This judgmental attitude continues to permeate the thinking of Jehovah's Witnesses.

Children would be the last book Rutherford would write. He was suffering from colon cancer and was very ill during the St. Louis convention, although the Witnesses in general were not unaware of that. He died January 8, 1942. His many books have passed into oblivion. Like his predecessor, Charles T. Russell, his prognostications and authoritative rhetoric were discredited by the outworking of world events.

As I write these things I feel a certain sadness as I reflect on the many Witnesses I have known and for whom I retain much affection. One such person is Ann Stepoway, now deceased. I was only a child when she came weekly to our home to study with my mother. She sometimes brought one of her two small boys with her. She was a pleasant, unassuming person with a ready smile. Her manner was so mild and warm. She radiated a certain calmness of spirit that I was drawn to and admired. Her religious background was Russian Orthodox. She lived on the West side in St. Paul. To get to our home on Maria Avenue on the east Side, she had to take a streetcar to downtown St. Paul and then transfer to another streetcar which would take her to the East side. In the evening this could take up to an hour or more each way. One bitterly cold winter night she came to our home wearing only a light spring coat and my mother asked her why she hadn't dressed warmer. She smiled and said that her husband had hidden her heavy coat to prevent her from going out. So she simply wore her lighter coat. This kind of self-sacrifice and dedication made a deep impression on me. Years later I was able to tell her how much I appreciated her ministry toward my mother and me.

There are many other Witnesses who occupy a place in my affections. And in the many years that I have touched the lives of believers outside of the Witness community, I have come to have an equally deep affection for them as well. I see in these people the same degree of dedication and selfless service that I saw in Witnesses like Ann Stepoway. Of course, not all Christians show the same degree of love, devotion and zeal. Some are quite content to do little to advance their perception of God's cause in Jesus Christ. But that was true of some Witnesses as well. Some, like Ann Stepoway, were very zealous; but there were others who were less so and still others who could only be described as nominal Witnesses, active only in a marginal way within the movement. I later came to see that variation in another community of believers.

The Witnesses think they are unique in their love for God. They are not. Their teachings and practices are unique, but as people they are not unique. The simple truth is that the same cross-section of people exists in all religious systems. As a Witness I experienced the deep feeling of brotherly love that flowed through our worldwide fellowship. I have experienced that same degree of intense love for one another with other believers since leaving the Witnesses. The primary difference between the two groups is that the latter do what they do on a more individual and spontaneous basis, while the former are more programmed and organizationally conditioned and controlled in their religious activity.

Chapter 4

An
Uncertain
Faith

When I reached 18 years of age in September of 1943, I registered for the military draft as a conscientious objector. I fully intended to "take my stand," as the Witnesses spoke of those refusing military service. My mother voiced concern about my resolve, but I assured her I would do what was right. The problem was—and my mother understood this better than I did—I was not living and acting as a committed Jehovah's Witness. My attendance at the Kingdom Hall was spotty at best, and I shared in the door-to-door ministry only when circumstances forced me into it.

An example of such forced circumstances was my being recruited by my mother to assist my aunt Lucretia in her public witnessing. She was a "pioneer," which meant she had made a commitment to the WBTS to spend a minimum of hundred hours each month in public preaching. At that time the Witnesses were using a portable phonograph machine which played messages produced by the WBTS to be used in their public ministry. The machine was rather heavy, so I was pressed into service to carry my aunt's phonograph machine for her from house to house. On one occasion a girl I knew socially answered the door. While my aunt spoke to her about God and his kingdom, the girl looked at me over my aunt's shoulder with a puzzled look on her face, as if to say, "What the heck is Ron doing?" I felt humiliated and embarrassed. I spent the few minutes we were there closely examining the condition of my shoes.

Despite my lack of enthusiasm and commitment to the Witness movement, I convinced myself that I would choose prison over military service when the time came. My mother had spoken to me against war and she instilled in me the conviction that it was morally wrong. Also, by nature I was mild-spirited and had a personal aversion to violence of any

27

kind. Sometime in the mid-1930s my mother took me to a movie titled: "All Quiet on the Western Front." Originally released in 1930, the movie was an American adaption of a book by German author, Erich Maria Remarque. Because of its anti-war theme the book had been banned in Germany. The movie depicted the brutality of war through the lives of idealistic German youth fighting protracted trench warfare in France during World War I. The utter horror of it all, the savage waste of young life and the devastating effects on the human psyche, were all graphically dramatized. That depiction of war, together with my mother's values, made an abiding impression on my young mind. I still remember the final scene where the main character, played by American actor, Lew Ayres, was stretching his arm out over the top of a trench to touch a beautiful butterfly. His hand inched toward the butterfly and when he had nearly reached it a shot rang out. His hand fell limply to the ground. That scene summed up the horror of war. I never forgot it.

But while I was sympathetic toward the Witnesses' view of war, and believed they were right in their understanding of the Bible, I was not morally or religiously dedicated enough to make the kind of personal sacrifice it would take to be identified with them. I was more concerned about what my friends would think than what God, my mother or the Witnesses would think. Even though I had been baptized as a Witness when I was 16, I had done nothing to cultivate a deep, personal faith—one that would sustain me in a time of testing. While I respected those men who did stand up for what they believed and were prepared to pay the price for that, I lacked their moral courage. I had good intentions, but those good intentions were not strengthened by a diligent Christian life. When I was ordered to report for induction at Fort Snelling, Minnesota, on November 30, 1943 I did what I usually did: I followed the line of least resistance. I reported for induction. It broke my mother's heart.

In January of 1944 I was sent to Camp Blanding, Florida for basic training. While I looked like everyone else, dressed like everyone else and drilled like everyone else, I was not like everyone else. I was a Jehovah's Witness—a delinquent one to be sure—but a Jehovah's Witness, nevertheless. By failing to act consistently with what I believed to be right, I had created an inner conflict that gave me no peace. In addition, I was tormented by a dreadful fear of God! For the first time, I felt under his judgment. I believed that Armageddon could break out at any moment, and here I was in the United States Army, of all places! I had been told that there were but two organizations on earth: Satan's organization and Jehovah's organization, and I certainly was not in Jehovah's organization. I would certainly be destroyed at Armageddon. There was no doubt in my mind about that.

In May of 1944 after finishing Basic Training, I was given a two-week furlough and ordered to report to Fort George G. Meade, Maryland, I knew Fort Meade was a port of demarcation for troops being sent to Europe. Time was running out for me, and I was growing more and more desperate about my situation. Soon after arriving at Fort Meade we were issued our oversea's gear and confined to barracks waiting for orders to board a troop ship. It would be only a matter of a day or two before I would be heading for Europe and the war. I was beside myself with anxiety and fear. The mental and emotional dissonance I had been struggling with for many months had reached a crisis stage. But what to do?

The morning following our confinement to barracks I became more and more agitated. I couldn't sit still. I began to pace back and forth, my mind whirled with an overpowering sense of desperation. We were on the second floor of a two-storied barracks and I recall thinking that the only thing I could do was to crash through one of the windows. I wasn't thinking of suicide, but thought if I injured myself seriously enough I could avoid being sent overseas. As irrational as that sounds, it was the only thing I could think of. A soldier friend whom I had known since basic training, had apparently been watching me pace back and forth. He must have realized that something was very wrong with me. The episode remains hazy to me but at some point I bolted for one of the windows, but my friend tripped me as I rushed pass him, and fell. At that point I lost all control of my emotions and began yelling, crying and thrashing about as he and others restrained me. I don't recall the immediate events after that episode.

I was taken to the base hospital for psychiatric evaluation. I was in the hospital for several weeks, during which time I was examined and interviewed by several army doctors. I told them about my being a Jehovah's Witness and a conscientious objector. I tried to explain why I could no longer be a soldier. I knew they couldn't begin to understand, and I had the distinct feeling that they didn't hear a word I said. The last doctor who spoke to me before sending me back to active duty said I should talk to a Chaplin when I got on the boat. The message was clear: my conviction in the matter was of no relevance. As far as the doctors were concerned, the matter was closed. But for me, the matter was not closed. I had passed the point of no return.

By the time I returned to active duty the former group I had been assigned to had been shipped out. I was placed in another unit which was awaiting its turn to be sent to Europe. I was back in the same situation I had left a few weeks earlier. I knew it would be pointless to speak to an officer about the matter any further. I decided to go AWOL (Absent Without Leave). I got a weekend pass and took a bus into Baltimore where I bought some civilian clothes. I found a public restroom and changed clothes, putting my uniform in the package that had held the civilian clothes. I went to the Bus Depot and purchased a ticket for St. Paul. The Depot was filled with soldiers, sailors, and a sprinkling of Military Police. Had I been stopped and questioned they would have quickly learned that I was going AWOL. Although I was 18 I looked more like 16. No one paid any attention to me as I boarded the bus. I got back to St. Paul a couple of days later and made my way home. My parents almost died! They convinced me that I must turn myself in at Fort Snelling, which I did the following day.

Learning that I was AWOL from Fort Meade, they put me in the stockade, where I remained for a week or so. During that time I was interrogated and I repeated my story once more. Then I was transferred to the psychiatric unit of the hospital in Fort Snelling The only doctor I remember clearly was a Major Schmouse I am not certain about the spelling of his name, but that was how it sounded. He was very military but with a doctor's demeanor. He spoke to me on several occasions and appeared to listen to what I had to say. I didn't know it at the time, but later learned that he had contacted my mother and asked her to come to his office at Fort Snelling. Apparently, he wanted to know more about my background and my reasons for not wanting to be a soldier. At some point in this interview he told her: "I have the authority to make or break this young man." He asked my mother whether she believed I was sincere about my religious objections to being a soldier. Honest woman that she was, she said, "I don't know."

One day the Major came to our ward and asked me, if he sent me back to Fort Meade, would I go willingly? He explained that if a Military Police escort were necessary, I would have the cost of that taken out of my pay. If I went back by myself, I could save that charge. I told him I would go back. That was a lie. I had no intention of returning to Fort Meade. But had I said I wouldn't go back voluntarily, I would have been sent there under guard. It seemed certain that I would end up being court marshaled and sent to prison.

A day or two after this conversation I was brought my uniform and told to get dressed. After getting dressed, I was taken to an office where several officers, including Major Schmouse, were seated. I was again questioned about my service record and my religious values. After a short while I was told to step outside and wait. A short while later, an orderly took me to another department to finalize my release from the hospital and preparation for my return to Fort Meade. I was asked to sign a few papers and given a cash voucher. The last document I signed had the word SEPARATION in its title. As I looked at the document, I gradually realized that I was not being sent back to Fort Meade. I was being separated from the Army! It was an honorable discharge based on poor health. I was in a state of stunned disbelief. Within a matter of minutes, I was outside in the afternoon warmth of an August sun, only a few miles from home. As I rode the streetcar to downtown St. Paul I still couldn't believe that what had just happened. Did it really happen? Up to the moment I signed that separation paper, I hadn't the slightest notion that I was about to be honorably discharged from the United States Army.

When I wrote the first draft of this chapter a few years ago, I was overwhelmed by emotion as I relived that traumatic period in my youth. It will ever remain one of the most incredible experiences of my life. To whom do I credit that remarkable deliverance? Was it God? Was it the Major? I still ponder that question. While I was in the hospital at Fort Snelling, I prayed many times to God through Jesus that he deliver me from the situation I was in, and I was delivered in the most remarkable way. Why hesitate then to credit God? My reason is that when I prayed for God's help I added a caveat: I told him that if I was only going to go back to being a delinquent Witness as I had been then I wouldn't expect him to help me. The sad truth is that after the euphoria of deliverance passed, I gradually slipped back into my former ways of life. It would be several years before I would begin serving my God with the kind of whole-souled commitment that has dominated my life from that time until now, nearly 60 years later.

One thing is certain: the circumstances of my release from the military bordered on the miraculous. I also know that Major Schmouse played a key role. To the extent that God worked in this matter he worked through this man. What prompted the Major to contact my mother and why he made it possible for me to walk away from the army in an honorably way? I can't be certain. Perhaps he saw something in me that gave him reason to believe I was sincere. I believe my mother played a role in his decision. He must have sensed the genuine quality of her faith and been impressed with her honesty and candor. Was it something within the man himself that prompted him to make the decision he made and convinced his colleagues to make? Perhaps it was a combination of all these things. I may never know.

The
Turning
Point

It was in 1948 that I finally committed myself to a consistent and de voted involvement with Jehovah's Witnesses. By that time I was married and the father of a little girl, Jamie, the only child my wife Mavis and I would have. I had married Mavis Christopherson, whose father, Thomas, and older sister, Laverne were both Witnesses. It was Mavis who first took the initiative to become active as a Witnesses. She began attending meetings regularly and took our daughter with her. In the summer of 1947 she was baptized. Her example had an influence on me but I still held back for a time.

I had lived on the fringe of the movement from the start of my teenage years but had never really applied myself or developed a personal belief system based on their theology. It had always been my mother's prompting and prodding that accounted for what little participation I engaged in prior to 1948. By this time, I was feeling a desperate need for God. My life had been dominated by a pursuit of personal pleasure and this had only served to create the duel demons of frustration and disappointment. Seeking God at this critical moment could only mean becoming a Jehovah's Witness. And because I had never applied myself to a studious approach to the religion, it was suggested that I have a personal Bible study with an older, more knowledgeable Witness. This seemed like good advice and the one that I decided I wanted to study with was Dr. Earl Seeliger, a chiropractor, who lived and worked in Minneapolis. We had known him for a number of years and I respected him as a professional and as a Christian. I contacted him and he was agreeable to conducting a study with me.

Earl had an office in the historic Foshay Tower building in downtown Minneapolis, and we agreed to meet there for our weekly study. I felt especially privileged to be helped by him because he was one of the "anointed." To understand why his being one of the "anointed" was significant to me, it is necessary to explain the unique gospel preached by the Witnesses. It is a gospel or good news that is radically different from the one preached by Jesus and his apostles. Its roots are to be found in the teachings of Charles T. Russell, who crafted a number of time feature prophecies in relation to the end of the world. While his prognostications have been abandoned by the organization he founded, his successors have retained his basic premise and reworked it with new date-setting speculations. It is on this shaky foundation that their doctrinal house is built. For those not familiar with Watchtower doctrine, I offer the following explanation.

The Watchtower Society teaches that there are two classes of Christians within their association: one class is very small and the other class is large. The small class in their midst is said to be the last members of Jesus' congregation or church. They teach that of the hundreds of millions of Christians who have ever lived, only 144,000 were destined to be approved by Christ Jesus to become members of his heavenly bride. This predestinated number, they say, was completely filled by 1935 A.D. The few Witnesses who claim to be of this predestined number represent less than 1% of the Witnesses as a whole. It is this small number in their midst that they refer to as the "anointed." They say that especially since the year 1935 another class of believers has been gathered by Jesus Christ, under the direction of the WBTS. These latter ones now number 6 million or more and are said to have an earthly hope of future life.

These two classes of Christians, according to the WBTS, are identified in Revelation chapter 7 where it speaks of 144,000 "sealed ones" taken out of the 12 tribes of Israel. (Rev. 7: 1-8) This, they say, identifies the complete number of spiritual Israelites—the Christian Church—and proves that it is limited to 144,000 members. The same chapter goes on to speak of a "great multitude which no man could number, from every nation, from all tribes, and peoples and tongues." (Rev. 7: 9,10 *RSV*) These are said to identify the ones who will inhabit the earth in the kingdom of God.

In 1948, when I began my studies with Dr. Seeliger began, there were about 25,000 Witnesses worldwide who claimed to be one of those "sealed ones" out of a total of 260,000 Witnesses worldwide. Such ones identified themselves by partaking of the bread and wine served on the evening of March 25, 1948 to commemorate the anniversary of Jesus' death. This yearly observance, which they call the Memorial, is said to be in keeping with the Lord's command: " This meant that only one out of every ten Witnesses claimed to be reconciled to God through Jesus Christ as that is explained in the New Testament. (Rom. 5: 1-3) Because they were viewed as the final members of that select body they were spoken of as a member of "the remnant." The vast majority of Witnesses attended that March 25th observance only as spectators because they were told they were not entitled to partake of the bread and wine which symbolized the Lord's body and blood. Concerning the two groups that made up the worldwide community at that time, *The Watchtower* said:

> By drinking the Memorial wine the remnant proclaim that they are bap-tized into Christ's death and that they bear about in their fleshly bodies the dying of Christ, and that they are thus having a common participation in his death for the vindication of Jehovah's name. (Rom. 6: 3,4; Mark 10: 38,39; 2 Cor. 4: 10; Phil. 3: 10) It does not mean that they have a part in the sin-offering or share in providing the ransom sacrifice. Jesus Christ only is the ransom sacrifice; he only can provide and has provided the sin-offering. But the communion in the reproaches, afflictions and death of Christ is something that has been given by Jehovah God through Christ Jesus to the 144,000 members of his body as an exclusive privilege. To them the promise is: "If we be dead with him, we shall also reign with him," that is, reign in his heavenly kingdom.—2 Tim. 2: 11,12

> For this reason the consecrated persons of good will [those said to have an earthly hope of life], the Lord's "other sheep," who are cordially invited to be present at the Memorial supper should not and do not par-take of the emblems. They respect the occasion and respect what it means by attending the celebration and observing what the anointed remnant do in obedience to the instructions of their Head. But they discern that they are not themselves anointed members of the body of Christ and are not baptized into his death nor called and destined to rule with him in his heavenly kingdom. They are seeking for everlasting life in human perfec-tion on earth under that heavenly kingdom. For them to partake of the em-blems would picture something that is not true with respect to themselves. Hence they do not partake. —*The Watchtower*, February 1, 1948, page 43.

Those above who are said to be excluded from the body of Christ, are also told that they are excluded from the new covenant. This means they do not come under the provisions of the new covenant which in-cluded having their sins completely removed and forgotten by God. (Heb. 8: 10-12) Their official statement on this matter is as follows:

> **Those for Whom Christ Is Mediator.** The apostle Paul declares that there is "one mediator between God and men, a man, Christ Jesus, who

gave himself a corresponding ransom for all"—for both Jews and Gentiles. (1 Ti 2: 5,6) He mediates the new covenant between God and those taken into the new covenant, the congregation of spiritual Israel. . .The total number of those who are finally and permanently sealed is revealed in Revelation 7: 4-8 as 144,000. —*INSIGHT ON THE SCRIPTURES* , 1988, vol. 2, page 362.

On the same page in the above dictionary published by the WBTS there is another article that seeks to comfort those in their ranks (nearly all of them now) regarding their spiritual security. The New Testament from which these arcane teachings are fabricated is a new covenant document. By that I mean it was written by, to, and for those who were called to become a part of the bride of Christ and to be glorified with him. As such the faithful Jews and Gentiles who became Christians—born from above, became the new "Israel of God." (John 3: 3-8; Gal. 6: 15,16) We are told that a feature of the law covenant mediated by Moses at Mount Sinai, was the Aaronic priesthood which functioned *exclusively* within it. When the time came for the law covenant to be replaced by a new covenant, it also came time for a different priesthood This is the argument that the writer of the book of Hebrews makes. "If, then, perfection were really through the Levitical priesthood, (for with it as a feature the people were given the law,) what further need would there be for another priest to arise according to the manner of Melchizedek and not said to be according to the manner of Aaron?" (Heb. 7: 11 *NWT*)

The writer then goes on to point out the superiority of our Lord's priesthood—both the efficacy of his once-for-all time sacrifice and his indestructible life—always remaining alive to plead for us! It was this priesthood that was to be the feature of the new covenant. "For the Law made nothing perfect, but the bringing in besides of a better hope did, through which we are drawing near to God. Also, to the extent that it was not without a sworn oath, (for there are indeed men that have become priests without a sworn oath, but there is one with an oath sworn by the One who said respecting him: 'Jehovah has sworn (and he will feel no regret), 'You are a priest forever,') to that extent also Jesus has become the one given in pledge of a better covenant." (Heb. 7: 19-22 *NWT*)

These words, together with the whole of the book, were written to and for those who were *in* the new covenant arrangement. The message was intended to remind these Jewish disciples that what they now had in Jesus Christ and his priesthood was far superior to what they left behind in the law covenant. The law covenant and its priesthood was not given to the world as a whole; it was given to the nation of Israel, and any

foreigner willing to abide by the law covenant came under the law covenant. Similarly, The new covenant is not given to the world as a whole
but to those who become a part of the Israel of God. 'Jesus' priesthood
functions *exclusively* within that covenant. When someone is told that
they do not have to be in the new covenant to claim Jesus as their high
priest they are being misled. Yet, the WBTS makes that very argument.

> **Blessings to Mankind in General.** While Jesus' mediatorship oper-
> ates solely toward those in the new covenant, he is also God's High Priest
> and the Seed of Abraham. In fulfilling his duties in these latter two posi-
> tions, he will bring blessings to others of mankind, for all the nations are
> to be blessed by means of Abraham's seed. Those in the new covenant are
> first blessed by Christ, the principle Seed (Gal. 3: 16,29) being brought in
> as associate members of the seed. Being made kings and priests by reason
> of the new covenant that he mediated. They will share in administering
> the blessings of Jesus' sacrifice and his kingdom rule to all the nations of
> the earth. . . There are, thus, others not of the 144,000 "sealed" ones who
> also pray to Jehovah God in the name of Jesus Christ, putting faith in the
> merit of his ransom sacrifice. This sacrifice is not only for those whom
> Jesus mediates the new covenant but also for all mankind expressing faith
> in Christ. (1 Jo 2: 2) These not in the new covenant also appreciate that
> "there is not another name under heaven that has been given among men
> by which we must be saved." (Ac 4:12) They, too, look to Jesus Christ as
> their great heavenly High Priest, through whom they can approach God
> and through whose ministration they can get forgiveness of sin. (Heb 4:
> 14-16). —*INSIGHT ON THE SCRIPTURES*, Vol. 2, pages 362,363.

While it is true, as the above quotation points out, that Jesus died not
only for his spiritual body, the church, but also for the life of the world,
they misapply how that is to eventuate according to the New Testament
Scriptures. The present age is the "day of salvation" for *all those* putting
faith in Jesus Christ as Lord and faithfully doing the Father's will by
keeping the Lord's commands. (2 Cor. 6: 1,2) Their sins have been forgiven because the terms of the new covenant under which they live with
Jesus as their mediator grants them complete forgiveness. (Heb. 8: 7-13)
The recipients of the letter of Hebrews were Jews who had become born
again believers and sharers in the new covenant which the Lord mediated and for whom he serves as high priest. The Watchtower Society
argues that those not in the new covenant can also claim Jesus as their
high priest. But the context in which he is presented as high priest in
Scripture clearly shows that it is *within* the new covenant that he acts as
high priest. There is no scriptural warrant for claiming there are others

outside of the new covenant arrangement, at the present time, for whom he also serves as high priest.

A cardinal rule of scriptural exegesis is determining what was meant by what was said to those to whom it was first written—how did they understand what was being said to them? Every statement is written within a certain context and interpretation must be determined by that context. And, as I said before, the New Testament is written to and for the church. The benefits extended to the church cannot be taken out of context and made to apply to another body of believers created by the genius of human imagination nearly two thousand years later. The benefits of Jesus' sacrifice and priesthood will be extended to humanity as a whole *in the age to come*—the millennium. It is *then* that the "healing of the nations" takes place, not before. (Revelation 21 & 22) Millions of Witnesses fail to understand this basic teaching of Scripture. Their misunderstanding is the result of the careful and persistent indoctrination that flows through the pages of *The Watchtower* magazine and kindred publications. Typical of such indoctrination which includes manmade date-setting, is the following:

> We note that up to the spring of the year 1935 the remnant of the spiritual Israelites who belong inside "this fold" were preoccupied with gathering into that fold, or pen, the final ones needed to make up the full membership of the 144,000 spiritual Israelites. These would be the last to be brought under the new covenant as mediated by the Fine Shepherd, who died as the Lamb of God to provide "the blood of an everlasting covenant." (Hebrews 13: 20; Psalm 50:5) What, then, happened in 1935?
> —*The Watchtower*, Feb.15, 1984, p. 18.

The scriptural reference to "this fold" in the above is taken from the *New World Translation* rendering of John 10:16: "And I have other sheep, which are not of this fold; those also I must bring, and they will listen to my voice, and they will become one flock, one shepherd." The context of Jesus' words clearly shows that he was talking to those Jewish disciples of his who were still under the Law. This was the sheep pen or fold in which they were enclosed. Gentiles were never under the Law and therefore not in that sheep pen. The time would come, however, when Gentiles would be included in the "one flock" arrangement under the provisions of the new covenant. The Gentiles, therefore, are the "other sheep" of which he speaks. Beginning with the Roman centurion Cornelius, Gentiles were brought into the new covenant faith under the direction of the Holy Spirit. (Acts 10) Without straining, that understanding fits well into the outworking of events as recorded in the New Testa-

ment. For the Watchtower Society to wrest John 10:16 out of its historical context and apply it to an obscure twentieth century event is arbitrary
and without scriptural warrant. Yet, that is what they do. Regarding the
significance of 1935 (from their myopic perspective) the article quoted
above went on to answer its own question: "What, then, happened in
1935?"

> On the second day of the convention, May 31, the then president of the
> Watch Tower Bible and Tract Society thrilled the conventioners with his
> address on Revelation 7: 9-17, regarding the "great multitude." (Revela-
> tion 7:9 *Authorized Version*) He explained that this foretold "great multi-
> tude" was to be made up of the "other sheep," those foreshadowed by
> Jonadab, or Jehonadab, the non-Israelite man who accompanied Jehu, the
> king of Israel, in a display of zeal for Jehovah and against the worshipers
> of the false god Baal. (2 Kings 10: 15-28; Jeremiah 35: 6-19) Thus Jehu
> showed "toleration of no rivalry toward Jehovah," or according to the
> *Authorized Version*, "zeal for the LORD." —2 Kings 10: 16.
>
> Hundreds of those who wanted to be like Jonadab and be among the
> "other sheep" of the Fine Shepherd responded to the published invitation
> and attended the Washington convention. To become modern-day
> antitypical Jonadabs it was Scripturally necessary for them to make a full
> dedication of themselves to Jehovah God through the Fine Shepherd and
> symbolize this dedication by total immersion in water, as the sheep be-
> longing to "this fold" had done. So it was that, on Saturday, June 1, 1935,
> there were 840 conventioners that got baptized in water, resembling the
> mass baptism that took place on the day of Pentecost of the year 33 C.E.
> at Jerusalem." —*The Watchtower*, Feb. 15, 1984 page 18.

This was how that new class of believers was created by the WBTS.
Where in Scripture is there any suggestion of such a thing? What proof
is offered that would scripturally validate it other than the president of
the WBTS simply saying that it was so? None! The grandiose manner in
which the baptism of those 840 people is presented as "resembling the
mass baptism that took place on the day of Pentecost," is clearly intended to give a scriptural flavor to the matter. Keep in mind that this is
said to fulfill John 10: 16. The reality is that John 10:16, was taken out of
context and woven into their date-setting theology. Their interpretation
of John 10:16 was read *into* the Bible, not *out* of it. That people claiming
to be Christians would think of themselves as "antitypical Jonadabs" is
ludicrous and would not be possible unless they had already been held
captive by a different good news. The above article then moved to the
present in 1984:

> Already they [the supposed "other sheep"] enormously outnumber the foreordained number of 144,000, which limited figure has been set for those brought into "this fold" that is reserved for the spiritual Israelites, the co-heirs with the Fine Shepherd in his heavenly Kingdom. This fact gives further evidence that they are not in "this fold" of the Fine Shepherd's little flock.—Luke 12: 32.

> Has the difference of hopes—the heavenly hope for the sheep in "this fold" and the earthly hope for the other sheep belonging to the recently provided other fold—influenced them into parting company from one another as if they have nothing in common? Developments since the year 1935 answer, Positively No! Jesus the Fine Shepherd, foretold that this would not be the case, for he went on to say: "And they will become one flock." (John 10:16) —*The Watchtower*, February 15, 1984 pages19, 20.

The apostle Paul, echoing Jesus' teaching, says that there is but one body of believers—all sharing the same relationship with God through Jesus Christ and having a common hope. "One body there is, and one spirit, even as you were called in the *one hope* to which you were called; one Lord, one faith, one baptism; one God and Father of all (persons), who is over all and through all and in all." (Eph. 4: 4-6 *NWT*) In this way the apostle Paul summarizes the one true good news or gospel. The whole of the New Testament is so clear on this matter that only someone approaching it with a different doctrinal agenda could possible misconstrue it. And that, unfortunately, is the case with Jehovah's Witnesses. Beginning with Charles T. Russell, a maze of "last days" scenarios and date-setting predictions have dominated the movement and introduced the radical "gospel" outlined above. John 10: 16 simply became a convenient text to twist and misapply in order to give some scriptural coloring for this destructive doctrine which is but one product of their date-setting prognostications which historical events have *repeatedly* refuted.

This matter is so important that it bears repeating: The obvious understanding of John 10:16 is that the Jewish disciples of Jesus Christ would be joined by other believers who were not a part of the law covenant "fold" in which they lived. Those spoken of as the Lord's "other sheep" would be those gentiles who lived outside of the Jewish "fold" but would be united with them in one flock under one shepherd—Jesus Christ. This perception of things is summarized by the apostle Paul in Ephesians 4:4-6. This conclusion does not strain related scriptures and is consistent with all that we read regarding the fact that Jews and Gentiles were brought together into one flock of believers. (Compare Eph. 2: 11-22)

But at the time, in 1948, I had no correct understanding of these matters. I was scripturally ignorant. So, when the opportunity came for me to be assisted in a Bible study by one of the "anointed," I considered myself greatly blessed. A Bible study conducted by one of Jehovah's Witness means using a publication of the Watchtower Society as a "guide" to understanding the Bible. Studying the Scriptures without such a "guide" is almost unheard of. So when Earl Seeliger agreed to study the Bible with me it was understood that we would be looking at the Bible through the matrix of one of the Society's books. Witnesses believe that it is only through such publications that the Bible can be understood. Typical of such assertions is the following:

> The Bible must be understood if it is to give us faith and if we are to be able to apply it in our lives. And to be able to understand it we need the help of God's holy spirit, for which we are told to pray. However, for God to answer our prayers for his spirit we must meet his conditions, among which is that *we recognize the visible channel he is using for that very purpose.* —The Watchtower, July 1, 1965, page 391, (italics not in original)

The "visible channel" referred to above was, of course, themselves. They unashamedly declare that God's Spirit is only available through them. When I began studying with Earl Seeliger, I was already convinced that Jehovah God was using the Watchtower Society as his exclusive channel of communication to people on earth. I was more than comfortable with that concept. In fact, I was most grateful to God for that channel. My approach to the study material was not to subject it to critical analysis but simply to understand it and accept it.

The book selected for our study was the first edition of *Let God Be True*, published in 1946. It was divided into twenty-four chapters, each one developing a particular scriptural topic. It covered the primary beliefs Jehovah's Witnesses held at the time. One chapter dealt with "The Lord's Return," in which it was argued that 1914 marked the year that Jesus Christ returned *invisibly* to begin judgment proceedings against his church and the world-at-large. Putting the matter into the Watchtower perspective the book declared:

> For many years prior to 1914 earnest Bible students understood that the year 1914 marked the end of the Gentile times. That date marked the end of Satan's uninterrupted rule, and therefore the time when Christ the rightful ruler of the world received control . . . Jehovah's time to assert his universal domination has arrived. Jehovah has become king. God's kingdom, pictured by a man-child, was born in 1914. —*Let God Be True*, 1946 ed. Page 191.

The teaching that Jesus Christ returned *invisibly* (undetected by the world) in 1914 was, and continues to be, the premise upon which the Society currently builds its authoritative structure and prophetic time-table. If you accepted that premise, and I did, then what they taught as corollary to that premise made perfect sense. The corollary doctrine was that after his invisible return, discerned only by his watchful and faithful servants, he would use them to direct a dividing work—separating people into approved and disapproved categories. And what would be the basis for such division? The dividing line would be whether one accepted the teaching that Jesus returned invisibly in 1914 and appointed those associated with the Watchtower Society to be his official channel of communication to people on the earth. This channel would be made up of the few remaining members of the 144,000 heavenly class of Christians who would dispense timely spiritual food to the worldwide association of true believers—exclusively Jehovah's Witnesses.

The reasoning on this matter is circular, and goes something like this: We are the only ones who know Jesus returned invisibly in October of 1914. Therefore, we must be the ones Jesus is using to direct the dividing work. If you do not believe that you are rejecting Jesus Christ himself. Rejecting Jesus means you are not one of his disciples because you can only be one of his disciples if you believe what we are preaching to you about his returning invisibly in 1914, and appointing us to have charge of all his earthly interests. *Let God Be True* put it this way:

> This clearly shows that the Lord would use *one* organization, and not a multitude of diverse and conflicting sects to distribute his message. The "faithful and wise servant" [Matt. 24: 45 *AV*] is a company following the example of their Leader. That "servant" is the remnant of Christ's spiritual brethren. . . From and after A.D. 1914 this "servant" class have delivered God's message to blinded "Christendom" still feeding on the religious traditions of men. The truth so proclaimed does a dividing work, as foretold, the ones accepting the truth being taken to the Lord's side, and the others left.—*Let God Be True*, 1946 ed., Page 189. (italics not in original)

I was more than open to accepting such teachings. I was eager to accept them. They filled me with a sense of meaningful pleasure and personal importance. Here I was, living in the very moment of time when all the grand purposes of the living God and his kingdom were reaching their fulfillment! I had this wonderful opportunity to serve under God's appointed "faithful and wise servant," and enjoy divine favor. What a magnificent time in which to live and have a share in the never-to-be-repeated work of dividing the nations—either for everlasting life on a paradise earth or for everlasting destruction at the battle of Armageddon! What made matters even more dramatic was that the time allotted for this dividing work was nearly ended! Time was rapidly running out for Satan and his world—his organization! Very soon now God would execute his judgments against an unbelieving world and his people, Jehovah's Witnesses, would be the only ones to survive into a cleansed "new heavens and new earth." What a time to be living! What a wonderful, fulfilling work in which one had the opportunity to share in the short time before Armageddon.

Suddenly, all the things my mother had talked about when I was a child came together to form a coherent pattern. I began to experience the transforming power of conviction. The urgency of the times could not be greater. The eternal destiny of people—the whole world—was at stake and time was rapidly running out. Those who had been privileged to come into association with Jesus' "faithful and wise servant" were morally and scripturally obligated to inform and warn everyone of the imminent danger and escape the rapidly approaching storm of Armageddon. Note how the matter was presented to me in the book:

> The destiny of all people living will *shortly* be determined. "For the Son of man shall come in the glory of his Father with his angels; and then he shall reward every man according to his works." (Matthew 16: 27) The final revelation of the King *draws near.* The disaster of Armageddon, greater than that which befell Sodom and Gomorrah, is *at the door. . .*Acceptance of the despised King and his kingdom is the only security for anyone.—*Ibid*, page 194. (italics not in original)

Once I accepted the teaching that Jesus Christ returned invisibly in 1914 everything else fell into place. Obviously, the Witnesses of Jehovah were the only ones preaching this truth, because they were the only ones who knew this! Building on this premise, it was also clear that those who refused to believe this truth must not be fitted for God's kingdom by Christ. That Jehovah God had revealed that 1914 was the *starting date* for the establishment of God's kingdom and the *beginning* of the generation that would live to see the end of the world, was quite remarkable to me. Concerning this, I read:

> The birth of the kingdom has been given wide publicity. As far back as 1884, under the Lord's direction, Jehovah's witnesses proclaimed, among other Bible truths, the importance of 1914.—*Ibid.*, pages 249, 250.

> So close was the world to its end, the book said: "Unbelievable as it may sound, many of these "other sheep" [earthly heirs of God's kingdom, including me!] *may never die.* They were foreshadowed by the family of

Noah, who, because of their faith and righteous works in the midst of a corrupt world, passed alive, with Noah, through the flood. . .Continuing faithful till Armageddon, the "other sheep" who seek meekness and righteousness, like the flood survivors of Noah's day, shall be hid in the antitypical ark, *God's organization*, and come through into an earth cleansed of evil."—*Ibid,* pages 260,261. (Italics not in original)

The 1914 date was the only date given currency in the book. It was clearly set forth as a date marked in Bible prophecy and only understood by the Witnesses as marking the end of the "Gentile times" and the birth of God's theocratic kingdom. To read that as early as 1884 they had proclaimed the importance of that future date was very impressive. Historically, 1914 marked the beginning of World War I, and that war was cited as proof that the beginning of travail Jesus forecasted in Matthew 24 began in that year. That the leaders of the WBTS had known these things decades before 1914 further confirmed my conviction that God had really chosen this group of people to serve as Jesus' "faithful and wise servant," to carry this kingdom message to the world. The desire to be identified with these people and share in the final phase of that grand worldwide witness took me captive. For the first time in my life I found a cause greater than myself—more important than self. Prior to this I was the center of my universe. I had no deep moral sense to guide my life. Now, I found the greatest of causes—God's cause in Christ Jesus! My life would never be the same. The importance of sharing in the proclamation of the timely message about Jehovah's kingdom began to consume me.

A personal benefit that came to me from becoming a Jehovah's Witness was the regimen of meetings (five each week), public witnessing and personal Bible study that required considerable discipline and the management of time. This was another area in which I was lacking. Moreover, these new moral and religious demands insisted that I break off certain associations and activities. While Mavis was well organized and possessed self-discipline, I needed an outside influence like the highly structured Watchtower system to make better use of my time. I welcomed the structured demands of that system. I never felt burdened by them. I recall thinking that every meeting I prepared for and attended was another step away from the old world in which I had wasted so much of my youth. I now had an enthusiasm for every aspect of life as one of Jehovah's Witnesses.

New friendships were being formed with those who shared my faith and strong desire to see Jehovah's name vindicated. I immersed myself in this organizational life. It was during this life-altering moment that I adopted certain values and a particular world view that has remained with me for a lifetime. Caught away with the majesty of the most high God Jehovah, and his anointed king Jesus Christ, I was taken captive to serving my God and my king. While the time would come when I could no longer live out that Christian quest as one of Jehovah's Witnesses, the flame that was ignited during that time has never burned out. There was a maxim presented in *Let God Be True,* taken from the Bible, that resonated with me in a powerful way and which I have never forgotten. From then until now I have tried to live by its guidance.

> To arrive at truth we must dismiss religious prejudices from heart and mind. We must let God speak for himself. Any other course would lead only to further confusion. What if men, religious and non-religious, have discredited and belittled the Bible and have placed their own or other men's opinions and traditions above the Bible? What if religious leaders have rejected the Bible's straight testimony? What if the highly esteemed clergy of "Christendom" have been found false and misleading? Do these shocking and disappointing facts change the Bible itself or its message of truth? Sound thinking assures us that the true and living God must have given searching mankind some inspired written revelation about Himself. That being so, then let our stand be that of one of the writers of the Bible who said: "What if some were without faith? Shall their want of faith make of none effect the faithfulness of God? God forbid: yea, LET GOD BE FOUND TRUE, but every man a liar; as it is written, That thou mightest be justified in thy words, and mightest prevail when thou comest into judgment." —*Ibid,* pages 8, 9.

I found this reasoning compellingly sound and worthy of acceptance. It etched itself into my consciousness. It became my mantra.. I accept its logic today as thoroughly as I did then. Little did I know that the day would come when the very principle articulated in the apostle Paul's words found in Romans 3: 3, 4 and enlarged upon in the above quotation would force me to reexamine the building blocks of my faith structure and force me to walk away from the religious organization and way of life that I deeply loved and in which I had invested the better portion of my fortune, my strength and my life.

Chapter 6

A
Life of
Ministry: Part I

By the close of 1948 I had become convinced that we were living in the final days of the "time of the end," that period of time between Christ's invisible return in 1914 and the end of the world in the war of Armageddon. That was how the matter was presented to us by the Watchtower Society. We breathed the air of urgency and expectation. It was not the time to be making plans for a future in a world about to be utterly destroyed. Very soon the whole world would be engulfed in flames. Planning for a future in this world was utter foolishness! The desire to spend those few remaining years in evangelical ministry became my preoccupation. I recall working at my drawing board in the art department of the company I worked for and thinking: "The world is coming to an end and I am drawing pictures." It seemed ludicrous to me.

My view of the world situation was not simply the product of my imagination. The urgency was coming from God's organization—his officially appointed servant entrusted with the final warning to be given to humanity. The persons writing the provocative articles that appeared in *The Watchtower* and other publications were personally unknown to us as no credits were ever given in those publications. We were taught that Jehovah God was using the Watchtower organization as his exclusive channel of communication and whatever appeared in its publications was produced under the direction of God's Spirit. Such direction was not to be taken lightly. What was written was "food in due season," as far as Jehovah's Witnesses were concerned. I was drinking deeply from that well of thought.

In the summer of 1949 we attended a district convention of Jehovah's Witnesses in Sioux Falls, South Dakota. It was there that we heard strong encouragement to enter the full time work. Those who contracted with the Watchtower Society to devote at least 100 hours each month to the public witnessing activity were called "Pioneers." I came home from that convention determined to get into the pioneer work. We had just settled into a home we had contracted for under the G.I. Bill. As a former serviceman I had been entitled to a low interest home loan. I had also attended a commercial art school under the same bill and was working in the advertising department of a wholesale grocery chain, Fairway Foods. Now, in 1949 our settled life was about to be changed in a profound way. It was a change that Mavis did not desire. She was inclined to be a homebody and live a balanced life. It was my persistence and her dutifulness that held the day. As I write this I realize how unwise it was of me to contemplate disrupting our lives so dramatically at this point in our marriage, but at the time I was convinced that only a relatively few years remained before the holocaust of Armageddon. My religious teachers had convinced me of that urgency.

Mavis did not share my enthusiasm for selling our home and moving into a small trailer. She was content to do what she could as a regular publisher. "Publisher," which was the in-house term used to identify anyone spending some time in public witnessing each month. But once the decision was made by me that pioneering was what we ought to do, she cooperated fully. She felt obliged to acquiesce to my decision because of the strong emphasis on male headship she had been taught. And while Mavis was not enthusiastic about contemplating this new way of life, once we entered it she was a fortress—making due with very little and never complaining. She selflessly set aside her personal desires and needs out of her belief that God would have her subject herself to her husband's religious leading. Without her cooperation and sacrifice we never would have been able to spend our many years in full time ministry.

Our Congregation Servant, the title used at the time to identify the principle leader of a local congregation, August Vogel, had done the pioneer ministry with his wife, Inez, and their only child, Carol. They lived in a trailer home August had built which was parked behind our Kingdom Hall on Hague Avenue in St. Paul. August was a carpenter and cabinet maker. I admired him as a Witness. He was an excellent speaker and teacher. Friendly by nature and endowed with a nice sense of humor, he became my mentor and role-model. I looked upon August and his family as the ideal Witness family. They lived a modest life and put kingdom interests first. That they had been able to pioneer with a child convinced me that we could also. Their daughter, who was several years older than Jamie, did not seem adversely affected by their austere lifestyle. To the contrary, she appeared to be a happy, outgoing, well adjusted girl. From the Witness point of view they seemed well balanced to me. This, too, made the idea of living in a trailer home more acceptable. I wrote the Watchtower Society inquiring about its opinion on subjecting our daughter to such a lifestyle with her parents serving full time in the ministry. They responded that it was a personal decision that we would have to make but pointed out that other couples with children had pioneered success-fully. There were members of our family who thought I was being un-wise, but I hardly heard what they said.

Late in 1949 we sold our house. We were able to sell it without a real estate agent and realized enough equity to have August build us a trailer. We moved in with my folks while it was being assembled in my parents back yard on Taylor Avenue. It was 8 feet wide and 22 feet long. And, as my wife often points out, that 22 foot measure also included the hitch! This provided a living space of less than 200 square feet. One end would serve Jamie, who was now four years old, with an elevated bunk bed and a clothes closet beneath the bed. The center housed a tiny kitchen and the other end served as dining room, living room and bedroom. A hideaway couch served as our bed. We ate at a table that folded down against the outer wall when not in use. This area was so small that the table could not be pulled up while the couch was extended into a bed. There was no toilet. This would be our home for the next 11 years.

Mavis and I lived in this tiny trailer for eleven years doing ministry work.

We moved into the finished trailer in De-cember of 1949. I re-member lying in bed looking at the light from our oil burning heater dance across the var-nished birch wood pan-eled walls and ceiling and feeling a deep sense of gratitude for our little home. I pondered with joyful expectancy what our future ministry in Jehovah's service would be like. I continued work-ing at Fairway Foods for some months, and Mavis also worked part time at a real estate and insurance agency. We remained parked in my parents' back yard, and they allowed us to use their bathroom.

The Watchtower Society arranged for an international assembly to be held in Yankee Stadium in New York, July 30 though August 6, 1950 titled: "Theocracy's Increase Assembly of Jehovah's Witnesses." We made plans to attend even though doing so taxed our meager resources. We didn't own a car at the time so we arranged to travel with another family and share expenses. Packed tightly in an automobile with several other people and driving several long hot days with no air conditioning was not comfortable, but it was a joy to contemplate the assembly. As we traveled eastward we were thrilled to see more and more cars displaying the special bumper sticker the Society had provided announcing the worldwide gathering. As we drove through the states of Pennsylvania and New York we encountered more and more such cars identified and a lot of waving and horn-honking went on. It was thrilling to see so many Witnesses converging on New York City.

The eight-day convention was remarkable in a number of ways. It was by far the largest assembly ever held up to that time and there were about 10,000 foreign Witnesses representing 67 countries in attendance. It was at this assembly that the Vice President of the Watchtower Society, Frederick W. Franz, delivered a talk on "New Systems of Things." In this talk he brought up the matter of the ancient Hebrew "princes" whom Rutherford had forecasted as "due any day now," 19 years earlier. Franz, given to dramatic flare, teased the audience that filled the stadium with the following words, forcefully delivered:

> Would this international assembly be happy to know that HERE TO-NIGHT, in our midst, there are a number of prospective PRINCES OF THE NEW EARTH? (*Jehovah's Witnesses in the Divine Purpose*, 1959, page 252. Emphasis in original.)

Delivered in an intense, high-pitched tone, the question sent shock waves through the massive audience that filled Yankee Stadium. One lady sitting near us got up and excitedly ran down an exit ramp shouting, "The princes are here! The princes are here!" Some heard him say that the long expected return of the ancient Hebrew prophets had taken place and they were now assembled with us in Yankee Stadium. He didn't say that. He only spoke of "*prospective* princes." He went on to explain that the "prospective princes" he was referring to were not the ancient Hebrew prophets but members of the present-day crowd of "other sheep," those prospective earthly heirs of God's kingdom who would eventually inhabit the "new earth." This was a tacit admission that their long-held expectation of the ancient prophets appearing on earth before Armageddon was now being set aside. No explanation was given for the change. They simply replaced the old view with a new one, a common Watchtower tactic.

It was at this international assembly, attended by over one hundred thousand Witnesses from around the world, that the Society released the New Testament portion of their Bible: *New World Translation of the Christian Greek Scriptures.* I recall the enthusiastic Witnesses hurrying to those locations in the stadium where hundreds of boxes of the new Bibles were about to be opened and sold. As they queued up, eager to be among the first to obtain the Bible, I remained seated, knowing that there was no need to rush. There would be Bibles aplenty. I silently thanked Jehovah God for it and thought that the best way I could show appreciation was to simply read it. I was developing a deepening love and appreciation of the Scriptures. My religious teachers had done a good job of convincing me that the Bible, and the Bible alone, was the authority in determining divine truth. I never dreamed that the time would come when those very Scriptures would challenge the very foundation of my faith.

I began my full time ministry in August of 1950 on the streets of Manhattan. Never having been to New York, I was amazed at the size, tempo and contradictions of that great metropolis. The streets were like canyons flanked by soaring skyscrapers. One moment you would see upscale New Yorkers striding down an avenue, and the next thing you might see was a derelict huddled in a doorway. And here I was, a young, unsophisticated Midwesterner, standing on the street advertising *The Watchtower* and *Awake!* magazines and the convention to blasé New Yorkers. The incongruity of it all did not escape me. A young man, still in his teens stopped and spoke with me one day and ended up inviting Mavis, Jamie and me to his apartment where we met his mother. They were very kind and seemed impressed with our sincerity of faith. He was a violinist and played for us. We invited them to the assembly, and they did come one day. That experience has remained one of the most precious of the assembly for me.

By the time the eight-day assembly ended on Sunday, August 6, there were 123,707 Witnesses in attendance either in Yankee Stadium or in the temporary tent/trailer facility that had been set up about forty miles away. Because the stadium seating would not accommodate the vast numbers on the last day, the ground keepers allowed thousands of Witnesses to sit on the grass in the outfield. This was very unusual as the baseball field was meticulously cared for. By loudspeaker the ladies were asked to remove their high heels so as not to damage the outfield sod. As I watched this mass of men, women and children flow onto the field, my eyes filled with tears of joy. Later, As we stood and sang a closing song I gazed around the stadium overwhelmed with love for God and his people. My voice quavered with emotion as I joined with this great chorus in singing praises to the almighty God Jehovah.

Back in Minnesota I continued my pioneer service and worked part time at a variety of menial jobs: dish washer, gas station attendant and door-to-door shoe salesman. Within a few months Mavis also joined the pioneer ranks. Spending 100 hours or more every month in some form of public witnessing was difficult. Most time was spent making "cold turkey" calls going from house to house or standing on street corners displaying *The Watchtower* and *Awake!* Magazines, and conducting home Bible studies in one of the Society's books. While it was not overly demanding physically, one spent a great deal of nervous energy confronting residents and business people with our unique biblical views. It was common to engage several hundred people in the course of only a month. There were many who resented our uninvited calls, but most often people were simply not interested. I found this disinterest the most difficult attitude to deal with. Sometimes there were heated debates with those who felt equally passionate about their religion. The Midway district of St. Paul, where we conducted our ministry, had a number of Seminary schools and we often debated highly motivated students who attended these various schools. I was emotionally drained by these encounters. In many respects I was still a novice, having been fully engaged in the movement for only about two years before entering the full time service.

It was customary for men to wear suits while engaging in public witnessing, and I would put pads in the underarms of my suits to help absorb some of the moisture. The excessive perspiration was due to the emotional intensity generated by the ministry. In addition to this there was the time needed to prepare for the five different meetings that were held each week. Soon there came additional time consuming responsibilities in relation to leadership in the congregation. In 1951 I was appointed the Assistant Congregation Servant in the West Unit of the St. Paul Congregation of Jehovah's Witnesses. About a year later, August Vogel was asked by the Watchtower Society to serve the South St. Paul Unit of Jehovah's Witnesses, and I was appointed to replace him as Congregation Servant in the West Unit.

Looking back on that appointment I realize I was not ready for that kind of responsibility. I was only 27-years-old and had been active as a Witness only a few years. There were men in the congregation who had been Witnesses much longer than I had and were more seasoned and balanced than I was. At the time I viewed it as an appointment from God through his earthly organization and a confirmation that I was making the right choices in my life. I was convinced that God's Spirit went with the assignment and made me qualified to carry out the oversight I had been given. Without consciously thinking about it, I was rapidly becoming an organization man.

I was rigidly focused on following Watchtower directives and guidelines which urged more and more public witnessing. This emphasis was a dominant force in our tightly controlled religion. Each Kingdom Hall had a chart displayed at the front of the assembly hall that presented the number of hours spent by the congregation in public witnessing. The average hours per Witness were shown along with the number of return visits made on those who showed some interest in our message. The number of Bible studies conducted in private homes were also displayed. Each congregation had numerical goals in relation to these activities. These figures and the need to improve them were constant topics presented from the podium. This constant tress on increased activity and productivity was frustrating for many who were given the impression that no matter how much time and energy they devoted to the religion, it was never enough. The lock-step mentality of the Watchtower-directed way of life often resulted in failing to meet the individual needs and emotional difficulties various ones were experiencing in their lives. I live with a measure of sadness where I believe I hurt people by being too organizationally zealous and failed to meet their emotional and spiritual needs.

Yet, for me, those organizational demands were not oppressive. I viewed them as coming from God himself through his earthly servant— his organization. Gifted by nature with a certain ability to speak publicly and to teach, I found much personal satisfaction in the opportunities to further develop these native skills. I was outgoing and comfortable in large gatherings, something Mavis did not enjoy by nature. I enjoyed the casual banter and camaraderie that our close knit community exhibited. Mavis often reminded me that we were usually the last people to leave the Kingdom Hall after a meeting because I talked so much. That was true. I also enjoyed the organizational structure and self-discipline it forced on me. It filled a need I did not have by nature. I was grateful too, for the Bible-based moral standard the organization rigidly enforced.

Serving in the ministry as one of Jehovah's Witnesses was a perfect fit for me. The demands were great, if one immersed himself in every facet of activity, and I was often weary in both mind and body. But the cause to which I was dedicated was always greater than the demands and frustrations associated with it. I have often reflected on the fact that being a Witness was the only thing I believed I was ever very good at. As I was given more and more organizational responsibilities I viewed them as confirmation of God's blessing. Only later did I learn that the approbation of men does not necessarily mean approval by God and Christ.

The picture of these early years would not be complete without pointing out that Mavis and I enjoyed many good things as Witnesses. We enjoyed many wholesome pleasures in the company of honorable people. We were part of a close-knit, caring family and we enjoyed being a part of that family. Many close friendships were developed that were to last for a long time. The dedication of the Witnesses to their understanding of God's truth was true and complete. Our efforts were prompted by a sense of responsibility; if people did not hear the truth which only we possessed, how would they learn the truth? As for our material needs, we were seldom in serious want. Jesus said that if we sought first the kingdom of God and his righteousness our material needs would be met, and they were. I believed that then, and I believe it now. We both worked at part time secular jobs to support ourselves and our families and others helped us in various ways. Sometimes a fellow Witness would give us an article of clothing, food or money to help us remain in the full time work.

Ron, Mavis and Jamie Frye in 1952.

What made it possible to accept such help was the belief that it was God's way of providing the help he promised and that people were rightly motivated in their giving. One could say we were poor on purpose. We set aside certain financial security in order to pursue the ministry. I remember a pair of dress shoes I bought and wore only in the house-to-house ministry. One morning I noticed that a hole had developed in one of the soles and I had a sense of satisfaction knowing that I had worn that sole out doing the one thing I felt was the most important work in the world.

While in St. Paul we had an addition to the family. My parents thought it would be good for Jamie to have a pet so they bought her a chihuahua puppy. We named him "Slipper." He was a delight to us and brought much laughter into our little dwelling. Over time he decided his preferences in people. While he was friendly toward everyone, he had a distinct order of preference. If he was being held by Jamie he would go to Mavis or to me but never the reverse. If I was holding him he would not go to Jamie but would eagerly go to Mavis. If Mavis were holding him he couldn't be enticed to go to either Jamie or me regardless of how much we coaxed him. He had decided that Mavis was his mistress and no amount of arguing ever changed his mind during the fifteen years we had him. Slipper hated it when we went to assemblies and left him with others. It was common to see him sitting on an open suitcase, hoping, I suspect, that we would take him along. Mavis shared in his misery of separation at these times. One time she was talked into leaving Jamie with her mother while we traveled to an assembly. Mavis was miserable the whole time and vowed never to leave her again. She kept that vow.

After pioneering in St. Paul for about four years I had a desire to work in areas where there were no Witnesses. Such areas were called "Isolated Territory." My mother's sister, LuCretia, had served in just such an area in Pennsylvania a number of years earlier as a "Special Pioneer." Special Pioneers were required to spend a minimum of 150 hours each month in public witnessing. They could *request* a pittance of money each month they made their quota of 150 hours of public witnessing. I believe my aunt received $25.00 a month when she performed her Special Pioneer service in the 1940s. A report had to be filled out at the end of each month, verifying that the hour quota had been made, together with other quotas regarding magazine placement—magazines sold or given away—the number of Bible studies conducted, and how many individuals were baptized as a result of one's ministry. This report also included space where the Special Pioneer could request all or part of the current stipend being given. When Special Pioneers were ill and failed to meet their quota of hours in any given month, they could only request half of the current stipend offered.

Special Pioneers were usually sent to areas where there was no Witness population, oftentimes not even a family or individual. This meant that those who shared in this work would be cut off from fellow Witnesses for months at a time. As demanding as it was (my aunt LuCretia, had suffered a nervous breakdown as a result of her Special Pioneer service), I desired to enter that service. I spoke to Mavis about it, but she was not enthusiastic about taking on an even more demanding ministry. But, as usual, my desire took preference over her desire to remain where we were. Once again, she surrendered her wishes to mine. Another factor that would later prove significant was her physical health. She developed an ovarian cyst in 1953 that required surgery. She recovered quickly and we felt the problem was behind her. We later learned that it was not. We applied for Special Pioneer service, were accepted and assigned to Alexandria, Minnesota in April 1954. Jamie was just eight years old. Our little trailer home was made road worthy and towed to Alexandria by a Witness friend, Harold Shelley, and his wife, Elaine. Harold was an amiable man, gifted mechanically and always willing to give of himself in the service of others. We parked in Antell's Trailer Park in Alexandria. When Harold and Elaine said their goodbye's we experienced that sinking feeling that we were suddenly alone. There were no Witnesses living in the territory we were assigned which included several other small communities in Douglas County. A sudden spring snow storm greeted us the morning we started our house-to-house work.

It was a fulfilling assignment but extremely demanding. The additional fifty hours of witnessing each month that special pioneering required above the regular pioneering quota of one hundred hours taxed us to the limit. Trying to engage people in Bible discussion all day—everyday—while encountering general indifference and occasional hostility had the accumulative effect of draining one emotionally. Yet there were encouraging moments with people who showed respect for the Scriptures and the work we were doing. Over and above that there was the sense that we were touching people with the good news, as we understood it, who would otherwise not be hearing it. I remember standing at a door one sunny morning in summer and thinking that I didn't want to be anywhere else doing any other thing. We spent more than a year in Alexandria and managed to start more than 24 home Bible studies. But one by one, after a few weeks or months people would cancel the study or simply not answer the door when we came at the scheduled time. It was in the home Bible study arrangement that foundations were laid for people to grow into dedicated Jehovah's Witnesses. Our inability to sustain such studies long enough for thorough indoctrination and develop the nucleus of a congregation was the biggest disappointment of all. This disappointment was accompanied by a sense of having failed people in some way. We had approached our assignment with great expectations but our labors failed to produce the desired results.

We enrolled Jamie in public school where she was the only Witness. Her summer school vacation was spent at her mother's side in the house-to-house ministry. She would take things to read or entertain herself with in the back seat of our car. She endured this with a good spirit. Like her mother, she was not a whiner. She developed a friendship with the children of the Antell family that owned the trailer park and played with them from time to time. We had some recreation and we were visited once in awhile by family and friends. Sometimes we would make trip back to St. Paul to visit our parents. These were refreshing moments.

Being isolated meant that the regular meetings carried on in congregations of Jehovah's Witnesses were condensed and gone over by the three of us in the trailer. We learned that there was a man named Peterson in Alexandria who had a Witness background and we began to have him in attendance for our Sunday study of *The Watchtower*. Terribly deformed from birth, he was unable to walk or dress himself. He was a resident in a nursing home in Alexandria. I would pick him up there and bring him to our trailer each Sunday. I would have to carry him into the trailer. What made it more difficult was that he had a rather disagreeable way about himself. Apparently, he had been cast off by his family as too difficult to care for and I believe this had embittered him. So in addition to his deformed body he had a rather unpleasant, underdeveloped personality. I confess that his presence did little to lift my spirits. A feature of the witness work in those years involved standing on street corners in business districts offering people copies of *The Watchtower* and *Awake!* Magazines. We would pick up brother Peterson and put him in a wheel chair so he could join us from time to time in this activity known as "street work."

After several months of isolation we were so hungry for association with other Witnesses that we drove to Fergus Falls, Minnesota which was the closest congregation of Witnesses at the time. What a joy it was to be in their company. However, this represented a round trip of nearly a hundred miles and we could hardly afford the cost of the gas for our car. At the time we were each only getting $25.00 each month. If one of us was ill and failed to meet the quota of 150 hours for the month, we could only request half of that amount. I was ill with influenza in the winter of 1954-55 and Mavis had to work alone for a week or more. Also, Mavis began to experience health problems during the year. Prior to our going to Alexandria she had an ovary removed along with some cysts. We thought that surgery had solved the problem but now she was beginning to have discomforts that indicated that the problem had returned. A doctor confirmed that the cystic problem had returned and she would have to face another operation. This brought a very sad end our first Special Pioneer assignment In the summer of 1955. After a brief visit to Mavis' sister Laverne and her husband, Leroy in Kellogg, Idaho, we moved to Forest Lake, Minnesota. Shortly after this Mavis had a hysterectomy. The surgery was performed by her family doctor at Midway Hospital in St. Paul. She was only 28 years old.

Chapter 7

A
Life of
Ministry: Part II

The year spent in special pioneer service had proved much more diffi cult than we had anticipated. It had drained us emotionally. Perhaps if we had been able to establish the nucleus of a congregation during that time things might have been different, but as it turned out we had noth- ing to show for our efforts. The effects of isolation, coupled with the rigid demands of the special pioneer service, and Mavis' declining health necessitated that we resign from that ministry. We moved from Alexan- dria and parked our trailer on a parcel of land we purchased from the Axel Johnson family, Witnesses who farmed near Forest Lake, Minne- sota. From 1955 to 1957 we associated with the Chisago City congrega- tion which was the one closest to Forest Lake. It was a small group of about twenty or so, but it was good to be in the company of other Wit- nesses in an established congregation once again. After we had been there a few months the Congregation Servant, Vernon Klunder, asked to be replaced; I was appointed to replace him.

At the time of Mavis' hysterectomy neither of us fully appreciated the long term effects that surgery would have on her emotional as well as her physical health. The hormonal imbalance created in the process led to on-going problems that would have proved difficult even in the best of situations. A positive person by nature, she began in subsequent years to struggle with bouts of depression. Also, the demands of the full time ministry were contrary to her natural desires for a family and a stable living situation. She had the need for a more balanced way of life, one that would allow her to pursue her many homemaking interests and skills. While she had set those natural desires aside in order to follow her husband's leading, it forced her to suppress much of what made her the unique individual she was, and deny herself things for which she had a natural need and right. Dealing with the daily tensions brought on by the confrontational style of our ministry, the absence of economic stability and sense of place were difficult enough in themselves. But given the additional health related factors, the difficulty was greatly multiplied. The combination of these factors would lead not only to further health problems but contribute to serious difficulties in our marriage. But what is very clear now was not clear to me at the time.

What made matters worse was the collective thinking among the Witnesses that those who were spiritually mature would be energized by God's Spirit to meet and overcome any and all challenges to their physical, mental and emotional well being that the ministry might bring. A text often cited in this regard was Isaiah 40:29-31: "He is giving to the tired one power, and to the one without dynamic energy he makes full might abound. Boys will both tire out and grow weary, and young men themselves will without fail stumble, but those who are hoping in Jehovah will regain power. They will mount up with wings like eagles. They will run and not grow weary; they will walk and not tire out." (*NWT*) The poetic hyperbole contained in those verses, so common in Hebrew poetry to dramatize God's unlimited ability and power, was often taken in a literal sense by Jehovah's Witnesses. So those who grew weary and were unable to continue in full time ministry were often viewed as lacking the right spirit. Unfortunately, Mavis was married to a man who shared that point of view.

The reality was that she was forcing herself too much, which caused her to expend herself far more completely than I did. Lacking that insight, I failed to realize the toll the full time ministry was taking on her. I was also subject to the weariness, discouragement and frustration that sometimes came from such a demanding ministry, but I was not forcing myself in the same way she was. I *wanted* to do what I was doing. Mavis was doing it out of *obedience* to what she believed God would have her do as my wife. Her sacrifice of obedience was much greater than mine. Another problem was that the more tired she became, the less able she was to sleep. This further compounded the difficulties she experienced.

Despite the need to stop full time service temporarily, I remained strongly committed to the preaching the good news, as I understood that good news to be. In my mind it remained the most important work one could possibly devote his life and energy to. So it was that after a few months after moving to Forest Lake, I applied for and was accepted again as a regular pioneer. A few months later Mavis also re-enrolled as a regular pioneer. I did not urge her to reenter the pioneer service. That was her decision. And I think it pointed to the strong determination she had to overcome her difficulties and succeed in the full time ministry. She felt as I did that this was important work Jehovah God would have us do and she wanted to be succeed in it. I confess that I was perplexed as to why she struggled so with our lifestyle. I sometimes spoke of her as my "Enigma," because over time it had become clear that in many ways she had greater strengths than I had and more self-disciplined. She was always more productive than I was. For those reasons I found it hard to understand why she would develop more serious problems of endurance than I did.

While we associated with the Chisago City congregation it grew in numbers, and a new Kingdom Hall was built which led to further growth. We also had an unusually high ratio of people in the regular pioneer service. Several young people fresh out of high school entered that service with us. While I enjoyed the ministry there I still had a strong desire to evangelize in areas not regularly witnessed to. The Witness practice of calling on the same people over and over again every few months took much of the joy out of the ministry for me. The end of the world as we knew it couldn't be more than a few years off at most, and it made little sense to me to be continuing to call on the same people year after year who showed no interest in our message when there were people in other areas of the country who hadn't had the same opportunity. Having tested the nature of special pioneering I was not under any delusion as to how difficult an assignment that was. Despite this understanding of the demands it brought, I was still passionately determined to try it again.

When Mavis appeared well enough to consider a special pioneering assignment again, I wrote the Society's headquarters to let them know we were willing to be considered for such an assignment again. The Society accepted us and we were assigned to Redwood Falls, Minnesota in August of 1957. As it turned out, we would not be isolated this time. There was a family living in Redwood Falls in which the wife was a Witness but the husband was not. They had three small children. Some time after we located in a trailer park on the western edge of the city, a young, newly married Witness couple moved into Redwood Falls. Also, a young Witness whom we had known from St. Paul, Jerry Haller, moved to Redwood Falls. We had known him and his family from our earlier association in St. Paul. His parents expressed concern about his lifestyle and asked us to contact him in Minneapolis. We did that and encouraged him to join us in Redwood Falls. Mavis had also invited a young girl, Geraldine Johnson, who had just graduated from high school in Forest Lake, to join us in the full time service as a regular pioneer. She was the oldest daughter of Alex and Margaret Johnson, from whom we had purchased the land where we parked our trailer. She lived with us for about two years. Jamie, who was now twelve years old, shared her bed and small quarters with Geraldine, without complaint.

Having other Witnesses to associate with made this assignment considerably more pleasant than the previous one. However, the responsibilities proved greater. Redwood Falls was assigned to the Olivia, Minnesota congregation of Jehovah's Witnesses and we were asked to support that congregation. So in addition to the 150 hours Mavis and I were obligated to spend in the ministry each month, there was the matter of

Ron, Mavis and Jamie at an Assembly in Milwaukee in 1957

preparing for and attending the five one-hour meetings each week—four of which required driving to Olivia, 20 miles north of Redwood Falls. Shortly after arriving in our new assignment the Circuit Servant visited the Olivia congregation and recommended to the Society that I replace the Congregation Servant, Bill Kurtz. Brother Bill was a kindly man but not particularly aggressive organizationally; he didn't push the congregation as hard in public witnessing as the Society would have him do. I know he was hurt by being replaced, but he never showed any resentment. He and his wife Irene had us over for meals many times, and we enjoyed them and their four daughters. It was their oldest daughter, LaVonne Reese, who lived in Redwood Falls. The Kurtz's had a young man from Minneapolis, Billy Moe, living with them while he pioneered there for a time. A short time ago I was asking Mavis a few questions about this period of time and she reminded me that Irene Kurtz wouldn't allow her to bring Slipper into their house.

Mavis had additional loads as well. She prepared meals for the four of us who lived in our trailer. When Jerry Haller moved to Redwood Falls, she invited him to have his meals with us. Gradually, after a year or so Mavis began to develop emotional difficulties that gradually became more and more apparent. The more tired she became, the less she was able to sleep. It was not uncommon for her to continue working late into the night while the rest of us slept. Over time it took its toll. Also, having a young woman living with us in such cramped quarters was not good. After a couple of years we had to ask Geraldine to return home.

At one point in our service in Redwood Falls the Society sent us a daily schedule form that divided a 12-hour day into 30-minute segments. We were instructed to fill this schedule out so that every moment of that 12-hour period would be accounted for. It is my recollection that we were told that the Circuit overseer would go over those schedules with us during his next visit. It is but a sampling of the rigid, almost mechanical way we were expected to live by the Society. We were allowed a two week vacation each year, but one week involved traveling to a district assembly of 4-6 days each year. This left only one week of genuine vacation. We found that it took at least a week to unwind from the arduous demands of the ministry, but then it would be time to jump back into it.

As I write these things many years later, I realize I was idealistically trying to live out a lifestyle that was unsustainable over a long period of time. It took many years for me to realize that being a Christian minister was not a hundred yard dash but a marathon in which a person must pace himself for endurance. I bought into the false notion that the end of the world was immanent; warning people of that fact and proving myself worthy of surviving into the world to come, was the most important work one could possibly do. Living a life people would consider normal was unthinkable to me under the circumstances. Time was running out for me and the world. And this thought was not just my private view of matters: it was an attitude preached by the men I looked to for religious guidance. A quotation from *The Watchtower* in the year I started pioneering illustrates the point:

> This is the acceptable time for you to join the pioneer ranks. Never was the need for them so great, *nor the time so short* and the harvest to be reaped so plentiful. . . The day of Jehovah is far spent and the night of Armageddon is *very near*. Do not be caught napping and in a state of indifference towards those in bondage. Hear the call for more and more pioneers of good news. Feel the urgent need, and then respond! —*The Watchtower*, April 1, 1950, page 108 (Italics not in original).

The above was the concluding paragraph in a lengthy article regarding the urgency and the propriety of being in the pioneer ministry. Mavis and I responded to that "urgent need" because the organization convinced us that the remaining time before Armageddon was so short. We had been told that the *final* generation of the present age began in 1914 and *within* the lifetime of that generation the world would experience its destructive end. We believed that. The thought of devoting one's life to ordinary pursuits in view of the world situation as portrayed by the Society, seemed derelict to us. We were convinced that we would never live to see old age in this system of things. Armageddon would be here long before that. Frankly, I was personally critical of those Witnesses who lived normal lives and concerned themselves about old age and retirement. Despite the Society's constant urging to the contrary, most Witnesses did live ordinary lives. They held full time jobs, owned homes and raised families. Such people were really the strength of all local congregations. Pioneers could come and go, which they often did, but those stable families who put down roots and remained in place were the enduring strength of a local fellowship. Over many years I observed that those most hurt by the Society's false teachings and directives were those who took them the most seriously.

By 1960, the accumulation of difficulties experienced in our assignment, coupled with Mavis' growing difficulties necessitated a retiring once again from special pioneer service. We returned to Forest Lake and parked our trailer on the same plot of land that we had used earlier. By now the cramped living conditions of our little home had become unbearable. Jamie was now becoming a young lady and needed more privacy. In 1961 we bought a commercially built mobile home. It was 50' x 8' with two bedrooms, a living room, full bath, kitchen and hot water! It was like a mansion to us. Jamie, who turned 16 that year, finally had a real bedroom. It represented so much luxury to us that we felt a twinge of guilt. We lived a more normal life for a few years but the idea of returning to full time service never left my mind. I remember scheming in my thoughts as to how I might be able to pioneer yet again.

Ron and Mavis in 1959

Mavis found work in St. Paul at an insurance agency and she traveled there daily, a distance of about thirty-five miles each way. I worked at a variety of jobs. For a time I worked at a sign company in St. Paul, I drove school bus in Forest Lake for several years, and later worked nights at a screen printing company in St. Paul. In this way we managed to settle into a more normal lifestyle while remaining very active in the local congregation. Jamie graduated from high school in Forest Lake in 1964 and entered the pioneer service. In the summer of 1965 I was asked to serve as the director of News Service at a district convention of the Witnesses in Duluth, Minnesota, and Jamie accompanied me there to work as a secretary in the pre-convention advertising program. It was here that she met her future husband, Frank Sciascia. Frank was serving as a traveling Circuit Servant and had been appointed as a chairman of the convention. They were married that following December. Frank left the Circuit work and they settled in Austin, Minnesota where they both continued in pioneer service. Frank was appointed the Congregation overseer a short time after moving there.

In 1966 our visiting Circuit Servant sounded me out as to my willingness to be recommended to the Society for the Circuit work, now that our daughter, Jamie, was out of the home. I indicated to him that I would be interested in such an assignment. A circuit consisted of 18 to 20 congregations. A Circuit Servant was assigned to spend a week with each congregation on a rotating basis. During his visit he would deliver several talks, meet with local elders and pioneers, deal with problems presented, take the lead in public witnessing and assess the general health of the congregation and offer counsel where improvement could be made. A primary function of the Circuit work was to make sure that each congregation was implementing and enforcing Watchtower directives. At the end of the week the Circuit Servant would write an evaluation of the congregation and send it to the Society's headquarters in Brooklyn, New York. Circuit Servants were the eyes and ears of the Society.

I had long realized that circuit work represented the most sustainable form of full time service. The Society provided no salary or pension plan for any of its full time workers. Regular pioneers were given Watchtower publications at a reduced rate and allowed to keep the extra money they received from the public for those publications, but this amounted to nothing more than pocket change. Even Special Pioneers were given only a small stipend that hardly covered the gasoline their cars burned in the ministry. Only in the Circuit work was provision made—not by the Society, but by the congregations served. The congregations provided materially for the traveling servant and his wife. Another advantage in this ministry was the complete nature of it. One's entire schedule was taken up with "theocratic" activity. This kind of full time service appeared to be ideal to me and I coveted an opportunity to do it.

While one could write the Society and ask to be enrolled in the Regular Pioneer service or Special Pioneer service, the matter of being appointed a Circuit Servant was only by invitation. The Society's branch offices had the authority to appoint local congregational servants and enroll pioneers, but only the President's Office determined who would serve in the capacity of Circuit Servant. It was an appointment recognized among the Witnesses as one of importance. To have an assignment in which one directly represented the very organization God and Christ were using in the "last days" was most honorable. Also, I believed that my organizational experience and years of full time service had trained me for such a responsibility. We had raised a child in the faith and were mindful of the difficulties families faced in this regard.

While the Circuit Servant had sounded me out regarding circuit work, he never committed himself to whether he would make such a recommendation. However, there were enough signals in our conversations to suggest that he would do that very thing. A few weeks after his visit I received a letter from the Society inviting me to attend their Kingdom Ministry School located near South Lansing, New York. This school was currently being used to give local servants training to improve their congregational leadership skills. The school was part of a larger facility known as "Kingdom Farm," where much of the foodstuffs were raised to feed the hundreds of workers serving at the world headquarters in Brooklyn, New York. The school portion of the farm had been used for the training of foreign missionaries but that school had been moved to Brooklyn. The school in upstate New York known as Kingdom Ministry School consisted of two weeks of instruction for about forty men at a time.

I arrived there in mid-December,1966. The daily schedule included doing some form of menial work along with attending classes. While there I was privately interviewed by Albert D. Schroeder, one of the instructors. Schroeder was a well known and respected man. He had worked at the world headquarters for many years and had served as branch overseer in England during World War II. When the Society's missionary school (Watchtower Bible School of Gilead) was created in 1942, Schroeder was appointed the school registrar, a position he held for 17 years. In 1974 he was made a member of the Society's Governing Body. During my interview he inquired at length about our years of full time service. I was certain that the reason for the interview was for him to evaluate my qualifications in relation to the Circuit work and forward his opinion to the President's Office, although the prospect of Circuit work never came up in our meeting.

Based on the tenor of our conversation, I returned home at the end of the two weeks reasonably convinced that brother Schroeder would make a favorable recommendation to the President's Office. I was filled with expectation and joy at the thought. Mavis made no secret of the fact that she did not want to be in the circuit work. We had many discussions about that and I was persistent that she at least give it a try. I convinced myself that she could learn to have satisfaction in this ministry. Most Circuit servants lived in the homes of the brothers during their week-long stay. But a few lived in travel trailers. I suggested that we get a travel trailer. This suggestion appealed to her as living in different homes week after week did not. We would be taking our noon and evening meals with the brothers and sisters which would free her of the chores of meal planning and preparation. I truly believed that the circuit work would be far less demanding of her than the other forms of full time service we had pursued. I knew she would be an excellent confidant, someone I could trust and whose observations and insights would be helpful in deal-ing with people and their problems. I knew ,too, that she would be well liked because there was nothing pretentious about her. I begged her to at least give it a try, and if it didn't work out we could leave that service. She realized that I was consumed with the idea and would have been impossible to live with if she didn't say yes. She reluctantly agreed that if I was appointed she would acquiesce.

January and February came and went in 1967 with no communica-tion from the Watchtower Society. I remember "haunting" the mailbox day after day and coming away disappointed. Finally, in March we re-ceived a letter from the Society informing me that I had been appointed a Circuit Servant and we were assigned to a Circuit in upstate New York. I can't find the words to describe the joy I felt. The door had been opened to a form of full time service that could be comfortably maintained over a period of many years; that was my dream. Before traveling to New York we were assigned to work for two weeks with an experienced Cir-cuit servant in Minneapolis. The first week was spent observing him and asking questions as he did his usual work. The second week I carried out the Circuit Servant duties while he observed and offered helpful sugges-tions. This was the extent of the training we received prior to going to our assignment. I had expected to receive something like a "Circuit Ser-vants Kit," which would outline practical directives gleaned over many years to further equip one for this serious responsibility, but no such "kit" arrived.

We outfitted our travel trailer which was about the same size as the one we had lived in earlier. The Circuit we were assigned to ran from North Syracuse north along the eastern edge of Lake Ontario, and in-cluded cities like Oswego, Watertown and Massena, near the Canadian border, and east to the beautiful Adirondack Mountains and then south again. It was April and the weather was pleasant as we settled into our weekly routine. We were warmly received in every congregation we served. The faith that Witnesses had in the central organization and its administrative role found a natural outlet in accepting its traveling representatives and according them respect and honor. This respect was not earned—it was a given.

An experience I had in one congregation illustrates this point. In a meeting with the local servants I called upon an elderly bother to open our discussion with prayer. This brother was in his nineties and a member of the "anointed" class of Witnesses. In his prayer he asked for Jehovah's blessing on our meeting and he also thanked God for sending me to them. Here was a brother who had served faithfully as a Witness longer than I had lived, and he was thanking God for providing them with spiritual direction through me! I found that most humbling. It wasn't me personally that he was grateful for because he didn't even know me. It was the arrangement that I *represented* that he had in mind. However, I would be less than honest if I did not admit that I found such organizational respect most satisfying. I felt truly blessed to be serving in Jehovah's organization in such a responsible position. Being absorbed in working with local servants and ministering to them was a labor of love. The daily public witnessing work was easier to perform because it was scheduled and arrangements were made each day for us to work with different ones in the door-to-door work and go to private home Bible studies with them. In this way we could give training and pass on our years of experience in these basic functions of all Witness congregations. I found it most satisfying and fulfilling. Spending each week with different brothers and sisters, getting to know them, working with them, dealing with questions and congregational problems, having meals in their homes and enjoying light moments of fellowship, left little to be desired from my point of view. I was in my element. The circuit work was all that I had hoped it would be and much, much more. I was where I wanted to be, doing the work I wanted to do.

Mavis' experience was much different. She wasn't being stimulated by the constant interaction with near-strangers in the congregational settings. While she had excellent teaching ability and was comfortable communicating our message to total strangers, she was less comfortable in large gatherings of the Witnesses. Years earlier, when we pioneered in St. Paul, she often complained that I was usually the last one to leave the Kingdom Hall. She would sometimes go to the car and wait for me there. Now, in the circuit work, the need to mingle with others after the meetings became a necessity for her because of who she was. Because doing these things seemed so natural to me I never appreciated how difficult they were for her and the accumulative toll such things took on her ability to cope.

I remember some of the stories she told about herself as a child which may give a clearer picture of Mavis' personality. She grew up near a little community known as Marine-on-the-St.Croix on the Minnesota side of the St.Croix River that separates Minnesota and Wisconsin. She attended a little country school about a mile from her home. While the other children would bring their lunches to school, Mavis would walk home each noon to eat her lunch with her mother rather than be with the other children. She said she liked school but she didn't enjoy the other children. Another story she told was of being offered a summer job when she was about 13-years-old. Her parents were too poor to buy her a bicycle and this summer job presented an opportunity to save up for a bicycle. Farm friends of her mom and dad sold vegetables at a roadside stand and they hired Mavis to work the stand. As it was a considerable distance from home she was to live with these folks during the weeks she clerked at the stand. She stayed one day and got so homesick she had to quit the job and forego the bicycle. So as a small child she had a very restrictive comfort zone. Even for a more gregarious person, the constant association could become a strain at time. I know I looked forward to Monday each week as that was the one day we had some measure of privacy. Because of her personality, her difficulty in these matters was much greater.

It is common for a Circuit servant to remain in the same circuit for several years; visiting the same congregations a number of times. Mavis looked forward to the second round of visits to the congregations which she felt would be easier for her. She kept a diary of names together with little descriptive observations of each one so that she could better relate to them on future visits. But this was not to be. We were barely through the circuit when we got a letter from the Society telling us we were being reassigned to a different circuit in New York which took us further into the Adirondack mountains that bordered the state of Vermont. It came as a serious blow to her expectations. She would have to integrate herself into another 18-20 congregations of strangers.

There was one thing about the circuit work that pleasantly surprised her. For some reason she had the feeling that no one would like her. She was wrong. People fell in love with her, and for good reason. Mavis did not have an "attitude." She was not impressed with herself or the fact that her husband was the Circuit Servant. As a consequence she didn't act the part of "first lady" in the circuit. She was simply herself and she was loved for her unassuming honesty and lack of pretentiousness. She was also effective in the ministry and gave good advice when asked for. Her years of pioneering had honed skills that were seldom matched by others. She sold (Witnesses would say "placed" rather than sold) many more Watchtower magazines and books than I ever did. When there was a campaign to obtain subscriptions to *The Watchtower* or *Awake!* magazines, she would always more than double the number that I would get. At one circuit assembly while we were in Redwood Falls the Circuit Servant had her pull, on stage, a coaster wagon filled with magazines which represented the hundreds of magazines she placed each month. One sister who worked with her in one of the New York circuits said, "She could talk a bear out of his fur!" In Rome, New York, one of the few congregations we visited more than once, two young ladies who were pioneering there, knocked on our trailer door one morning and when Mavis answered they literally pulled her out of the trailer and gave her enthusiastic hugs. Such spontaneous displays of affection convinced Mavis that she was liked for herself.

I especially depended on her because she was observant and discerning. She often saw things that I would miss. I also felt comfortable asking her opinion about a particular matter or situation to get feedback, knowing I could trust her confidentiality. I had hoped that she would become more comfortable in this particular ministry and she gradually did, but it was a matter of too little too late. By the winter of 1967 the stress Mavis was experiencing had completely undermined her ability to function. Some months earlier, a retired Witness medical doctor had given her a prescription for a certain drug that would serve as a stimulant. He probably felt she was going through a temporary phase of adjustment and this drug would help her through it. The drug did gave her a temporary high but then she found it difficult to sleep. So she had to take something to bring her down. This vicious cycle continued for some weeks and it became clear to me that this simply was not going to work.

I wrote two letters of resignation but Mavis talked me out of mailing them; she wanted to overcome her problems so I could remain in a work she knew was so important to me. But, by the end of the year it was clear that continuing in the circuit work was out of the question. In one of my phone conversations with the Society's Service Department head, Harley Miller, he suggested that Mavis fly back to Minnesota for a few weeks rest. Mavis wouldn't hear of it. I composed a third letter of resignation and mailed it. While I was genuinely concerned about Mavis' mental health, I was also dealing with the loss of something that was very important to me. Perhaps too important.

Chapter 8

The
Year
1975

Following the demise of our circuit work in 1967, we moved back to Minnesota and settled in Austin, where our daughter and her husband were living. Jamie's husband, Frank, was the Congregation Servant there and shortly after our arrival I was appointed the Assistant Congregation Servant. My mother and father were also living there along with my aunt LuCretia. In 1969 we moved to Owatonna, Minnesota where I was appointed Congregation Servant. Mavis continued to have serious emotional problems and descended into bouts of clinical depression which, at times, required hospitalization. It would be years before she would be able to take control of her life. Our relationship had suffered in the process of leaving the circuit work and this, too, took time to heal. I was resentful towards her for having to resign from the work, and she blamed me (rightly) for causing her to overdo and bring on her emotional problems. My self-pity and resentment for her inability to do what I wanted us to do, added to her difficulty to recover. Only later did I come to realize how selfish and unloving I was at the time.

I did accept the fact that full time service was no longer a practical reality. I decided that I would never again exert pressure on Mavis regarding the ministry. I would do what I was able to do and she could do what her limitations allowed. I still wanted to be as active locally as possible within the limits of my circumstances. Soon, that organizational zeal would be seriously challenged. It was during the winter of 1970-1971 that a casual conversation with a long-time friend, led to an investigative process that would forever change my religious convictions. To grasp the significance of that conversation, it is necessary to understand the background that led up to it. It takes in the years 1966 through 1975.

This period of time was especially dynamic for Jehovah's Witnesses. There was wide spread speculation among the Witnesses as to what the year 1975 would bring. This speculation was triggered by remarks made in the book *Life Everlasting in Freedom of the Sons of God*, published by the Society in 1966. The opening chapter titled, "Why Human Creation Will Yet Be Set Free," discussed the ancient Israelite law which decreed that any Israelite who had fallen on hard times and was forced to sell themselves or their ancestral property, could redeem themselves and their land inheritance during the year of Jubilee, which occurred every fiftieth year. (Lev. 25:8-17) Known as the Jubilee Law, the fiftieth year was also a sabbath year during which crops were not to be planted and what grew of itself was not to be harvested. It marked a year of liberation for those who had been forced to sell themselves into servitude to another Israelite. The book asserted that this ancient law was prophetic of what Jehovah God would yet do in the modern world. This was followed by a five-page chart which set forth a chronological timetable from Adam's creation to 1975. Based on the information presented it said:

> "According to this trustworthy Bible chronology six thousand years from man's creation will end in 1975, and the seventh period of a thousand years of human history will begin in the fall of 1975 C.E.—*Life Everlasting in Freedom of the Sons of God*, page 29.

Why would this appear significant to Jehovah's Witnesses? Watchtower teaching was that each of the six creative days mentioned in Genesis chapter one were 7,000 years long. Adam and Eve's creation concluded the sixth creative day. It was argued that the seventh day to follow would also be 7,000 years long. If true, this meant that we were still living in the seventh day. (Gen. 2: 2,3) The timetable provided by *Life Everlasting in Freedom of the Sons of God*, argued that the first 6,000 years of that seventh day would end in 1975. This would leave but one more 1,000 year period to fill out the 7,000-year-long Sabbath day of God. Why this was exciting news is made plain by the following quotation which presented the Society's view.

> There is, as we have seen, good reason to believe that the days of creation were each 7,000 years long. Now the fact that we are living at the end of six thousand years of the seventh "day" *is of greatest interest and importance to us*. When Jesus Christ was on earth, he performed many of his miraculous cures on the sabbath. To those who were offended by this he pointed out that he was "Lord of the sabbath." By this he was pointing forward to *the sabbath of a thousand years* during which he will bring back mankind to perfection of body and mind. He will do for all mankind

what he did for his people Israel back there. This will include even the raising of the dead, for "all those in the memorial tombs will hear his voice and come out."—*The Watchtower*, 1970, page 120. (italics not in original)

This understanding of the length of the days of creation, and that the last 1000 years of the seventh day of rest would correspond with Jesus' millennial reign, had been taught for many years prior to the publishing of *Life Everlasting in the Freedom of the Sons of God,* in 1966. In 1968 the matter was further reinforced by another argument presented in *The Watchtower*:

> According to reliable Bible chronology Adam was created in the year 4026 B.C.E., likely in the autumn of the year, *at the end of the sixth day of creation*. Then God brought the animals to man to name. . . Adam's naming of the animals and his realizing that he needed a counterpart would have occupied *only a brief time* after his creation. Since it was also Jehovah's purpose for man to multiply and fill the earth, it is logical that he would create Eve *soon* after Adam, *perhaps just a few weeks or months later in the same year,* 4026 B.C.E. After her creation, God's rest day, the seventh period, *immediately followed.*

> Therefore, God's seventh day and the time man has been on earth *apparently run parallel.* . . Thus, eight years remain to account for a full 6,000 years of the seventh day. Eight years from the autumn of 1967 would bring us to the autumn of 1975, fully 6,000 years into God's seventh day, his rest day.

> After 6,000 years of misery, toil, trouble, sickness and death under Satan's rule, mankind is indeed in dire need of relief, a rest. The seventh day of the Jewish week, the sabbath, would well picture the final 1,000-year reign of God's kingdom under Christ when mankind would be uplifted from 6,000 years of sin and death. (Rev. 20: 6) Hence, when Christians note from *God's timetable* the approaching end of 6,000 years of human history, *it fills them with anticipation*. Particularly is this true because of the great sign of the "last days" has been in the course of fulfillment since the beginning of the "time of the end" in 1914. And, as Jesus said, "this generation will by no means pass away until all these things occur."—*The Watchtower*, 1968, pages 271, 272 (italics not in original).

It was against this background of understanding that *Life Everlasting in Freedom of the Sons of God* was written. We had been taught that the generation that witnessed the events of 1914 would not pass away until the complete end of the world. That end would mark the beginning of Jesus' millennial reign and the transforming of the earth into a global paradise. So the idea, carefully outlined and argued for by the Society, fit nicely into this chronological scheme. You will note in the above that these things were spoken of in relation to "God's timetable." To be told that 1975 would end 6,000 years of God's rest day and that the final 1,000 years of that day would see the restoration of all things lost to the human family by Adam's disobedience, did indeed, fill the Witnesses with anticipation. The suggestion was presented in an almost titillating manner in the book.

> How appropriate it would be for Jehovah God to make of this coming seventh period of a thousand years a sabbath period of rest and release, a great Jubilee sabbath for the proclaiming of liberty throughout the earth to all its inhabitants! This would be most timely for mankind. It would also be most fitting on God's part, for, remember, mankind has yet ahead of it what the last book of the Holy Bible speaks of as the reign of Jesus Christ over earth for a thousand years, the millennial reign of Christ. Prophetically Jesus Christ, when on earth nineteen centuries ago, said concerning himself: "For Lord of the sabbath is what the Son of man is." (Matthew 12: 8) It would not be by mere chance or accident but would be according to the loving purpose of Jehovah God for the reign of Jesus Christ, the "Lord of the sabbath," to run parallel with the seventh millennium of man's existence.—*Life Everlasting in Freedom of the Sons of God,* page 30.

While the *Life Everlasting in Freedom of the Sons of God* did not specifically say the end of 6000 years of human history in 1975 would mark the beginning of Jesus' thousand-year rule, it provided all of the ingredients for the Witnesses to conclude exactly that. They argued that each of the creative days were 7,000 years long and Adam and Eve were created at the very end of the sixth creative day. Therefore, they concluded that the seventh day of 7,000 years ran parallel to mankind's time on earth. This meant that when 6,000 years of human history came to a conclusion in 1975 that would also mark the end of 6,000 years of the seventh day of God's rest. There would remain, then, according to their chronology, only 1,000 more years for God's day of rest to see the completion of his purpose for the earth. And that final 1,000 year period was to correspond with Jesus' 1,000 year reign by which God's purpose would be fulfilled. When such speculative reasoning was being given by the one looked to as Jehovah's spokesman to the world, such reasoning took on great significance.

Coupled with that was the corollary doctrine that the generation of 1914 would not pass away until all these things had taken place, including the end of the present world order. That the 1914 generation was passing away was pointed to as proving the remaining time must be short. So, the combining of Watchtower chronology in relation to the days of creation and 1914 as marking the beginning of the generation that would live to see the end of the world, provided a strong conviction in the minds of the Witnesses that the end of the world was only a few years away. This was not the view of a few radical Witnesses. This was the Society's view carefully cultivated through its official publications, one being a book published in 1968:

> But there are people still living who were alive in 1914 and saw what was happening then and who were old enough that they still remember those events. This generation is getting up in years now. A great number of them have already passed away in death. Yet Jesus very pointedly said: "This generation will *by no means* pass away until all these things occur." Some of them will still be alive to see the end of this wicked system. This means that only a short time is left before the end comes!—*The Truth That Leads to Eternal Life*, 1968, page 95. (Italics in original)

In this way the Society continued to pump up enthusiasm and expectation regarding what 1975 might bring. And while they did not flat out say that 1975 *would* see the end of the present world order, they did everything short of that to convince the Witnesses that it would. I personally found such talk disturbing. In the first place, I realized that the evidence for the 7,000-year creative day speculation lacked Scriptural support. I learned that fact the hard way many years earlier. While Mavis and I were special pioneering in Redwood Falls, Minnesota in the late 1950s we offered the public a book titled, *From Paradise Lost to Paradise Regained*, published in 1958. In this book the 7,000 year theory was presented as a settled truth. It was not presented as a mere possibility. It said:

> The time had now come to start getting the earth ready for the animals and humans that would later live on it. So a period began that the Bible calls the "first day." This was not a day of twenty-four hours, but was instead 7,000 years long. —*From Paradise Lost to Paradise Regained*, Page 10.

When speaking of the human creation at the end of the sixth day, the book added:

> It was near the end of the sixth creative day. This means that nearly 42,000 years had passed from when God said: "Let light come to be." Five creative days of 7,000 years each had gone by and now the sixth day was almost finished. The ending of his sixth day, or period, would mean

that God would stop making things for the earth. Therefore the Bible says: "And by the seventh day God came to the completion of his work that he had made, and he proceeded to rest on the seventh day from all that he had made." —Genesis 2: 2 *Ibid,.* Page 18.

One family that had purchased a copy of the book from me had their minister attend one of my return visits in which he asked me where the Bible taught that the creative days were each 7,000 years along? I used the Society's explanation of certain verses in the Bible to prove the point, but the reality was that such texts required a sectarian interpretation in order to make them say that each creative day was 7,000 years long. The more I argued for it, the more I realized I had a very weak case. The truth was that the Scriptures simply did not explicitly say how long each day was. I came away from that discussion resolved never to argue that point again. I was also forced to acknowledge to myself that I believed something not because the Bible taught it, but because the Watchtower Society taught it. That realization didn't shake my faith in the Society, but I realized for the first time that I accepted a teaching that the Bible was silent about. So, when I read *Life Everlasting in Freedom of the Sons of God* in 1966, I could not get excited about speculations based on the 7,000-year "day" theory.

It wasn't long after the appearance of the book in 1966 that Witnesses began talking openly about 1975 and the possibility of its marking the beginning of the Lord's thousand year reign. While we were in the circuit work in 1967 many were already convinced of what the year would bring. One example: the district overseer and I visited a Witness family not currently attending meetings. In the course of the discussion which was intended to encourage their getting back to attending meetings at the Kingdom Hall, the district overseer said, "We *know* that the kingdom will be here by 1975." I could hardly believe what I was hearing. Here was a man highly positioned in the organization touting 1975 as early as 1967! In fact, he and another brother who was serving the same assembly said that at the headquarters the speculation was that the end might come a year earlier (in 1974) because there were some factors present in relation to the Jewish calendar that argued for the earlier date.

As I served the congregations I counseled them against saying *anything* to the public about 1975. I realized that once people heard that date in relation to the possible end of the present world order they would assume that that was what Jehovah's Witnesses believed. Also, this assumption could lead to serious disappointment as well as generate wrong motives for serving the Lord. As we traveled from congregation to congregation I would include a quotation taken from *The Watchtower* that instructed being careful about what was said about what 1975 would bring. At a district assembly in Baltimore in the summer of 1966 the Society's Vice President, Frederick Franz, addressed questions about the date.

> At the Baltimore assembly Brother Franz in his closing remarks made some interesting comments regarding the year 1975. He began casually by saying, "Just before I got on the platform a young man came to me and said, 'Say, what does this 1975 mean? Does it mean this, that or any other thing?'" In part, Brother Franz went on to say: "You have noticed the chart [on pages 31-35 in the book *Life Everlasting—in Freedom of the Sons of God*]. It shows that 6,000 years of human experience will end in 1975, about nine years from now. What does that mean? Does it mean that God's rest day began 4026 B.C.E.? It could have. The *Life Everlasting* book does not say it did not. The book merely presents the chronology. You can accept it or reject it. If that is the case, what does that mean to us? [He went into some length showing the feasibility of the 4026 B.C.E. date as being the beginning of God's rest day.]
>
> "What about the year 1975? What is it going to mean, dear friends?" asked Brother Franz. "Does it mean that Armageddon is going to be finished, with Satan bound by 1975? It could! It could! Does it mean that Babylon the Great is going to go down by 1975? It could. Does it mean that the attack of God of Magog is going to be made on Jehovah's Witnesses to wipe them out, then Gog himself will be put out of action? It could. But we are not saying. All things are possible with God. But we are not saying. And don't any of you be specific in saying anything that is going to happen between now and 1975. But the big point of it all is this, dear friends: Time is short. Time is running out, no question about that."
> —*The Watchtower*, Oct. 15, 1966, page 631. (Emphasis not in original)

I read the above during my concluding remarks at each congregation in the circuit, especially emphasizing the sentence I underlined. But the "cat was out of the bag." And, while using a few words of caution, Franz made a point of concluding, "Time is short. Time is running out, no question about that." So from 1966 to 1975 there was a growing conviction within the Witness population that 1975 would see the beginning of Jesus' millennial reign.

Initially I was not critical of the Society for what it had postulated in the *Life Everlasting* book regarding 1975, but as I heard more and more Witnesses making plans with 1975 in view, I realized that the published information was fueling unsubstantiated hopes. I concluded that the Society should have known better. I was also surprised that so many Witnesses were convinced that 1975 would probably bring the end of things. I believed that we had grown beyond looking to dates, but I was wrong. It became common to hear many Witnesses talking more and more strongly about the world ending by 1975. I had more than a few discussions with various ones, including members of my own family, about my reservations.

At a circuit assembly in Minnesota in the winter of 1970-1971, an elderly sister whom Mavis and I had known from our special pioneering days, approached me and inquired about Mavis' health. I explained that she wasn't doing very well. She responded, "Well, she has only months to put up with that." She had calculated the number of months from the present to October 1975 but I don't recall the exact number. I said, "We don't know about that." She gave me an incredulous look and rather indignantly replied, "*Well*, you certainly believe *that* don't you?" I glanced at my aunt LuCretia standing by me and her expression told me she shared this dear sister's view. She was very concerned about my lack of faith.

It was this brief exchange, together with the increasing ground swell of conviction among the Witnesses that 1975 would mark the end of the world that prompted me to ask my long-time friend, August Vogel, also attending the assembly, what he thought about the excitement over the year 1975. His response to me was, "Ron, there was more reason to believe that 1925 was a significant date than to think 1975 is a significant date." His answer confirmed my reservations about the date but raised another question regarding the year 1925.

I had always been interested in the roots of our movement and read everything I could get my hands on that dealt with our history. In all of my reading I couldn't recall anything being said about 1925 being of some prophetic significance. So I asked him what was so important about 1925. He said it was explained in the book, *Millions Now Living Will Never Die*. His words piqued my curiosity. I knew we had that book in our library. Mavis' father died in 1953 and his widow, Lillian, had given us a number of his older Watchtower books. *Millions Now Living Will Never Die* was one of them. I decided that when I got back home I would read it. Little did I know that reading that book would shatter much of my confidence in the Society's biblical insight and integrity.

Chapter 9

A
Painful
Discovery

Returning home from the circuit assembly I got the book *Millions Now Living Will Never Die* and began reading it. It had been published in 1920 by International Bible Students Association of Brooklyn, New York, which was another corporation of the Watch Tower Bible and Tract Society. Its pages were yellow with age but still intact and easily readable. The arguments I was now reading sounded very much like the ones I was hearing currently. They had to do with the ancient Israelite law regarding the 50-year Jubilee observance that commanded the return of land lost due to misfortune and the release from servitude to another Israelite. This remarkable and loving provision guaranteed that no Israelite would suffer such losses in perpetuity. The Jubilee year was also a sabbath year. Besides the weekly sabbath there was a sabbath year every seven years. After seven of such sabbaths (7 x 7) or 49 years, there was to be on the 50th year, another year-long sabbath. It was this latter sabbath year that was designated a year of liberty and jubilee. (See Lev. 25)

The book argued that the ancient Jubilee arrangement in Israel was typical, that is, a shadow of things to come and due for fulfillment now in the early twentieth century. The book was attributed to Joseph F. Rutherford, second president of the Watch Tower Bible and Tract Society. The book was published in 1920 but much of what it contained had already been given in lecture form by Rutherford since 1918. The scheme set forth was that seventy Jubilee periods (70 x 50) was to transpire before the antitype or reality would take place. What that would mean for the world was clearly stated in the book:

> A simple calculation of these jubilees brings us to this important fact:
> Seventy jubilees of fifty years each would be a total of 3500 years. That

period of time beginning1575 before A.D. 1 of necessity would end in the fall of the year 1925, at which time the type ends and the great antitype must begin. What, then, should we expect to take place? In the type there must be a full restoration; therefore the great antitype must mark the beginning of restoration of all things. The chief thing to be restored is the human race to life; and since other Scriptures definitely fix the fact that there will be a resurrection of Abraham, Isaac, Jacob and other faithful ones of old, and that they will have the first favor, *we may expect 1925 to witness the return of these faithful men of Israel from the condition of death*, being resurrected and fully restored to perfect humanity *and made the visible, legal representatives of the new order of things on earth.— Millions Now Living Will Never Die*, 1920, page 88. (italics not in original)

On the following page this was added:

As we have heretofore stated, the great jubilee cycle is due to begin in 1925. At that time the earthly phase of the kingdom shall be recognized. . . Therefore we may confidently expect that *1925 will mark the return of Abraham, Isaac, Jacob and the faithful prophets of old*, particularly those named by the Apostle in Hebrews chapter eleven, to the condition of human perfection.—*Ibid*, pages 89,90. (italics not in original)

The resurrection of the Hebrew prophets in 1925 was to inaugurate the earthly phase or reign of God's kingdom by Christ. This was to result in massive benefit to the human family. It meant that people living in 1925 would be the first to benefit from this new, theocratic rule administered by the ancient Hebrew prophets. Those who responded in faith to this new earthly administration would have the blessing of continuing to live on the earth and never die—hence the name of the book: *Millions Now Living Will Never Die.* Jesus' words were enjoined to support this prediction:

Again he [Jesus] said: "Whosoever liveth and believeth in me shall never die." (John 11:26) Do we believe in the Master's statement? If so, when the time comes for the world to know, then they who believe and, of course, render themselves in obedience to the terms *have the absolute and positive statement of Jesus that they shall never die.—Ibid*, page 97. (italics not in original)

There was nothing in *Millions Now Living Will Never Die* to suggest that this remarkable prediction was merely a suggestion or possibility. Rutherford wrote with great conviction and, for those associated with him, with great authority. The dramatic declaration quoted below drove home the summary of 97 pages devoted to constructing Rutherford's prophetic utterances:

> Based upon the argument heretofore set forth, then, that the old order of things, the old world, is ending and is therefore passing away, and that the new order is coming in, and that 1925 *shall mark* the resurrection of the faithful worthies of old and the beginning of reconstruction, it is reasonable to conclude that millions of people *now on the earth* [in 1920] will be still on the earth in 1925. Then, based upon the promises set forth in the divine Word, we *must reach the positive and indisputable conclusion* that millions now living will never die.—*Ibid.* Page 97. (italics not in original)

I was not prepared for what I found in *Millions Now Living Will Never Die.* I was shaken by what I read. I knew, or thought I knew, that some mistakes in understanding of God's Word had been made in the past regarding what the end of the gentile times would bring in 1914, but those mistakes were said to be minor in significance and were not repeated. Yet now I was forced to realize that only six years after 1914 (actually only four years if you consider Rutherford's lectures on the topic beginning in 1918) they were again advancing a date:1925. The emphatic conclusion published was that "1925 shall mark the resurrection of the faithful worthies of old and the beginning of reconstruction." The matter was not presented as a mere possibility. After 1925, when the date failed to produce what was predicted, it would be said that what was stated in the book was only a "suggestion." Those who put their confidence in Rutherford's prediction and were stumbled by its failure would be accused of reading into the book more than it had said. This "blaming the victim," I gradually learned, was a hallmark of Watchtower apologetics.

Since 1948 I had had a deep interest in our organizational past and read with keen interest those articles in *The Watchtower* and kindred publications that discussed our history as God's people. I had been told about Charles T. Russell and what a fine student of Scripture he was. While never having read anything he wrote, there were, from time to time, brief quotations from things he had written in support of concepts appearing in current publications. He was credited with having restored biblical Christianity, and I had great respect for him.

In 1959, the Society published a history of Jehovah's Witnesses covering the period from 1870 to 1959. It was titled: *Jehovah's Witnesses in the Divine Purpose.* Having carefully read that history, I wondered why I had failed to take note of the great significance that had been

placed on 1925? How could I have missed that? To satisfy my puzzle-
ment I dug the book out and reread the time period between 1920 and
1925. I found the section that mentioned the *Millions Now Living Will
Never Die* book and discussed its value. The book presented a glowing
report of how successful the "Millions Campaign" was. The "Millions
Campaign" referred to the worldwide publicity and public distribution
of the *Millions* book. In connection with the "Millions Campaign" mention
was also made of another book known as the "Seventh Volume." Charles
T. Russell had written six books or volumes which detailed his theologi-
cal beliefs, and after his death another book was published which claimed
to be the posthumous work of Russell, and thus labeled the "seventh
volume." The actual title of the book was *The Finished Mystery*, which
was a commentary on Ezekiel and Revelation. It had been published in
1917.

> The Seventh Volume had been distributed extensively when the *Studies
> in the Scriptures* [what Russell's six volumes were collectively called]
> were still encouraged for use. Then in connection with the distribution of
> these publications a new work opened up that was called the "Millions
> Campaign." This was actually a public-speaking program beginning Sep-
> tember 25, 1920, designed to stir the attention of millions of people. It
> centered around the lecture published in the book *Millions Now Living
> Will Never Die*, published late in 1920. This was the lecture that Brother
> Rutherford had given for the first time February 24, 1918, with such ex-
> citing results in California. The book was also translated and published in
> Dano-Norwegian, Finnish, Swedish, French, German, Hollandish, Yid-
> dish, Greek, Arabic, Russian, Polish, Malayalam and Burmese.—*Jehovah's
> Witnesses in the Divine Purpose,* 1959, page 98.

A glowing report is presented about how wonderfully successful
the "Millions Campaign" had been:

> The campaign lasted a couple of years. In addition to distributing the
> 128-page *Millions* book, large billboard advertisements were erected in
> all the big cities with streaming letters, "Millions Now Living Will Never
> Die." Newspaper advertisements were used also. This campaign of ad-
> vertising was so extensive that this spectacular slogan almost became a
> byword, and many persons we meet today [in 1959] still recall this cam-
> paign." —*Ibid*, page 98.

No mention was made anywhere in the book regarding the *message*
contained in *Millions Now Living Will Never Die.* I now understood
why the year 1925 had not made an impression on me when I first read
Jehovah's Witnesses in the Divine Purpose, back in 1959. They totally

ignored the contents of the book and Rutherford's prediction regarding 1925. Now I was presented with another disappointment, namely, that the Society was not completely forthcoming about its past. This lack of editorial candor shattered another confidence that I had which was that the Society readily acknowledged any mistakes they may have made. Instead, this *official* historical overview glossed over Rutherford's prediction. The vast majority of Witnesses reading *Jehovah's Witnesses in the Divine Purpose* in 1959, would have no knowledge of or even access to *Millions Now Living Will Never Die*. If I hadn't had that chance conversation with August Vogel in the winter of 1970-71, I would probably never have read the *Millions* book. Despite the fact that nothing that Rutherford dogmatically argued for in the book ever happened, notice what they had to say about it:

> From 1922 through 1925 Jehovah God helped his people to wait or endure, carrying on his kingdom preaching on a widening scale. This resulted in bringing into the sanctuary many more to be members of this remnant consecrated by Jehovah. This was evident from the increasing attendance at the annual celebrations of the Lord's evening meal, 32,661 participating in1922; 42,000 in 1923; 62,696 in 1924; and 90,434 in 1925.
>
> Evidently, however, there were some who did not "wait" with the Lord's faithful remnant. In 1926 there was a reported decrease in the attendance on March 27 at the Lord's evening meal to 89,278. *The year 1925 especially proved to be a year of great trial to many of Jehovah's people. Some stopped waiting and went with the world.* Those who did survive this *critical time* were happy indeed with the blessings Jehovah had in store for them from May, 1926, forward.—*Ibid.* Page 110. (italics not in original)

I found this evaluation of matters quite remarkable. Great increases were being shown from 1922 to 1925 and then suddenly, for no reason at all, "some stopped waiting and went with the world." Why? It is said to have been a "critical time." Why? No mention is made about the fact that 1925 failed to produce that which had been boldly predicted as "positive and indisputable." The great drum-roll of the hyped slogan, "millions now living will never die," faded into shameful silence. It is little wonder that many lost confidence in Rutherford as a true prophet of God. That the Society would blame the victims in this instance, was another blow to my perception of the organization. Reading of the growth that took place with 1925 in view, reminded me of what was now taking place—unusual growth taking place with 1975 in view.

The vast majority of those Witnesses who read *Jehovah's Witnesses in the Divine Purpose* were, like myself, ignorant of what had been written in *Millions Now Living Will Never Die,* and this ignorance provided the Watchtower Society with editorial immunity to present matters as they did. When I first read about the Society's publishing history in *Jehovah's Witnesses in the Divine Purpose*, I had no reason to question its veracity. Now, I was learning something different. Their presentation of *Millions Now Living Will Never Die*, was clearly dishonest—no other word fits.

Was this an aberration—an anomaly, that never happened before? This question naturally suggested itself to me. Were there other facts in the Society's history that had been misrepresented to me? How much did I *really know* about Charles T. Russell and what he taught? Virtually nothing. I decided that I owed it to myself and to my God to find out. My father-in-law had copies of Russell's *Studies in the Scriptures* that had also been given to us, so I decided that I would read them and find out first hand what he had to say.

I was not prepared at this point to walk away from an organization and a doctrinal concept that I had believed and preached for more than twenty years. I had invested all that I had to offer in the way of time and effort to this movement that I truly loved and admired. I had many friends whom I loved dearly who were also Jehovah's Witnesses. My wife and daughter and her family, my mother and her sisters were all Witnesses. My whole social structure—my world—revolved around this religion. Moreover, I did not want to believe that I had been misled and had misled others. Yet, I had discovered something that put it all into question.

Would I now allow fear of discovery prevent me from making a closer examination of those things I had been carefully taught? Would the loving thing be to ignore what I discovered? Would it be in the best interest of others to gloss over this error? I decided that the search for truth is neither unloving nor contrary to the best interests of anyone. On the contrary, one should have the courage to seek truth and follow it wherever it leads. Only error has reason to fear truth. I remembered the words that so impressed me in *Let God Be True,* regarding how we are to arrive at truth: "To arrive at truth we must dismiss religious prejudices from heart and mind. We must let God speak for himself. Any other course would lead only to further confusion." I always honored that view of matters. I tried to live my life in harmony with that principle. Now that principle was compelling me to test the truthfulness of those who first brought that principle to my attention. The irony did not escape me.

Chapter 10

One
Set of
Weights

In ancient Israel it was forbidden to have two sets of weights or measures: an honest one and a dishonest one. Only an accurate measure or weight was to be used in business transactions. (Lev. 19: 33,34; Prov. 11: 1) Until now, at the start of 1971, I had always given the Watchtower Society the benefit of the doubt in matters pertaining to Bible teaching. If I read something in their literature that didn't seem clear or well supported by Scripture I would always acquiesce to their explanation. I reasoned that they were divinely guided and knew much more than I did, so it would be presumptuous of me to question any of their conclusions.

When I read material published by other religion organizations, however, I did so with a critical eye. I would carefully critique everything—especially those teachings that contradicted what I had been taught to believe. In effect, I was guilty of using two different weights: one that lacked criticism, and another heavy with criticism. I now decided I should use but one standard of evaluation for *all* biblical exposition—including that produced by the Watchtower Society. My reading of Scripture seemed to support this conclusion. The apostle John had written: "Beloved ones, do not believe every inspired expression, but test the inspired expressions to see whether they originated with God because many false prophets have gone forth into the world." (1 John 4: 1 *NWT*) How could any one test such spirits unless they examined them in the light of the Scriptures? Another biblical injunction tells us to "Make sure of all things; hold fast to what is fine." (1 Thess. 5: 21 *NWT*) And speaking of the need to advance in scriptural understanding in order to mature as a Christian, the writer of Hebrews had this to say:

> For, indeed, although you ought to be teachers in view of the time, you again need someone to teach you from the beginning the elementary things of the sacred pronouncements of God; and you have become such as need milk, not solid food. For everyone that partakes of milk is unacquainted with the word of righteousness, for he is a babe. But solid food belongs to mature people, to those who through use have their perceptive powers trained to distinguish both right and wrong.—Hebrews 5: 12-14 *NWT.*

The ability to *distinguish* right from wrong means to perceive a difference, and a number of English Bibles use *discriminate* here instead of distinguish. To distinguish or discriminate one must examine something carefully in order to discern right from wrong. Such discrimination involves the ability to carefully analyze a matter; to look at it from various perspectives with the objective of determining what is true and what is untrue. Such scrutiny is absolutely necessary to the learning process. And as the above scripture indicates, we are *commanded* to exercise such scrutiny. This mental process works no harm toward those who profess to speak for God, nor does it reflect a disrespectful attitude. Only those who are arrogant or have something to hide would take offense if someone approached their utterances or writings in a discriminating way.

As a Jehovah's Witness I often urged people of other religions to compare their church's teachings alongside the Bible in order to arrive at truth. I didn't feel that I was doing anything wrong when I did that. To the contrary, I felt I was giving them good advice. And the Watchtower Society felt free to encourage non-Witnesses to carefully examine their religious organization's teachings.

> We need to examine, not only what we personally believe, but also what is taught by any religious organization with which we may be associated. Are its teachings in full harmony with God's Word, or are they based on the traditions of men? If we are lovers of the truth, there is nothing to fear from such examination. It should be the sincere desire of every one of us to learn what God's will is for us, and then do it.—*The Truth That Leads to Eternal Life*, 1968, Page 13.

Of course the above advice was not given to Jehovah's Witnesses, who were told they already had the truth. The advice above was intended for others. For a Jehovah's Witness to question something the Society taught and to make a critical examination of it would be considered presumptuous, ungrateful and unloving. But there was no exclusion clause in the excellent admonition presented above. The advice to examine "what is taught by *any* religious organization" in order to determine if its teachings are in harmony with truth or not, insists (by implication) that

Jehovah's Witnesses do the same. It is a matter of using but one accurate scale or measure. Something else I found encouraging in the above quotation was the statement: "If we are lovers of the truth, there is nothing to fear from such examination." Witnesses would agree in principle that this is true but in practice they would not feel free to critically examine their own belief structure because they have been conditioned to believe it would be wrong to do so. I had to overcome a considerable degree of organizational fear in order to continue the critical examination of my religious roots. Would I prove to be a lover of truth, or not? I decided that I couldn't allow the fear of man to hinder the search for truth.

I knew from my early indoctrination that Charles T. Russell was the founder of the Watch Tower Bible & Tract Society, and that his writings were accepted as revealed truth to those early believers known as Bible Students. I decided the best way to pursue my search would be to read his writings we had in our personal library. I spent much time in the two years following my discoveries about the "Millions Campaign" researching these volumes. I was amazed at the intricately detailed threads of thought he wove into his doctrinal schemes. Basically, he argued that the Bible contained a number of types and antitypes that determined the outworking of God's divine plan of restoration. These types and antitypes were linked to corresponding time periods that determined not only what would happen but also when it would happen. Russell concluded that he was living in the "time of the end," and that all prophesy regarding the end times would be fulfilled by 1914. Hundreds upon hundreds of pages were devoted to establishing these things and arguing for their accuracy. By combining chronology with Bible prophesy he was able to assemble an interlocking pattern that buttressed his dispensational theme. Frankly, I found his writings most impressive even though the outworking of world events proved him wrong.

Here is not the place to go into great detail about such things but a summary of them is important and will give the reader a general idea of Russell's teachings regarding the end of the present world. One book of his was titled: *The Time is at Hand*, written in 1889. It was the second book in *Studies in the Scriptures* series. This book set forth Russell's understanding of time features in relation to the end of the world. He calculated that 6,000 years of human history ended in 1872 A.D. The next 1,000 years, he said, would be the thousand-year reign of Jesus Christ. Russell calculated that Jesus Christ began this rule in 1874 when he returned invisibly to judge his church and the world. About this he wrote:

In this chapter we present the Bible evidence which indicates that six thousand years from the creation of Adam were completed with A.D. 1872; and hence that, since 1872 A.D., we are chronologically entered upon the seventh thousand or the Millennium—the forepart of which, the "Day of the Lord," the "Day of trouble," is to witness the breaking into pieces of the kingdoms of this world and the establishment of the Kingdom of God under the whole heavens.—*The Time is at Hand,* 1910 edition, page 33.

The "Day of trouble" that Russell here described was the forty-year period between 1874 and 1914. These forty years were viewed as the first years of Christ's millennial reign. They were but a part of a much larger time frame he called "The Time of the End." Concerning that larger time period he wrote:

The careful student will have observed that the period designated "The Time of the End" is very appropriately named, since not only does the Gospel age close in it, but in it, *all prophecies relating to the close of this age terminate, reaching their fulfillments.* The same class of readers will have noticed, too, the special importance of the last 40 of those 115 years (1874-1914) called "The End" or "Harvest."—*Thy Kingdom Come,* 1917 edition, age 121. (italics not in original)

Russell was not timid about asserting that this 115-year period called "The Time of The End" would see the close of the present age. Nor was he vague about how the year 1914—the final year of the 115-year period (1799-1914)—would conclude. He wrote:

In this chapter we present the Bible evidence proving that the full end of the times of the Gentiles, *i.e.,*the full end of their lease of dominion, will be reached in A.D. 1914; and that that date will be the farthest limit of the rule of imperfect men. And be it observed, that if this is shown to be a fact firmly established by the Scriptures, it will prove:

Firstly, That at that date the Kingdom of God, for which our Lord taught us to pray, saying, "Thy Kingdom come," will obtain full, universal control, and that it will then be "set up," or firmly established, in the earth on the ruins of present institutions.

Secondly, it will prove that he whose right it is thus to take the dominion will then be present as earth's new Ruler; and not only so, but it will also prove that he will be present for a considerable period before that date; because the overthrow of these Gentile governments is directly caused by his dashing them to pieces as a potter's vessel (Psa. 2: 9; Rev. 2: 27), and establishing in their stead his own righteous government.

Thirdly, It will prove that some time before the end of A.D. 1914 the last member of the divinely recognized Church of Christ, the "royal priesthood," "the body of Christ," will be glorified with the Head; because every member is to reign with Christ, being a joint-heir with him of the Kingdom, and it cannot be fully "set up" without every member.

Fourthly, It will prove that from that time forward Jerusalem shall no longer be trodden down of the Gentiles, but shall arise from the dust of divine disfavor, to honor; because the "Times of the Gentiles" will be fulfilled or completed.

Fifthly, It will prove that by that date, or sooner, Israel's blindness will begin to be turned away; because their "blindness in part" was to continue only "*until* the fulness of the Gentiles be come in" (Rom. 11:25), or, in other words, until the full number from among the Gentiles, who are to be members of the body or bride of Christ, would be fully selected.

Sixthly, It will prove that the great "time of trouble such as never was since there was a nation," will reach its culmination in a world-wide reign of anarchy; and then men will learn to be still, and know that Jehovah is God and that he will be exalted in the earth. (Psa. 46:10)

Seventhly, It will prove that *before that date* God's Kingdom, organized in power, will be in the earth and then smite and crush the Gentile image (Dan. 2: 34)—and fully consume the power of these kings. Its own power and dominion will be established as fast as by its varied influences and agencies it crushes and scatters the "powers that be"—civil and ecclesiastical–iron and clay. —*The Time is at Hand*, 1910 edition, pages 76-78. (Italics in the original)

In view of this strong Bible evidence concerning the Times of the Gentiles, *we consider it an established truth* that the *final end* of the kingdoms of this world, and the full establishment of the Kingdom of God, will be accomplished at the end of A. D. 1914.—*Ibid*, page 99 (italics not in original).

Not one of the seven things Russell postulated that the terminus date of 1914 would *prove* concerning his 115-year end times prophecy took place! The whole of it was like a series of dominos, with 1914 serving as the last domino. When 1914 failed to fulfill the promises made, it toppled, and with it all of the preceding dates and events associated with the 115-year prophecy toppled with it. The only date that could have provided empirical evidence of truthfulness—1914—failed to produce that evidence. Self-delusion came face-to-face with reality in 1914. Russell had been a product of the Adventist movement of the nineteenth century, and got caught up with his own importance as a prophet. He was critical of other Adventists who had concluded that the second coming of Christ would occur in 1844, a date set by William Miller and his associates. Addressing their error and contrasting it with his own views he said:

> Their attempts to apply prophecy to their false expectations often lead to twisting, stretching or whittling, according to the necessities of the case, in the endeavor to get all the prophecies to terminate at some one date. These friends should awake to their error in this direction; for one after another their expectations have failed, while we and they know that some of the prophecies they have used cannot be stretched into the future, but are in the past, and are now abandoned by them. They are fulfilled, but differently from what they expected, and they know it not.
>
> On the contrary, the prophecies here presented, and those yet to be considered, are unstrained, and without twisting or whittling. We simply present them as we find them in God's Word; and, having correct expectations from God's great "Plan of the Ages," it is easy for those seeing it clearly to note how the various prophetic chains fit to it and measure it. They mark it, some at one important point and some at another; and to such as see this much, this parallelism of the Jewish and Christian dispensations shows *and proves beyond reasonable doubt the correctness of all the others.—The Time is at Hand*, 1910 edition, page 244 (italics not in original).

Russell's certainty regarding his own calculations proved presumptuous. The outworking of history demonstrated that he was as much in error as were those he had criticized. As I read this official and published record I marveled at Russell's ability to weave all of his many arguments into a cohesive whole. I came to realize that because many things can be made to fit together in a comprehensive scheme of things, it does not prove that the scheme is correct. Of a more immediate and personal concern for me was the fact that the Watchtower Society had so blatantly misrepresented Russell's prognostications in relation to the year 1914. What had been taught in *Let God Be True* back in 1948, was a clear misrepresentation of the historical facts. Russell and his associates did not believe that 1914 would mark the *beginning* of end-time events. They believed those end-time events began in 1799 and would be fully consummated by 1914! The clear implication given in *Let God Be True* was that 1914 was understood to mark the *starting point* for the end-times. It was in this context that the chapter on "The End of the World" declared:

> The birth of the kingdom has been given wide publicity. As far back as 1884, under the Lord's direction, Jehovah's witnesses proclaimed, among other Bible truths, the importance of 1914.—*Let God Be True*, (1946) pages 249,250.

I now knew that statement to be grossly misleading. The importance attached to 1914 by Russell was totally different from what *Let God Be True* had implied. That none of Russell's predictions, including what was to happen in 1914, came true was made inconsequential. The obvious intent of *Let God Be True* was to impress the reader with Jehovah's Witnesses' prophetic vision. But in so doing they took liberties with the truth and misled people like myself. I was now, in the 1970s, being forced to acknowledge that my confidence in their spiritual insights and Christian character was unfounded.

Russell had taught that Gentile rule of the earth would completely end in 1914. Rather than acknowledging that this prediction was an error, the Watchtower Society came up with the novel idea that the Gentile nations reached the end of their *legal right* to rule the earth in 1914. So, from 1914 onward the Gentile nations would continue to have dominion over the earth and even grow in number, but their *legal right* to rule had officially ended in 1914. This tenuous interpretation allowed the Watchtower Society to salvage the 1914 date. They moved the year of Jesus' *invisible* return from 1884 to 1914 and started a whole new "end times" scenario.

As I was discovering what Russell really taught about these things, I was able to discern when current articles glossed over his many errors. The tactic used was not to overtly lie about the record, but to present only enough information to misrepresent the record. An example of this can be seen in the quotation from the *Let God Be True* above. No mention is made regarding the *context* in which the date 1914 was considered in the nearly forty years prior to 1914. The current reader, in the 1940s, would have no way of knowing that historical context. I certainly did not. When things don't happen the way they say they will, the Society glosses over such errors— -never assuming full responsibility for the seriousness of such errors. But such misrepresent God and Christ, and stumble thousands of sincere believers who look to them for divine guidance. This practice began with Russell himself. Notice what he had to say in 1916, shortly before his death that year, about the failure of 1914 to see the end of the present age:

> The author acknowledges that in this book he presents the thought that
> the Lord's saints might expect to be with Him in glory at the ending of the
> Gentile Times. This was a natural mistake to fall into, but the Lord over-
> ruled it for the blessing of His people. The thought that the Church would
> all be gathered to glory before October, 1914, certainly did have a very
> stimulating and sanctifying effect upon thousands, all of whom accord-

ingly can praise the Lord—*even for the mistake.*—Author's Forward, written October 1, 1916 for reprinting of *The Time is at Hand,* (italics not in original).

Russell betrayed no sign of remorse for having misled many thousands of people. No shame is expressed here for having misrepresented God and misusing his Word. This misleading of sincere people was repeated by Rutherford in the book, *Millions Now Living Will Never Die,* which promised deliverance in 1925.

Despite these sad discoveries, I hoped that things might change. Witnesses who saw the need for change in certain areas were told to "wait on Jehovah," and in his due time, if something needed to be corrected he would correct them through his channel, the Watchtower Society. There was still a lingering hope (wishful thinking?) that this would prove true. Besides, where would I go? While I was growing more and more suspect of some of the Society's teachings, there were things I felt worth holding on to. I believed they taught correctly that the Father, Jehovah God, was the Most High God and not part of a Triune deity. I believed the Bible taught that human souls were mortal and hope for future life rested in the resurrection hope. I agreed with the Society's teaching that the wicked would not experience unending, conscious torment, but experience total annihilation. Another factor was that I had developed a dependance on them and that dependance continued to have a strong hold on me. But, because my faith in the organization was being severely tested, the result was that I was losing my zeal to advance its doctrinal agenda. Outwardly, my routine remained the same. I continued to attend meetings and share in public witnessing in a limited way but that was becoming a growing struggle. The "pioneer spirit" that I had had for so many years was slipping away. I was losing my enthusiasm for convincing people they needed to become one of Jehovah's Witnesses. Having been a Witness for so many years made it easier to follow the line of least resistence, but without much joy.

In 1972 the Society instituted a new elder arrangement in the congregations which did away with the former position of Congregation Servant. When that went into effect I was appointed an elder. From that time forward the congregations would be locally supervised by a body of elders who would serve as presiding servants on a yearly rotating basis. I welcomed the change as I felt it fit the biblical model of the early church better than the former one.

Matters came to a head one Saturday morning in January 1973. I was preparing to share in magazine work that day, offering *The Watchtower* and *Awake!* magazines from door-to-door. I was looking through the current magazines for something to use as a talking point in recommending the magazines to householders. In the *Awake!* magazine I saw an article titled, "Who Can Accurately Predict Man's Future?" I thought this might pique someone's interest so I began to read it. Near the end of the article there was a subheading that read: "Jesus' Accurate Predictions for Our Day." The first paragraph under this heading read:

> Of all men used by God to prophesy, Jesus is outstanding. Based on what he said, along with the words of Daniel and John, Jehovah's Witnesses pointed to the year 1914, decades in advance,* as marking *the start* of the "conclusion of the system of things." (Daniel 4; Matthew 24; Mark 13; Luke 21; Rev. 6: 1-8) Within the period of one generation, outstanding war, food shortage, pestilence, and other terrible conditions were predicted to strike before God destroyed this system and replace it with a new order.—*Awake!*, January 22, 1973, page 8 (italics not in original).

Reading that paragraph literally made me ill. It was a complete misrepresentation of the facts. Russell had clearly taught that 1914 was the *concluding year* of the 115-year "Time of the End." The reference to *The Bible Examiner* of October 1876, as a confirming reference was a safe thing to do because no reader would have access to that hundred-year-old publication. It was an editorial device often used by the Society to make a statement appear authentic and historically credited. But in the Kingdom Hall libraries such historical material did not exist. Over the years the Society had systematically removed all of Charles T. Russell's writings from such libraries. Even the works of its second president, Joseph F. Rutherford were expunged. Why? Because to make them accessible for reference would have revealed the sad history of repeated miscalculations and false prophesies.

The reading of that material made it impossible for me to share in the public ministry that day. I phoned the family I was supposed to work with and told them I was too ill to join them. I didn't explain matters to them. I shared my upset with Mavis who was the only person I could confide in on these matters. She said that if I felt so strongly about the matter perhaps I should write the Society and explain my concerns. I took her advice and wrote a lengthy letter in which I outlined the discoveries I had made regarding the numerous false prophecies made by the organization over a period of a hundred years. I said that the record clearly showed the organization had acted as a false prophet, as that term is

---

* See, for example, the *Bible Examiner*, Vol. XXI, No. 1 (Whole No. 313), October 1876, pages 27, 28.

defined in Scripture. (Deut. 18:20-22) In their written response they took issue with my conclusion. What was taught in the past that proved to be a mistake simply demonstrated how Jehovah God was directing them. About this, they quoted what had been written in the December 15, 1962 issue of *The Watchtower*, on page 762:

> God's spirit operates on his dedicated servants today, not to inspire them, but to move them gently in the direction of increased understanding. It permits them to make mistakes as they grow in understanding of God's Word, but in time it helps them to see their mistakes, which they gladly correct. In this manner they progress along the path of the righteous ones, with the light of Scriptural understanding steadily getting "lighter and lighter until the day is firmly established." (Prov. 4: 18) This progress in Scriptural knowledge might be likened to an overcast sky that is gradually breaking up. As the openings between the clouds grow, more and more light comes through. Sometimes a truth is seen and then is obscured by a misunderstanding, just as a passing cloud momentarily obscures some rays of the sun. Later this truth returns in greater clarity when the misunderstanding is removed. God's spirit is evident upon the organization from the progress it is making along the path of Scriptural truth.

> Regarding the charge that Jehovah's Witnesses have been false prophets in connection with some points made that have proven to be in error as progress in understanding has been made down through the years, this point is made in the same issue of The Watchtower on the same page: "Since their comments on the Scriptures are not inspired, they can at times make mistakes. Does this make them false prophets? Not at all! A false prophet does not correct himself. He persists in proclaiming a wrong view even though he knows it is wrong. But these students of God's Word correct misunderstandings when they discover them. They are interested in the truth, not in self-justification. Their mistakes do not mean God's spirit does not operate upon them; it does, just as it did upon Peter despite his mistakes." —Letter from WBTS with the code EF : ES, dated March 9, 1973, pages 2,3.

I got no comfort from the above remarks or the letter as a whole. The rationalizing and self-serving interpretations they presented were arguments I had heard many times. The misuse of Proverbs 4:18 was one example of this. The Proverb contrasts the outcome of the wicked and the righteous. The righteous will prosper but the wicked will not. Charles T. Russell was the first to take it out of context and apply it to his own "mistakes," and has been used over and over again by the organization to justify its "mistakes." As for their assertion that they "correct misunderstandings when they discover them," the truth is that in regard to their false predictions, it is only when the outworking of history proves them wrong, that they address the matter. Then they brush the failure aside with, "Oh, the truth gets brighter and brighter over time." This organizational rationalization to mask false prophecy was not acceptable to me.

Over the years I read about different Witnesses who had taken issue with the Society over one thing or another; and such ones were always described as lacking appreciation for all they had received through Jehovah's organization. I had believed that evaluation of matters and now I was confronted with the same problem. It took considerable self-examination and a continual reviewing of the facts to find the moral strength to continue my quest for truth. There was a little country cemetery not far from where we lived and I sometimes walked in this lonely place and spoke to myself *sotto voce* about all the facts I had been gleaning from official Watchtower records and how those facts seriously discredited the claims the Watchtower Society made about how it was being used by Jesus Christ. It was as if I had to hear these things in my ears and argue with myself about them. It was an extremely difficult and upsetting process. I had to continually remind myself that I was not sinning by doing this. I hadn't been *looking* for fault; but once serious fault was uncovered, how could I in good conscience ignore it?

Chapter 11

A
Personal
Failure

I remember standing in our living room looking out over a snowy taciturn landscape on the morning of January 1, 1973. Speaking partly to my wife and partly to myself, I asked, "I wonder what this year will bring?" Little did I know that in a matter of days there would arise a situation that would very nearly destroy me. Even before these events began to unfold I was already greatly distressed. Mavis and I were still struggling with our relationship, and after five full years removed from the circuit work she was still seriously ill with depression. I am reasonably certain that her hormonal imbalance brought on by her earlier surgery created additional difficulties for her. It would be several more years before she would regain a measure of emotional balance.

Then there was the matter of my faith. The previous two years of research and discovery had created an upheaval in my evaluation of my religious teachers. It wasn't only the discovery that the organization had been a constant prophet of false expectations; they had covered over these errors with misinformation and half-truths. The deep respect I once felt for them had given way to a feeling of confusion, betrayal and anger. The religious assurance and comfort I had felt for so many years was eroding. Much of what I had accepted as truth and preached to others as truth was proving to be nothing more than human wisdom that had taken on a sacred status in my thinking. Since 1948 I had thought of myself in the very center of God's activity in the world through Jehovah's Witnesses. Now that world view was being seriously challenged. Had I really been serving Jehovah's interests by advancing the message preached by the Witnesses? I was no longer certain of that. As bad as things were, they were about to get worse.

1973 would prove to be the darkest year of my life. Not only would I continue to struggle with my faith but I would also fail a test of moral rectitude. During the first days of January a sister in our congregation approached me to say she had a problem she wanted to discuss with me privately. As I was one of the five elders in the congregation this request was not unusual. Moreover, she and her husband were close friends of ours. In fact, she was Mavis' closest friend. Mavis had confided in her, discussing some of her problems. Since they both were experiencing some emotional difficulties, they formed a special bond of friendship and seemed to be helping one another cope with their respective problems. Their relationship helps to explain why this person sought me out with her problem.

She wanted to meet me privately so we agreed to meet at a restaurant. I learned what her problem was: she had romantic feelings toward someone other than her husband and she asked me if that was wrong. I said something to the effect that we can't always control our feelings toward someone, but that we couldn't allow such wrong desires to be nourished in our thoughts. As I spoke I recalled a similar conversation we had in the Kingdom Hall library a month or two earlier. At that time she had asked essentially the same question and I had responded as I was now doing. After reflecting on that earlier exchange, I faulted myself for not attempting to find out who it was she had these feelings for. Was it someone in our congregation? Perhaps knowing that would prove helpful in avoiding a future problem. Now, she was bringing the matter up again. So after repeating the same counsel of impropriety of such a thing as I had before, I made an attempt to draw her out as to who this "mystery man" was. She was reluctant to say. I pressed the matter by suggesting a couple of men who I thought it could be but she said no to each of them. Something about her demeanor prompted me to ask if it was me, and she said, "Yes." She hastily added that she had never intended to let me know that it was me. But, having said that, she went on to explain what she found attractive about me.

I can honestly say that I had no indication that she felt this way, and I had no such inclination towards her. We were simply friends. Now, suddenly, everything about that friendship was being threatened. I made it clear that this was something that could go no further. Our discussion concluded with her making me promise not to tell her husband. A day or two later she phoned again and asked me to meet with her again. It was at this point that I should have brought the matter to a firm conclusion. Had I done that, I would have saved her, Mavis, myself and many innocent people a great deal of hurt. But I didn't do that. In addition to not wanting to be unkind, I was flattered by her interest in me. She was an attractive woman and about ten years younger than myself. That she found me attractive fed my vanity. I agreed to meet her at the restaurant again, feeling confident that I could handle the situation and prevent it from getting out of control. I couldn't have been more wrong.

Looking back on the matter, I realize that she had tapped into a vulnerable area of my character, one that was now being tested as never before. Her words of love and desire excited a preexisting vulnerability. My feelings were quickly conflicted. Another factor was that I was too trusting in my ability to avoid serious problems. I thought I could control the situation without cutting her off abruptly. This false sense of self-confidence and kindness allowed me to take another step in the wrong direction. I agreed to meet her a third time.

Each time we met she was more forthcoming about how much she cared for me. She also revealed that some of the things Mavis had said about me actually attracted her to me. She said she saw some of herself in me. I was soaking these things up like a thirsty sponge. I was flattered by her words and I lacked the moral strength to resist responding to them. There was a strong desire welling up in me that did not want to let go of this attraction. Rather than taking flight from the situation I unwisely delayed and was soon overcome by my own wrong desire, just as the Scriptures say. (James 1: 13-15)

I knew that what we were doing was wrong but I couldn't resist becoming more and more involved with her. Talk evolved into gestures of affection; a touch, a hug, a kiss. These brief pleasures were followed by deep feelings of guilt and a sense of uncleanness, and yet I was unable to pull away. She had aroused feelings and responses in me that I didn't realize I was capable of having. They were delicious to savor, but in alternate moments I was repelled and disgusted with myself. After a number of weeks of these brief, emotion-charged encounters I realized that I was powerless to end a relationship that appeared to be leading to adultery. At the time I believed that I could never be forgiven should that happen. The truth was that I was already guilty of that sin, according to our Lord's evaluation. (Matt. 5:27,28)

This emotional roller coaster continued for a number of weeks. At one point I phoned her to say I was too emotionally torn to continue meeting with her. She responded by threatening to harm herself if I broke it off. The thought that she might do that terrified me. I tried to sooth her and ended up backing off from my resolve. I finally decided that the only way to end the matter was to confess it to my fellow elders. I convinced her and her husband ,who had become aware of what had been going on, that this was what needed to be done. They finally agreed. I must say here that my decision to confess to the elders at this point was not an act of repentance; it was an act of desperation.

The elders met with us individually. She was privately reproved and counseled not to have any contact with me again or she would be subject to being disfellowshiped. In my meeting with the elders I was reproached for having taken advantage of a sister seeking my help. They accused me of taking advantage of her and worming my way into their family. They removed me as an elder and decided that I should be publicly reproved. Being publicly reproved meant having your name announced during a congregational meeting as one "guilty of conduct unbecoming a Christian." This took place in February of 1973. Mavis was devastated. Betrayal by her husband and her best friend on top of her already weakened condition was just too much for her. She decided she needed to get away from it all, so she arranged to go stay with her older sister Laverne. A few weeks after arriving in Idaho, Mavis filed for divorce.

The next few months were extremely difficult. Left alone, I felt more vulnerable than ever. I also felt abandoned by God. I had dishonored him and broken a sacred relationship. Writing about it more than thirty years later, is still painful. I wrote in a journal at the time that my spirit was like "lifeless, coagulated blood." I had ruined my way. I had acted in a manner that contradicted everything I thought holy and good. I had hurt everyone I loved. Yet, despite these self-condemning thoughts, another part of me was reluctant to let her go. Sometimes I would seek her out and other times I would run from her. She was perplexed by my contradictory behavior. In fact I was a contradiction! I was like a man driving an out of control automobile sliding on ice, violently swerving from one ditch to the other. This irrational conduct went on for several months. It was only later, when I was able to put some perspective on the matter, that I was able to make some sense of my irrational behavior during that time. Sin, once it is given the breath of life, must run its course. Recovery would not come in an instant. Regaining self-respect and a measure of control of my life proved to be a painfully slow process.

It wasn't until August 1973, a full six months after the start of the illicit affair, that I mustered up enough moral courage to make a final break with her. In a phone call in early August, I told her I could not see her again. She was distraught and once again threatened to harm herself if I did that. This time I held firm and did not allow that threat to influence a change of heart. It was finally over. As it turned out, this was at this very time that Mavis had returned to Minnesota. She had taken a job in St. Paul, and had arranged to move there. Instead of proceeding directly St. Paul she and her sister stopped to see our daughter and son-in-law in Austin, Minnesota, which was about 30 miles south of Owatonna. My mother informed me of this and encouraged me to go to Jamie's house to see Mavis. I was reluctant. Mavis had convinced me that I was responsible for her problems and I didn't want to continue being responsible. If she felt that the only way out for her was a divorce, I wasn't going to try and talk her out of it. But, despite my reservations, I decided to make the visit.

At our daughter's home I saw Mavis, together with the other members of our family. We decided to go for a walk so we could talk privately. I let her know that my involvement with this other sister was over, but I stopped short of asking her to come back. When she asked why I had not protested the divorce, I told her I did not want to obstruct her from getting away from the source of her problems—me! As we talked it became clear that there was hope of a reconciliation, which I thought was a better option than a divorce. By the end of our walk we had decided to reconcile. Thus began the difficult task of rebuilding a trusting and loving relationship.

The news of our reconciliation traveled quickly. When the woman I had been involved with learned of it she experienced some kind of emotional upset that prompted her to discuss the matter with another Witness who recommended that she speak to the local elders. In this way the elders learned that we had had contact in the months following our first meeting with them. Their response to her confession was to promptly disfellowship her. I was unaware of this at the time. A couple of days after Mavis and I had reconciled I got a phone call from one of the elders telling me they wanted to talk to me. They arranged a meeting time and let me know that they knew what had been going on. I told them I had broken off the affair and that Mavis and I had reconciled, but that appeared irrelevant to them. One of the questions they asked me was, "Why didn't you come to us ?" I said, "I knew what you would do had I done so; you would have disfellowshiped me." The fact that they did that very thing with the other party who did go to them convinced me that I had been right. They disfellowshiped me as well.

To be disfellowshiped as a Jehovah's Witness is to become *persona non grata* in that worldwide community. No one is allowed to speak to such a person, not even to say a greeting. Even family members are to avoid all unnecessary contact with such persons. I knew of a situation within a family where the disfellowshiped member of the family was not allowed to eat at the same table with other members of the family. If a disfellowshiped person decided to continue attending meetings at the Kingdom Hall, he or she would not be greeted or otherwise acknowledged. Nor would there be any effort on the part of the congregation elders to help the individual seek repentance and reconciliation. Mavis and I would have to struggle on our own without any outside assistance. Even family members would now be hindered from offering support. When my mother or other family members visited our home, I would absent myself to avoid their having to see me.

During the time I was disfellowshiped, which was about six months, I continued to attend meetings at the Kingdom Hall. Despite my growing suspicion that the Watch Tower Society was not being used by God as they claimed it was, I gave no thought of pulling away from the organization—not now, not in this way. And besides, where would I go? I knew of nothing better. As humiliated and as shameful as I felt, there were important lessons being learned. I now realized how quickly one's good record of faithful service could be destroyed in a moment by sin. My twenty-five years of devoted service and unblemished record did not prevent me from stumbling into sin nor could that record of service be offered up to God as proof that I deserved mercy. Sometimes a well-meaning friend would remind me that God had forgiven certain ones named in the Bible who had served him but were overcome in some transgression. I took no comfort from that. I knew then as I know now that no one can presume upon God's mercy. At no time did I feel that I could do what I was doing and get away with it by later turning to God and asking forgiveness.

Being in the Kingdom Hall as an outcast was not easy. I would walk into the Hall when I knew the meeting was due to start and take a seat in the rear. As soon as the meeting was over I would go to our car and wait. Now it was my turn to wait for Mavis. This went on for about three months. Then I learned that the other party had been reinstated by the elders. This surprised me because those disfellowshipped were usually not reinstated for at least a year, sometimes longer. When I learned of her reinstatement I felt encouraged to seek my own and asked to meet with the body of elders. They did meet with me and I was hopeful that I would also be accepted back into the congregation, but they rejected my appeal for reinstatement. I was crushed by that refusal. I had by this time truly repented and my life was showing evidence of that. I had approached God in prayer seeking his forgiveness and was confident that he would honor true repentance. I had also sought and obtained forgiveness from the sister's husband. When the elders withheld their forgiveness it was like being disfellowshiped all over again. I felt a great despair.

The very next day a man representing the Owatonna Canning Company stopped by my sign shop regarding some signs he had ordered. The man was Otto Strelau. Otto was the supervisor of plant maintenance for the canning company and I had done business with him for a number of years. Otto was also a Christian associated with the Owatonna Assembly of God, and we sometimes discussed scriptural matters. We agreed on some things and disagreed on others, but there was always a spirit of mutual respect shown in these discussions. I could see his obvious devotion to God along with his forthright and kindly manner. He once said I was the only Jehovah's Witness he was ever able to have a meaningful conversation with. He had also shared something of his family's experiences in Germany as they fled the communists during World War II. They immigrated to Canada and then later to the United States. He had served as a pastor for the Assembly of God in Canada but was now serving as an elder in the local church.

I grew fond of Otto, and I respected him as a believer. He was honest, fair and helpful in our business dealings and he had a nice sense of humor and a ready smile. Without realizing it, he was challenging my perception of people claiming to be Christians who were not Jehovah's Witnesses. I had been carefully taught that only those who were associated with Jehovah's Witnesses could have a relationship with God. I found myself unwilling to judge him as not acceptable to God. How dare I say that his faith in Jesus Christ was invalid and not acceptable to God because he was not a Witness? That I was unable to judge Otto, was a clear indication of how dramatically my religious thinking was changing.

That morning, as Otto and I conversed, I became overwhelmed with sadness over having been rejected by the body of elders the evening before. I began to weep. I asked him to forgive me as I tried to get my emotions under control and compose myself. I explained to him what had happened and why I was so distraught. He listened kindly and patiently. When he finally spoke he said, "Ron, it is obvious to me that you are repentant of whatever sin you were guilty of." Then he quoted a scripture from memory: "If we confess our sins, he is faithful and just to forgive us our sins and to cleanse us from all unrighteousness." (1 John 1: 9 *KJV*)

He went on to say that men are often slow to forgive and cited an example drawn from his own life. But men's slowness, he continued, did not prevent God from extending forgiveness. He reassured me that I could trust God's promise. As he continued to comfort me, I felt a release of pain and sadness that I hadn't experienced for a very long time. His ministry to me that morning, using the Scriptures and treating me as a brother in Christ, was a healing experience. I had approached God in faith and asked his forgiveness earlier, but the elders judgment against me was like God saying no to me. Without their forgiveness, I could not be forgiven. Otto, convinced me otherwise. A number of years later, after I had completely separated myself from the Witnesses, I was able to stop by his home and share with him how important that brief conversation we had together that morning had been for me. It gave me hope and renewed my spirit.

If I were to point to a defining moment when listening to what God had to say in the Scriptures became more important than the views of men, the conversation with Otto would be the moment. It was the beginning of losing the fear of men. Witnesses do not think of themselves as being able to have a good relationship with God apart from the Watchtower organization. Jesus does not stand alone between them and Jehovah God. The organization stands between them and Christ. Apart from them there is no access to Jesus Christ. I am certain that this is the case in many if not most authoritative religious organizations..

It was not that Otto had quoted a Bible text that I had never given consideration to before. I knew and believed the truth contained in those words from 1 John 1:9. But on another level I still had the need for organizational approval and forgiveness. This need had been carefully taught by the Watchtower Society and was deeply ingrained in my subconscious. I had to hear those precious, hope-instilling words from someone else. I will always be grateful to God and Christ for bringing Otto into my life. I decided that I would not approach the elders again regarding reinstatement. I would continue to attend meetings but was prepared to remain indefinitely in the disfellowshipped state. I no longer felt the need for their forgiveness. While I retained a deep sadness over my infidelity I lost the sense of guilt that had burdened me so. Another three months would go by before one of the elders approached me and said the body of elders would like to meet with me. This time they agreed to reinstated me.

The term Reinstatement is somewhat misleading. It comes with certain restrictions attached to it. I was told that the privilege of participating in meetings by making comments would not be mine for an unspecified period of time. Making comments, like answering questions in a study, is open to anyone who attends meetings at the Kingdom Hall.

Calling on someone who raises their hand to speak is at the discretion of whoever is leading the particular meeting. One does not have to be a baptized Witness in order to be called upon. So to be told this "privilege" is not yours means that you are welcomed back into fellowship one rung below an unbaptized Witness. It would be a full six months after being reinstated before I was told I could now volunteer comments at the meetings.

When I had been initially reproved, a year earlier, the right to comment at meetings had been taken away from me. Then, six months later I was disfellowshiped and another six months of silence was imposed. After being reinstated an additional six months of not being permitted to participate vocally meant that I was mute for 18 months during 1973 and 1974. This forced silence was not all bad. Although it had the effect of stigmatizing me, it also allowed for an opportunity to simply listen and observe. While it was not a pleasant experience, I did benefit from it in a number of ways. I found that being an observer rather than a participant helped me be more objective in evaluating what was being said and taught in the Kingdom Hall.

1973 was the darkest hour of my life. Four very serious problems were being dealt with at once: (1) my wife's emotional health; (2) our troubled marriage; (3) my crumbling belief structure; and (4) my serious moral failure. Yet, there had been some good things that came out of the year. I had experienced a release from condemnation apart from organizational forgiveness. A foundation was being laid which gave promise of a more direct and personal relationship with Jehovah God through Jesus Christ. I had learned a sobering lesson regarding my own weaknesses. I had a certain confidence (self-righteousness?) born of 25 years of commendable service as one of Jehovah's Witnesses. I had served as a presiding overseer in five different congregations, pioneered many years and had served as a circuit overseer. That I could so easily have slipped into such sinful conduct shattered my self-image.

I also learned how vital genuine faith is. Being separated from God is no big deal for a person who has never experienced a relationship with God. But when serving God has been your reason for being and having his approval means everything to you, separation from him is a big deal! The principles I violated were principles I truly believed. I can't describe how terrible the realization was that I had violated what I held sacred. The sense that God had withdrawn from me was the deepest sense of abandonment I have ever felt. Would God, could God, ever forgive me? It takes genuine faith to trust God's promise that if we turn away from our sin he will forgive us. Only my faith that *God is faithful* enabled me to seek his forgiveness through our Lord Jesus Christ, even when I felt personally condemned. So while 1973 was the darkest of hours, it was also a dawning of promise based on God's faithfulness.

1975:
Another
Disappointment

As 1975 approached, expectations ran high within the worldwide community of Jehovah's Witnesses. At a District Assembly in Duluth, Minnesota in the summer of 1972, one of the speakers, a circuit overseer, announced to the assembly that we were so close to the end of the world that the time remaining was like that instant between the little "click" one hears just before the alarm clock goes off. Such expressions of confidence regarding what 1975 would bring were commonplace at this time and spurred many to greater religious activity. Some Witnesses were quitting jobs and entering the pioneer service with 1975 in view. Others were cashing in retirement funds, putting off needed medical attention and in other ways gauging their lives and resources with 1975 in view.

The tsunami wave triggered by the speculation advanced in *Life Everlasting in Freedom of the Sons of God*, continued to grow and overwhelm rational thinking. What began as a possibility based on Watchtower chronology quickly grew into something much more certain—fueled by many published articles which argued for certainty. The years leading up to 1975 began to show significant increases in witnessing activity and the ranks of the Witnesses grew proportionately. In 1975 alone, 295,073 people were baptized. By comparison,1965, the year before the speculation regarding 1975 was first published, only 64,393 were baptized. But 1975 came and went without anything happening and the wind escaped from the balloon.

The number baptized in 1976 fell to 196,656, nearly 100,000 fewer than the previous year. An even greater decline was recorded in 1977 when the number baptized slowed to 124,459, more than 170,000 fewer than two years earlier. The high-water mark of baptisms experienced in

1975 would not be equaled for another 15 years. In 1990 there was a reported 301,518 baptized. But by then there were twice as many Witnesses engaged in the proselytizing witness work. In 1975 there were a little more than 2 million Witnesses worldwide, while in 1990 there were 4 million. The hours spent proselytizing in 1975 were 382,296,208 worldwide, compared to 895,229,424 hours spent in 1990. So, in 1990 it took twice as many Witnesses triple the amount of time to accomplish what had been accomplished in 1975. Obviously, the false momentum that had been created by speculations regarding 1975 was the primary factor. It reminded me of the increases experienced with 1925 in view, as heralded by *Millions Now Living Will Never Die.*

I had sincerely hoped and even expected that this latest casualty to the Society's efforts to pinpoint a date in the outworking of God's purposes would lead to a display of genuine repentance and some doctrinal reformation as well. Perhaps now, after a hundred years of failed predictions, the Society's leaders would reevaluate themselves as to how much they really knew about time features regarding the establishment of God's kingdom and the end of the world. There needed to be a reexamination of the evidence regarding how closely Jehovah God was directing their efforts. I fully expected the Society to take responsibility for publishing the speculative theory they had advanced in 1966 which dishonored God and resulted in so much disappointment and disrupted many lives. None of those things happened.

Obviously, the Society had to address this latest disappointment but in doing so they continued an organizational pattern: they blamed the Witnesses for taking them seriously. *The Watchtower*, of July 15, 1976 officially discussed the matter in two articles: "Keeping A Balanced View of Time," and "A Solid Basis for Confidence." While the year 1975 was never mentioned in either article, it was obvious that they were addressing that year and the disappointments that ensued. The first piece pointed out that from time to time Jehovah God revealed some specific time features, but at other times he had not done so. About this the article said:

> So, when Jehovah God makes known a certain time for the outworking of some feature of his divine purpose, his faithful servants can rely implicitly on the exactness of the published schedule. But when he has not made such announcement, then it remains beyond their ability and power to determine the time of the realization of that purpose.—*The Watchtower*, July 15, 1976, page 433.

These were wise words even though they clarified the obvious. The paragraph following this one set forth another obvious reality:

> Should we think it strange that God would retain certain knowledge for himself in this way? As far back as the time when the Israelites were approaching the Promised Land, the prophet Moses recorded these inspired words at Deuteronomy 29: 29: "The things concealed belong to Jehovah our God, but the things revealed belong to us and to our sons to time indefinite, that we may carry out all the words of this law." Yes, all that we really *need* to know to serve Jehovah God faithfully, and that we need in order to sustain us in our hope and conviction, this, God reveals to us. But where it accomplishes his purpose better, he can also conceal matters, with no hurt or lack to his servants.—*Ibid.*, (Italics in original) Page 434.

The destruction of Jerusalem in A.D. 70 was next considered, with the article going on to point out that Jesus told his disciples what conditions would exist leading up to that destruction. He also said, "this generation will by no means pass away until all these things happen." (Mark 13:30) This was important for the readers of this material to understand. Why? Because the destruction of Jerusalem that came upon *that* generation was said to be a small scale example of what was to occur now, in *this* generation. Accordingly, they continued to insist that knowledgeable persons witnessing the events of 1914 would not pass away until the final end of the present world system. Concerning the 1914 generation which was already 70 years old (even if you were born in that year) the magazine said:

> Just as surely as the generation that experienced a fulfillment of his [Jesus] words, *just as surely* will this generation—the generation seeing the major fulfillment of his "sign" identifying the last days of this system of things—be the generation to experience the global tribulation due to come.—*Ibid.,* page 435. (Italics not in original)

I found that a remarkable statement! What was being said was that their interpretation of the 1914 generation as being the generation that would see the end of this system of things, was *just as sure* as Jesus' inspired pronouncements regarding the destruction of Jerusalem in his generation! It was evident that the editorial arrogance of the Society had not changed; in fact it seemed to have hardened. Perhaps it was felt that strong assertions at this point in time were necessary in order to shore up the growing lack of confidence in them. The writer went on to explain that some of the fine points of why we cannot know the precise "day and hour" for the coming destruction had to do with when the sixth creative day really ended and the seventh day began.

The premise for the Society's speculation rested on the belief that each of the creative days were exactly 7,000 years long, and it had been argued that 6,000 years of the seventh day would end in 1975. This would leave1,000 years remaining for the seventh day and would run concurrently with Jesus millennial reign. This was the Society's argument. This meant that the seventh day of rest would conclude with all things restored under Christ's kingdom according to God's purpose. However, the millennium did not begin in 1975.What was the problem? Addressing this matter the article continued:

> But that great rest day [the seventh day] did not begin immediately after Adam's creation. Other events took place after Adam's creation but before the close of the sixth creative day. One of these is of great importance to all of us. That is the creation of the first woman, Eve . . .How much time elapsed between the creation of the man and that of the woman? The Bible does not reveal this . . . we do not know whether it was a brief time such as a month or a few months, a year or even more. But whatever time elapsed would have to be added to the time that has passed since Adam's creation in order for us to know how far along we are within God's seventh "day" his grand day of rest.—*Ibid.,* July 15, 1976, pages 436,437.

What they were now doing by saying these things was buying time for their seven-thousand-year-day of creation theory. Earlier, in 1966, they had managed to reinforce their speculation that God's seven-thousand-year-day ran *concurrently* from Adam and Eve's creation. The first six thousand years of this 'day' they said would end in the fall of 1975, which, according to their arithmetic, ended 6,000 years of man's habitation on earth. Now, they were saying that the sixth day did not expire as quickly as they had argued just as few years earlier. It was but a small example of how the Bible could be treated to say what you wanted it to say. There was no real scholarship present in either argument. When you approach the Scriptures with a pre-conceived idea you can make it fit almost any doctrinal framework. Scriptures used a decade earlier for one argument were now being used to refute that argument.

The Society had insisted that they knew the exact generation of mankind that would see the end of the world. What they didn't know, they said, was the "day and hour" it would conclude. It occurred to me that the whole argument about not knowing "the day or hour" was a ridiculous one. The meaning of the expression clearly meant not to know the time—period! It didn't mean you could know 99% of the time but not the remaining 1%—the *literal* day and hour! Had not Jesus said that neither he nor the angels of heaven knew the day or hour but only the Father? (Matt. 24: 36) Did Jesus mean he knew everything about the future generation that would see the end of the world except the *exact day and hour* it would end? Did that mean he knew what year it would end, the month it would end, the week it would end, but not the day or the hour? If that is what he meant, all I can say is that it wasn't much of a secret.

Date-setting by the Watchtower Society has kept the Witnesses in a constant state of frantic expectation. Yet Jesus clearly stated that the end would come when the disciples were *not expecting.* (Matt. 24: 44) And didn't he tell his disciples that it was not for them to know "the times and seasons" regarding the restoration of the kingdom of Israel? (Acts 1: 7) Once the Lord said that it was not for them to know such things, it put the matter in the category of "things concealed." (Deut. 29: 29) To continue to try and uncover what is only known to God constitutes an act of disobedience, and can only lead to miscalculation and disappointment. Christian history is replete with efforts by many false prophets who thought they knew when the end would come and preached their theories boldly. Jehovah's Witnesses are not the only ones guilty of this disobedient and destructive practice, but they have stood out as one of the foremost false prophets in both the 19th and 20th centuries. While the Witnesses bristle at being called a false prophet, the Scriptures are clear on this matter:

> However the prophet who presumes to speak in my name a word that I have not commanded him to speak or who speaks in the name of other Gods, that prophet must die. And in case you should say in your heart: "How shall we know the word that Jehovah has not spoken?" when the prophet speaks in the name of Jehovah and the word does not occur or come true, that is the word that Jehovah did not speak. With presumptuousness the prophet spoke it. You must not become frightened at him. (Duet. 18: 20-22 *NWT*)

The next article: "A Solid Basis for Confidence," that followed the one discussed above, pointed out that the Scriptures provide a sure basis for faith in God's promises and used Israel's deliverance from Egypt and eventual entrance into the promised land as an example of God's faithfulness to his word. From there a link was made to the present situation regarding their understanding of which generation was to see the end of the present system of things. Seeking to build confidence in *their word* they continued to assert that the generation of 1914 would see the end of the world.

> Similarly today, we have God's precious promise concerning life in a new system of righteousness. We have heard his "word" that the generation living in this "time of the end" will be the generation that will experience the 'great tribulation." —*Ibid.*, page 439.

Note that the speculative theory regarding the 1914 generation is spoken of as "his word" on the matter. It is clear that they present themselves as bringing forth Jehovah's word in their speculation regarding 1914 and its generation. A great deal of arrogance would have to be in place to say such a thing! Then, to top matters off, the article went on to reprove those who had been looking to a specific date:

> It may be that some who have been serving God have planned their lives according to a mistaken view of just what was to happen on a certain date or in a certain year. They may have, for this reason, put off or neglected things that they otherwise would have cared for. But they have missed the point of the Bible's warnings concerning the end of this system of things, thinking that Bible chronology reveals the specific date. —*Ibid.*, page 440.

It was unconscionable for the publishers of *The Watchtower* to put matters as they did. No mention was made as to *why* people may have done the things they mentioned in regard to the 1975 date. No responsibility, not even a little, was taken by the very ones who had planted the false expectations in the minds of Jehovah's Witnesses in the first place. It was another example of the Society's practice to parry responsibility for their words by blaming the victim. They did this after the 1925 disappointment, and now they were doing it again. Nothing had changed.

But the response represented in the July 15, 1976 *Watchtower* did not appease many Witnesses who were offended by the magazine's remarks. Had the leadership come clean at that time perhaps things would have been different, but because they did not, they made a bad situation worse by easing themselves of any responsibility in the matter. It was one of those moments of truth where the organization had an opportunity to accept responsibility for its words and humbly seek the forgiveness of God and those they misled. They had the opportunity to repent and show that repentance by not continuing to advance such theories. When an organization claims to be spirit-directed and claims spiritual authority, as the Watchtower Society does, it multiplies its reprehensibility before God and men, making repentance all the more urgent. That the moment was not seized was most discouraging.

Talk to most Jehovah's Witnesses today and they will tell you that 1975 was never a date looked forward to as being of some significance by them. It never happened. They take this view either through ignorance, because they were not Witnesses at the time and have been misinformed, or through self-delusion because they did experience it but have blocked the matter out of their collective memory. But it did happen and finally, after nearly five years of silence, the WBTS acknowledged their culpability in the matter:

> With the appearance of the book *Life Everlasting—in Freedom of the Sons of God*, and its comments as to how appropriate it would be for the millennial reign of Christ to parallel the seventh millennium of man's existence, considerable expectation was aroused regarding the year 1975. There were statements made then, and thereafter, stressing that this was only a possibility. Unfortunately, however, along with such cautionary information there were other statements *published* that implied that such realization of hopes by that year *was more of a probability than a mere possibility*. It is to be regretted that those latter statements apparently overshadowed the cautionary ones and contributed to a buildup of the expectation already initiated.—*The Watchtower*. March 15, 1980, page 17. (Italics not in original)

Then directing attention to their comments made earlier in the July 15, 1976 *Watchtower,* they said:

> In its issue of July 15, 1976, *The Watchtower*, commenting on the inadvisability of setting our sights on a certain date, stated: "If anyone has been disappointed through not following this line of thought, he should now concentrate on adjusting his viewpoint, seeing that it was not the word of God that failed or deceived him and brought disappointment, but that his own understanding was based on wrong premises." In saying "anyone," *The Watchtower* included all disappointed ones of Jehovah's Witnesses, hence including *persons having to do with the publication of the information* that contributed to the buildup of hopes centered on that date.—*Ibid*, page 17,18. (italics in the original)

The above confirms how serious the matter remained in 1980. It also confirms that published statements projected the 1975 date as more *probable* than possible as the year that would see the end of the present world. The above confession was forced upon them because the repercussions of the 1975 disappointment refused to go away. Many thousands had simply walked away from the organization after 1975 and there was a lack of enthusiasm among many more thousands who remained Witnesses but were depressed in spirit. All things considered, the Society's acknowledgment of culpability was an example of too little, too late. As their published rhetoric in 1976 confirmed, they continued to insist that the end *must* come within the generation of 1914. They simply cannot accept full responsibility for the terrible harm they have done and continue to do. Nor have their many failures caused them to desist from prophetic speculation into matters that have not been revealed. They fit the description of those who are said to be "always learning and yet never able to come to an accurate knowledge of truth." (2 Tim. 3: 7 *NWT*)

Chapter 13

No
Comfort
Zone

For one to develop a critical attitude within a religious system that does not tolerate criticism, makes for an incompatible marriage. In order to endure the emotional discomfort that created, I had to continually remind myself that it was not wrong to reexamine what I had been taught religiously. In truth, the concept of reexamining was not foreign to the thinking of Jehovah's Witnesses. We were trained to urge others to do that very thing. In our house-to-house ministry we routinely challenged others to critically examine their religious ideas and to compare what they had been taught with the Bible. A sampling of scriptures often used in such argumentation are shown below:

> Now the latter were more noble-minded than those in Thessalonica, for they received the word with the greatest eagerness of mind, carefully examining the Scriptures daily as to whether these things were so. (Acts 17: 11 *NWT*)

> Make sure of all things; hold fast to what is fine. (1 Thess. 5: 21 *NWT*)

> Beloved ones, do not believe every inspired expression, but test the inspired expressions to see whether they originate with God, because many false prophets have gone forth in the world. (1 John 4: 1 *NWT*)

> But solid food belongs to mature people, to those who through use have their perceptive powers trained to distinguish both right and wrong. (Hebrews 5: 14 *NWT*)

112

Of the four texts quoted above, three were written to believers! The counsel represented here was not primarily for those who were not Christians, but for those who already were. When witnessing, I often used such texts to encourage them to reexamine their beliefs and the things taught them by their religious leaders. I did this in good conscious. I didn't think I was encouraging disloyalty. If they voiced an objection to this kind of reasoning I would remind them that if they had the truth they had nothing to fear, as a careful examination would establish that truth even more clearly. The Society articulated this approach in a book the Witnesses distributed widely:

> We need to examine, not only what we personally believe, but also what is taught by *any religious organization* with which we may be associated. Are its teachings in full harmony with God's Word, or are they based on the traditions of men? If we are lovers of the truth, there is nothing to fear from such an examination. It should be the sincere desire of every one of us to learn what God's will is for us, and then to do it. — *The Truth That Leads to Eternal Life*, 1968, page 13. (Italics not in original)

Noble words, these. The problem was that the publishers of those words had other people in mind, not Jehovah's Witnesses. Of course, most Witnesses would say, "We have already examined our religion and we know we have the truth. We have no need to examine it further." I had heard that line of reasoning from Catholics and others over the years. It represents a rationalization that serves to free one from taking personal responsibility for what they ultimately believe. I believe it also serves the interest of those fearful of making a critical examination of what they believe, for fear of what they might find. I understood that fear, as I was struggling with that very thing. One part of me said that I was not a wicked person for trying to carefully reexamine what I had been taught and accepted as biblical truth. But another part of my consciousness condemned me for doing it. This inner conflict robbed me of peace of mind and a sense of direction. Still, as difficult as this process was proving to be, it had to be carried through to a final solution. There was no way I could walk away from it.

I realized that my religious perspective was undergoing a major change. For the first twenty-five years as a Witness my primary goal was to always be in some form of full time service. Now I had lost the intense zeal to convince others that they must become Witnesses if they were to be saved. Field service became more and more difficult. I could no longer strongly recommend *The Watchtower* and *Awake!* magazines without reservation because there were some things in them that I was no longer convinced were true. Sometimes I would just go from door-to-door with the Bible and discuss certain passages from it to make a point. I was more comfortable doing that. But this was viewed as unorthodox by loyal Witnesses who were taught to feature the literature of the Watchtower Society. I am sure that some thought I felt superior and above using the Society's literature. The truth was I did it to preserve a good conscience. Understandably, my Witness companions were perplexed by my behavior.

I had also lost my desire to serve in any kind of leadership position. From time to time, in the years following my reinstatement, a well meaning brother would encourage me to reach out for that responsibility again. Sometimes a traveling circuit servant would remind me that I could be much more helpful to the congregation if I were more zealous in the ministry. The fact was I was no longer able to do those things others expected of me. I still had a desire to be helpful so I focused on individuals who were less prominent in the congregation and could use some encouragement. Even this was misconstrued by the elders. One brother told me that it was said that I was trying to influence the weaker ones in the congregation. This criticism implied that I was trying to undermine the faith of weaker ones, not build them up.

Not prepared to walk away from the religion that had been my life, I was struggling to remain with it as best I could, but finding a comfort zone was proving futile. Someone might ask, "Why didn't he simply walk away?" The simple truth was that I was not able to handle that decision. For nearly thirty years of my life I had followed a strict regimen of activity: meeting attendance, preparing for meetings, field service, preparing for field service, studying *The Watchtower* and reading the Bible. It was easier to continue this routine, dysfunctional as it was, than to break it off. In effect, I was following the line of least resistance.

My wife, my parents, most of my relatives (at least the ones I kept in contact with), and all my friends and social contacts were Jehovah's Witnesses. I had no identity—no life, apart from being a Witness. It would not be like someone deciding to stop going to one church and start attending another church down the street. Leaving the Witnesses would change my life in a profound and irrevocable way. It would cost everything: family, friends and my social structure—my world. In addition to these things, there were a few things I continued to agreed with. These were, in my opinion, beliefs that withstood the test of Scripture. None of these beliefs originated with the WBTS. They had been believed in centuries past by other Christians. Such true teachings cannot be franchised. They do not belong to any single group or organization. Sometimes, to offset their many miscalculations and false predictions, the Society reminds the Witnesses that they have learned many good things that have withstood the test of time.

> When we look at what has been published by Jehovah's organization through the pages of *The Watchtower* and other publications for the past century, we find wholesome spiritual food in abundance. Early in this period, basic Bible truths were made clear, and they remain clear until this day. Our viewpoint on hell, Trinity, purgatory, the soul, where the dead are, the ransom, the resurrection, earth's destiny, the Kingdom and other key doctrines has undergone very little change during 100 years. The truth has always been truth, though at times, our understanding of it has required adjustment.—Compare John 16: 13.—*The Watchtower*, July 1, 1979, page 28.

There is some truth in the above. The Watchtower Society had freed itself of certain erroneous doctrines that were adopted by the institutionalized church over many centuries. The problem is that while abandoning some of these wrong teachings, the Witnesses proceeded to create their own unique errors that have become part of *their* tradition. And these errors have resulted in a whole new way of salvation—a way not taught by Jesus and his disciples. The few good teachings that have not been corrupted by their new gospel do not purify the errors that they teach along with those few correct doctrines. Like those religious systems they regularly condemn, the Witnesses have blended truth with error and corrupted the message of the Bible.

These things are clearer to me today than they were in the time period of the late 1970s. But as I was gradually coming out from under the ether of organizational control, I could see that much of what we saw in ourselves was delusional. We were told, for example, that only we had that quality of love which Jesus said would identify his true disciples. (John 13: 34,35) Because they are repeatedly told this, most Witnesses assume it is true. But it began to occur to me that we talked about love much more than we practiced it. And what I concluded then has been confirmed by my experience since leaving the Witnesses. I have seen remarkable love shown among other Christians. I don't say this to discredit the measure of love that the Witnesses have for one another; I say it to merely point out that there is nothing extraordinary about their love for one another.

We were also told that, unlike other religions, we had no clergy/laity division. I concluded that this was also untrue. According to the definition of a clergy class we are told they represent, "a group ordained to perform pastoral or sacerdotal functions in a Christian church."— *Webster's Ninth New Collegiate Dictionary.* On the other hand, a laity represents those associated with a church who are "distinguished from its clergy."—*Ibid.* Was it really true that we did not have both classes represented in our Kingdom Halls? Because the Witnesses have no salaried ministers, they tend to think of themselves as not having a clergy class. But there is more to it than that. Because someone is not paid for his services and does not wear certain religious garb or have the title of Reverend, does not prove he is not a clergyman. The question is: does he function in an ordained or appointed position that gives him the right to perform certain religious duties that are denied to someone who has not been similarly ordained or appointed? If he does, he is functioning as a clergyman, whether he thinks of himself as such or not. The fact is that the clergy/laity division among Witnesses is more pronounced than in most mainline protestant churches.

The congregations of Jehovah's Witnesses are strictly controlled by a group of men who are appointed elders. Another group of men are appointed to serve under their direction as ministerial servants, a position comparable to deacon in other churches. Only these men can give public talks (sermons) in the Kingdom Hall. In this regard they are more clergy-like than many churches which may have an ordinary member of the church give a sermon from time to time. Only elders can sit on judicial hearings. Nor are ministerial servants allowed to sit on such committees. A committee of three or more elders can excommunicate (disfellowship) a fellow Witness. The congregation cannot participate in this procedure and is not privy to the evidence or the reasoning behind the judgment—a judgment that is an organizational death sentence. Nor can Witnesses question the decision made by such a committee even if they happen to know the particulars in the case. This degree of clergy power is not present in most churches and, more importantly, it does not represent the Christian model presented in Scripture.

In most Protestant churches, the body of believers can and does vote as to who will serve as their pastor. Elders and deacons are also voted into positions of service in most churches. And the congregation can have a pastor removed by voting him out of that position. Such input by the rank and file members in congregations of Jehovah's Witnesses does not exist. They have no voice in such matters whatsoever. And, as for salaried ministers, I see evidence in Scripture for some financial support for those who perform the work of pastors (shepherds) and teachers. (1 Cor. 9: 4-14) The context of the text cited shows that Paul made a *personal decision* not to accept anything from the Corinthian church—not because he did not have a right to that assistance. To the contrary, he argues that it is appropriate that material assistance be provided for those who labor in the Christian ministry.

Another distinctive feature of the Witness movement is that everyone is charged with the responsibility to do some form of proselytizing—primarily, door-to-door visitations, unless they are physically unable to do this. It is this activity that non-Witnesses are most familiar with. That it takes conviction and a measure of courage to engage in such activity cannot be denied. I can speak from experience in this regard, as I spent about 15,000 hours in such activity during my many years as a Witness. However, I came to question that every Christian should be active in this form of ministry, along with the requirement to report such time spent to the local congregation. For one to be officially counted as an active Witness, he or she must record and report the number of hours spent each month in some form of public witnessing. Only those who regularly report such time are considered active Witnesses. I mentioned at the outset of this book that the point was made of my mother at her memorial service that during her fifty years as a Witness she *never* failed to report some time each and every month!

In the early church there were those who served as evangelists but not everyone did. (Eph. 4: 11) We all have different abilities and we are to use these abilities to advance God's cause in Christ. The lock-step activity orchestrated by the WBTS bears no resemblance to the activity of the early church. And there certainly is no evidence in Scripture to suggest that time spent speaking to others about one's faith was duly reported and recorded as part of that Christian's record. But in the Witness community unless one is active in public witnessing in one form or another—and *reporting* that time, they are not viewed as a faithful Witness. Moreover, if one fails to share in this organized activity when their circumstances permit it, they are led to believe that they will not be saved through the coming battle of Armageddon.

The Bible teaches that there are many ministries within the Christian community that are God-ordained. (Rom. 12: 4-8) Most of these have to do with ministering to the needs of others within the Christian community itself. In the city of Joppa, there was a disciple named Tabitha, who was well known for her good works and ministering to the poor. She became ill and died. The Apostle Peter was in the nearby city of Lydda and he was sent for. When Peter arrived they showed him the robes and other clothing that she had made for others. Peter raised this woman to life. (Acts 9: 36-43)

The point is that there were many forms of ministry within the Christian church, and all of them were God-ordained and honored. Tabitha, ministered to the needs of others by her needle work. And while Jehovah's Witnesses do acts of kindness to one another and their neighbors, such works and the time engaged in such works is not recorded. The end result of this arbitrary practice is to invest too much value in those hours spent going from door-to-door with Watchtower literature and not enough value invested in those hours spent helping people is other ways. I found this policy increasingly discriminatory. If the "left hand is not to know what the right hand is doing," why attach a name to *any* reported activity? Why keep a printed report card on every individual's activity in the house-to-house work? I submit that if the Society discontinued keeping a record of *individual activity* in this work, the amount of time spent in it would drop precipitously. Why? Because it would cease to be a significant factor in measuring the worth of people.

As I reflected on these things I gradually came to realize that we had created a system of organization and worship that was more the product of human wisdom than divine wisdom. And we used our organizational model to condemn other models. We had developed our own "language'" and could tell instantly whether someone was "in the truth" by his or her use of certain buzz words. Little by little, I was peeling away the many layers of arbitrary evaluations created by the Watchtower system and finding that they often lacked spiritual substance. The weekly meetings were repetitious and lacking in creativity, individualism and spontaneity. Nor was there ever a simple celebration of Christian joy. Everything was focused on the business of witnessing. Every talk and presentation was developed in Brooklyn, New York and regurgitated in the local Kingdom Hall. Witness elders never create their own talks (sermons). They are given detailed outlines as to what they will present and what little research might be done is confined to what the WBTS has already published on the matter.

This "one size fits all," approach to congregational life works very well in promoting conformity and keeping the association "on message," but I was finding that it lacked spirituality and not nourishing to genuine faith. The mindset was that if you fell into step with the program, all other areas of life would be healthy. This approach failed to meet the needs of many people. I often returned home from meetings more discouraged than encouraged. Mavis had stopped attending meetings before I did and when she saw me so upset by what I had heard at the Kingdom Hall, she would ask me why I continued to go there. I didn't have a good answer for that.

Chapter 14

Moment
of
Decision

By the spring of 1980 I could no longer continue stumbling along trying to find a comfort zone within a religious system that demanded complete, unquestioning obedience and submission. One Sunday morning in May while driving home from the Kingdom Hall after having attended a public talk and the Watchtower study, I thought of something Jesus had said and was recorded in Matthew, chapter 11. I pulled the car onto the shoulder of the road and stopped. I picked up my Bible and found that text and read it silently to myself:

> Come to me, all you who are toiling and loaded down, and I will refresh you. Take my yoke upon you and become my disciples, for I am mild-tempered and lowly in heart, and you will find refreshment for your souls. For my yoke is kindly and my load is light. (Matt. 11: 28-30, *NWT*)

As I drank in our Lord's humble and inspiring invitation to discipleship, I was struck by the contradiction my life reflected. Why wasn't I experiencing the refreshment Jesus had promised? Something was terribly wrong. Either I was guilty of loading myself up with burdensome cares that robbed me of joy, or someone else was doing so. As I pondered this matter one thing seemed clear: the burden was *not* coming from the Lord Jesus. He promised that his yoke of servitude and his load of responsibility would be light, pleasurable and satisfying. I sincerely believed what he said was true.

In that quiet moment of reflection, I decided that I would not associate with Jehovah's Witnesses again unless I could do so with full confidence that Jehovah God was truly using the organization as I had been led to believe he was. Continuing in my present half-hearted way satisfied no one, including myself. I needed time to sort matters out in a calm and reasonable way. I needed some space to more objectively evaluate my religious orientation as a whole. Perhaps I could then make a more balanced and measured judgment as to how to live out my life as a Christian disciple. That Sunday morning in May 1980 would be the last time I walked into a Kingdom Hall until my mother's memorial in January of 1996.

At this very moment in time, unknown to me, events taking place at the world headquarters of Jehovah's Witnesses which would have an impact on me and Jehovah's Witnesses everywhere. A number of respected and influential members of the Watchtower Society's headquarters staff were being aggressively investigated as apostates, and a few would be subsequently punished for privately discussing religious views that put into question some of the Society's foundational teachings. These differing views were the product of private studies by small groups of individuals at headquarters in which the Bible alone was used as the authority. This was a spontaneous, unorganized happening, perhaps triggered by the failure of 1975 and the official response to that failure. In any event, something unprecedented was happening at the world headquarters of the WBTS.

A few years earlier, in 1977, a Witness elder living in Sweden, Carl Olof Jonsson, had forwarded to the Brooklyn headquarters a carefully researched treatise that challenged the accuracy of the cornerstone doctrine of Jehovah's Witnesses known as "The Gentile Times." This treatise added fuel to the problems growing in Brooklyn. The treatise was later published in book form under the titled: *The Gentile Time Reconsidered*. It presented a serious challenge to the Society's core teaching regarding the Gentile times. I have already pointed out that 1914 marked the *terminus date* in Charles T. Russell's 115-year "end times' (1799-1914) calculations. The year 1914, according to his view would bring an end of what he called "The Gentile Times." It was an intricate component in Russell's "end times" tapestry. Russell had drawn the term "Gentile times" from Luke 21:24 "And they [the inhabitants of Jerusalem] shall fall by the edge of the sword, and shall be led away captive into all nations: and Jerusalem shall be trodden down of the Gentiles, until the times of the Gentiles be fulfilled." (*Authorized Version*). As to the length of those "times" Russell had used Daniel, chapter 4, to argue that those "times" amounted to 2,520 years: extending from 606 B.C. to 1914 A.D.

In Daniel 4, we are told that king Nebuchadnezzar of Babylon, lost his sanity for a period of "seven times," after which he regained his sanity and was restored to his kingdom. Russell saw in this a much greater prophecy. He understood the "seven times" in Nebuchadnezzar's case to be seven literal years. Then applying the formula of a "day for a year," he come up with his time feature of 2,520 years (7 x 360). A lunar year of twelve months of thirty days each explains the number 360. The concept of a "day for a year" in prophecy can be found in Ezekiel, but it is not found in Daniel. Russell's starting date of 606 B.C. was later changed to 607 B.C. because there was no "0" year between B.C.- A.D. The 606 B.C. date resulted in only 2,519 years. The Society later moved the 606 B.C. date to 607 B.C. to compensate for the one year shortage.

Now, in 1977, Carl Olof Jonsson's research was being read by a few prominent men at the Brooklyn headquarters and giving them pause regarding this cornerstone doctrine. Jonsson's carefully researched material was disturbing because, if true, it could destroy the very foundation upon which the organization was given birth, together with its claim of divine authority. This sent a shock wave through the headquarter's organization. In what can only be described as a witch hunt, the leadership lashed out at everyone they thought might be harboring "apostate" views. Before it was over, one of the Governing Body members, Raymond Franz would be removed from office. One prominent member of the writing staff, Edward Dunlap, a former registrar of the Watchtower's missionary school and lifelong Witness, was disfellowshiped. Other members of the headquarter's family (staff) were interrogated and some were disfellowshiped. It would only be a matter of weeks before the shock waves of these events would be felt around the world. The first tremor would be felt at the district assemblies held in the summer of 1980.

While I was not attending the local Kingdom Hall at that time, I did assist my mother to attend the district assembly of the Witnesses that summer at the Civic Center in St. Paul, Minnesota. I was in the audience of this assembly when a talk was given titled: "Confident In A World Of Doubts." This talk was later published in *The Watchtower*. The thrust of this talk was to paint doubting in an extremely negative light. Doubting was linked to the philosophy of scepticism, and ridiculed as "worldly" thinking. The Bible, by contrast, was held up as a source of a confident message; one that could be completely trusted and in which there was no room for doubting. Jehovah God was trustworthy and so was his Word, the Bible. This premise was summarized by the following statement:

> Strong confidence in Jehovah, in his Word *and in his organization* eliminates paralyzing doubts and brings real happiness. This is the path of true wisdom."—*The Watchtower,* August 1, 1980, page 16. (Italics not in original)

I had observed this tactic many times in the past. The Society would set forth an obvious or unquestioned truth and then link that truth to whatever it was they wanted to be accepted as truth without question. It was "truth by association," similar in concept to "guilt by association"—validating as trustworthy whatever they had to say on a given matter. They were doing it now in relation to doubting. It was not that those sitting in that audience or those who would later read the same words in print were likely to be doubting God or the trustworthiness of the Bible. The leadership's concern was having the Witnesses doubting *them!* No attempt was made to distinguish between reasonable doubts and frivolous ones. All doubting in relation to what the Witnesses were being told to believe was categorically wrong. The assembly speaker read from a manuscript that was later published in *The Watchtower*:

> If insidious doubts ever begin to creep into mind, the Christian would do well first to weigh the situation and ask himself a few pointed questions:

> Where did I learn that God's name is Jehovah, what that name means, what is God's loving purpose for mankind and why he has allowed suffering to go on so long on earth?—Ps. 83: 18; Rev. 21: 3,4; 2 Pet. 3: 9,13.

> Who taught me that Jesus Christ is not a second part of a Trinitarian godhead, but Jehovah's only-begotten Son, and who was it that helped me to understand the full meaning of redemption from sin through Christ's ransom sacrifice?—John 3: 16; 14: 28; 1 Cor. 15: 27,28.

> What religion cleared up in my mind the question of the holy spirit, not a personal "Holy Ghost," but Jehovah's active force, and where have I found a group of persons who sincerely endeavor to produce the fruitage of the spirit?—Acts 2: 33; Gal. 5: 22,23 Col. 3: 12-14.

> Which religious organization set me straight on the ancient pagan idea of the immortality of the human soul, proving from the Bible that the soul is mortal and thus giving real meaning to the Bible doctrine of the resurrection and freeing me from the God-dishonoring dogma of hellfire?—Ezek. 18: 4; Acts 24: 15; Rom. 6: 23.

> Who has been preaching God's kingdom as mankind's only hope, and who has helped me to become aware that we are living in the 'last days' and that we should "keep on the watch" for the coming of the Son of man?—Mark 13: 10,33-37; Luke 21: 34-36; 2 Pet. 3: 3-7.

> With whom have I found a real purpose in life, "the peace of God," protection from the temptations and pitfalls of this world and practical wisdom in solving life's problems?—Matt. 24: 45-47; 1 Tim. 3: 15; Phil. 4: 6-9.

Finally, what group of Christians genuinely have "love among themselves" (John 13: 34,35), really respect the principles outlined in John 17: 14,16 and Isaiah 2:4, and are persecuted, not because they meddle in politics, but simply "on account of Jesus' name," that is, for being real Christians?—Matt. 24: 9; John 15: 18,19.

For over 2,000,000 persons living in more than 200 lands and island groups, the candid answer to those questions is: Jehovah's Witnesses, as fed spiritually by the "faithful and discreet slave" class and its governing body.—Compare Luke 12: 42-44—*The Watchtower*, August 1, 1980, page 14.

I believed a few things presented in that question format, but there were other things on that list that had been highly radicalized and distorted. At that moment in time I hadn't fully comprehended the degree to which they had denigrated the Lord Jesus and changed the gospel. But, even if *everything* mentioned on that list were true, would that, in itself, make it inappropriate to question or doubt *anything* they taught? I think not. And another thing, any truth gleaned from the Scriptures does not originate with modern men and their organizations. What truth Russell may have had he received from others before him. He also received considerable error from others as well. I couldn't help but contrast this arrogant, self-exalting posturing with the modesty shown by the apostle Paul who faithfully served as an ambassador of Christ. When certain men were being exalted and especially looked to as leaders, Paul was moved to say, "What after all, is Apollos? And what is Paul? Only servants, through whom you came to believe—as the Lord has assigned to each his task. I planted the seed, Apollos watered it, but God made it grow. So neither he who plants nor he who waters is anything, but only God, who makes things grow." (1 Cor. 3:5-7 *NIV*) And in a subsequent letter to the same church he added, ""We have no wish to Lord it over your faith, but to work with you for your joy, for your stand in the faith is firm." (2 Cor. 1:24 *NJB*)

Unlike the spirit shown by the apostle Paul, the Society dominates the Witnesses and continually reminds them of how much they are indebted to it. Any doubting or questioning of any item of "food" being served up by them is indicative of a bad heart condition. The discourse drew attention to the fact that some of Jesus' disciples were slow to believe that he had really been resurrected and what Jesus had said to them in this regard:

Why are you troubled, and why is it doubts come up in your hearts? Yes, that is where doubts begin—in the heart. So if disturbing doubts ever start troubling us, we should begin by examining our motives. Are our doubts genuine, or are they a pretext for slowing down.?—*The Watchtower*, August 1, 1980, pages 14,15.

    I could hardly believe the way the Bible was being used in this presentation. That some disciples initially doubted the resurrection hardly compared to the doubts that the Society was dealing with. Furthermore, Jesus took steps to produce convincing evidence that he truly had been resurrected. Thomas, one of those who had such reservations, was accommodated by Jesus to know that he was truly alive once again. Jesus didn't hide his wounds and say to Thomas, "Trust me, Thomas. I tell you this is the same body that died." Nor did he assign bad motives to Thomas. Rather, he showed Thomas the wounds and invited him to touch them. (sec Luke 24; John 20) Clearly, the Society was "stacking the deck" against any doubting or questioning of them. They mentioned that doubting begins with the heart, and that is true, but the fact that doubts arise in the heart does not, in itself, imply bad motive. Surely, the disciples did not have bad motives in questioning Jesus' resurrection.

    All too often, a bad motive is assigned to those who register doubts or raise troubling questions. If you can delegate a bad motive to someone's questioning you can more readily feel free to dismiss the question and the questioner as not deserving of an answer. Because the Society now felt threatened they developed a siege mentality. After the summer of 1980 there would be an intensified effort to flush out any and all persons who dared question or doubt the organization in any way. It would be only a matter of months before Mavis and I would become targets of the purge.

Chapter 15

The
Separation
Made Complete

After the District Assemblies in 1980, there was a heightened concern regarding "apostates" in the midst of Jehovah's Witnesses. Articles appearing in *The Watchtower* regularly defamed those who would dare question the truthfulness of things being taught by the "faithful and discreet slave." This descriptive title was taken from the Watchtower's Bible translation of Jesus' words at Matthew 24: 45-47 "Who really is the faithful and discreet slave whom his master appointed over his domestics, to give them their food at the proper time? Happy is that slave if his master on arriving finds him doing so. Truly I say to you, He will appoint him over all his belongings." Similar to the way the Roman Catholic Church uses Matthew 16: 18 to validate their teaching that Peter was the first of a line of popes, the Witnesses moved a few chapters forward in the gospel to lay claim to being the successor of the "faithful and discreet slave." According to their interpretation, this "slave" constituted the Christian congregation as a whole which was directed by a governing body located in Jerusalem. This composite "slave" began his appearance at Pentecost and was to have a continuous existence until Christ returned. So, when Watchtower publications intone the phrase, "the faithful and discreet slave," it represents the organizational *imprimatur* of authority. Typical of the character assassination that continuously flowed from Watchtower printing presses is the following:

> Thus, the one who doubts to the point of becoming an apostate sets himself up as a judge. He thinks he knows better also than the "faithful and discreet slave," through whom he has learned the best part, if not all that he knows about Jehovah God and his purposes. He develops a *spirit of independence*, and becomes "proud in heart . . . something detestable to Jehovah." (Prov. 16: 5) Some apostates even think they know better

than God, as regards his ordering of events in the outworking of his purposes. Two other causes of apostasy are therefore *ingratitude* and *presumption.*—*The Watchtower*, August 1, 1980, pages 19,20 (italics in original).

The above is typical of the rhetorical torrent that gushed forth in the Society's publications and from the mouths of their traveling representatives. There developed what can only be described as a siege mentality as regards any and all persons who would voice criticism of the leadership. The word "apostate" was used to include mere questioning or doubting something the Society taught. It wasn't necessary to be teaching some contrary thing to receive this label.

There is no *honorable* way one can walk away from the Watchtower system of religion. Once people are baptized as Witnesses the system owns them! It is not necessary to speak out against some teaching or some policy in order to be defamed as a person. Nor is it necessary to have committed some grievous sin. If one simply decides he no longer wants to be a Witness, for any reason, he is treated *exactly* as one disfellowshiped for immorality. This means he will be shunned by those members of his family and friends who remain Witnesses. This harsh policy was also a product of the paranoia that seized the organization in 1980. Regarding the treatment of those who made it known that they no longer wanted to be considered a Jehovah's Witness, they declared:

> One who has been a true Christian [def: baptized Jehovah's Witness] might renounce the way of the truth, stating that he no longer considers himself to be one of Jehovah's Witnesses or wants to be known as one. When this rare event occurs, the person is renouncing his standing as a Christian, deliberately disassociating himself from the congregation. The apostle John wrote: "They went out from us, but they were not of our sort; for if they had been of our sort, they would have remained with us." —1 John 2: 19
>
> . . . Persons who make themselves "not of our sort," by deliberately rejecting the faith and beliefs of Jehovah's Witnesses should appropriately be viewed and treated as are those who have been disfellowshiped for wrongdoing.—*The Watchtower*, September 15, 1981 page 23.

When you consider that most of those who decide they no longer wish to be known as a Jehovah's Witness have been such for many years, you can appreciate the cost this decision imposes on them. In effect, one stands to lose family, friends and social network in a near total way. As a result, there are many Witnesses who do not agree with the Society on certain matters but out of fear of losing family and friends, remain in the organization. I have spoken with many such persons over the years, some of them elders, who are greatly disenchanted with the organization but "hang in there" for the reasons stated. The leadership of the organization has distorted the biblical concept of disfellowshiping in order to intimidate and silence dissenters. This cruel, unchristian policy, proves to be most effective.

As events began to unfold, it was only a matter of months before Mavis and I would find ourselves among those described above: ingrates, having a spirit of independence, ingratitude and presumption It began in February of 1981 with a phone call from a local elder in the Owatonna congregation, who said the elders would like to arrange a meeting with us. When I pressed him as to the nature of the meeting he told me that someone had reported to them that we had said things that disturbed them, and there was a concern that apostasy might be involved. I asked who brought the matter to their attention. He said he couldn't tell me that. I asked why the party in question had not come to us first in keeping with Jesus' counsel in such matters?—Matt. 18: 15-17. I said that if we wanted God's blessing in a matter it seemed appropriate that we abide by the directives contained in Scripture as to how such investigations should proceed. His reply was, "It isn't necessary in this case."

We responded to their request to meet with them at the Kingdom Hall in Owatonna, not knowing who it was that was making a charge against us or what the charge actually was. We were free to bring witnesses to the hearing but not knowing who or what the matter was about, prevented us from preparing in any way to defend ourselves. We decided to invite a friend, a man who had served at the world headquarters for a number of years and shared some of our concerns, and we also asked our daughter, Jamie, and our son-in-law, Frank, to join us.

When we arrived at the Kingdom Hall on the night the hearing was scheduled, we learned for the first time who our accusers were. It was a husband and wife whom we had met only once about a month earlier at the home of another Witness couple with whom we were close friends. Actually, there was but one accusing witness present, the husband, who said his wife was ill and couldn't come. We were told that the elders had a letter from her that substantiated the charge being brought against us by the husband. We were not shown the letter and its contents were not shared with us. In this way they were able to technically follow the dictum that "out of the mouth of two or three witnesses" a matter should be resolved.

On the particular night, several weeks earlier, that we had first met this couple we had decided not to discuss our doubts with these people.

Such discussion only led to strained relations. However, after dinner, our host, Glen Porter, brought up the matter of our having doubts about the Society's prophetic role and drew us out as to the basis for that. Because he raised this issue in the presence of the other couple we assumed he felt comfortable having us discuss matters in their presence. We did present the historical facts relating to our misgivings about the organization's history of failed predictions and that cast doubt on the extent the organization had been spirit-directed in its history. There was no indication that anyone present was disturbed by what we said. We returned home and gave no further thought to the matter.

Most Witnesses at this time were ignorant of the Society's true history of failed prophecy. What little information they had been given about the historical record in current publications either omitted previous errors or whitewashed them with half-truths that concealed the true magnitude of those errors. Kingdom Hall libraries were void of Watchtower publications produced during the first 60 or 70 years of their history so that a Witness could not check these things out for themselves. What we were sharing with people was not coming from outside sources but from the archives of the organization's official publications. We were not embellishing that record. There was no need to, the facts were damning enough. We didn't feel we were undermining people's faith by revealing these historical facts, facts that seriously challenged the Society's presentation of its history, its claim of spiritual authority and its role in proclaiming the outworking of God's purposes in the last days.

Because the faith of Jehovah's Witnesses in God and Jesus Christ is so entwined with their faith in the organization it is nearly impossible to separate them in their minds. Challenging their faith in the organization is to challenge their faith in God and Christ. They have been carefully taught and indoctrinated with the belief that they do not have Jesus as their mediator. Their "mediator," is really the organization. Without the organization they have no standing with God and Christ. It is this mindset that creates such a barrier to objectively reasoning on matters. As soon as it is detected that an individual is questioning or doubting "the slave" organization red flags unfurl and reasoning ability shuts down. This explains the extreme sensitivity they have about anything that would cast a shadow on the organization—even if what is said is true. Loyal Witnesses consider it an unloving act to mention anything negative about the Society's past that would disturb the sacred status of it and its leadership. It has become irreproachable as God and Christ are irreproachable. In other words, it is unloving to say, "the emperor has no clothes."

This is the general attitude that prevails among the Witnesses and it was the attitude that prevailed at our hearing that night in February, 1981. Incidentally, Glen Porter, our host, had been asked to testify against us but he refused. I don't recall specifically what the husband had to say, but I remember his comments were a fair recollection of the conversation we had that night. Mavis recalls that he said she "hated the elders," and this could not have been true. Mavis was extremely disappointed with the elders in our congregation, as they provided no spiritual support for her but she never said she disliked or hated them. In fact, she was inclined to excuse them to some extent because she realized they were acting out of a basic ignorance of her condition. But she always assigned good motives to them. Of course, her denial carried little weight. In reconstructing part of what I had shared with this couple and our host that evening in question, I explained briefly how my conversation with August Vogel in the winter of 1970-71 about the significance of 1975 and his response that there seemed to be more evidence that 1925 would be a significant year than 1975. I produced an original copy of the book, *Millions Now Living Will Never Die,* Vogel had alluded to and read Rutherford's prediction regarding 1925 from page 97:

> Based upon the argument heretofore set forth, then, that the old order of things, the old world, is ending and is therefore passing away, and that the new order is coming in, and that 1925 shall mark the resurrection of the faithful worthies of old and the beginning of reconstruction, it is reasonable to conclude that millions of people now on earth will be still on the earth in 1925. Then, based upon the promises set forth in the divine Word, we must reach the positive and indisputable conclusion that millions now living will never die.

After reading that to the elder committee, one of them, Lorice Wilkie, asked, "Why bring that up?" In other words, what relevance does that have to what we are dealing with here? The same brother inquired if I had gone back to brother Vogel to let him know the *harm* he caused by directing me to the *Millions Now Living Will Never Die,* book? I said I had talked with him afterward but the idea that he had done me a disservice by bringing it to my attention never occurred to me. To be sure, I was upset by what I found in the book, but at the same time I was grateful to have been made aware of it. But their view was that what he had done was an unloving act.

This underscores the problem that exists among the Witnesses. If a person is struggling with their faith in the organization there is no forum available to openly discuss such struggles. If they go to an elder with a serious objection he risks being told that he must have a bad heart, otherwise he wouldn't be having such "apostate" thoughts. If he presents sound evidence for his doubts he is likely to by asked if he believes in "the faithful and discreet slave?" This is a loaded question because if he says yes, then he accepts the organization's claim of being spirit-led and he must "wait of Jehovah." If something needs changing Jehovah God will correct matters in his due time. If he says no to that question, then he is already an "apostate" and, unless repentant, will be disfellowshiped. Much of the responsibility for questioning on the part of many Witnesses at this time was the fault of the Society itself. So much expectation had been created by them regarding the year 1975 and when that expectation failed, many were upset and angry about it. So it wasn't like there weren't reasons to be discussing *past* failures of the Society. In fact, the presence of many past failures clearly showed a *pattern* that was very significant. The disappointment over 1975 wasn't just a momentary "blip" on the radar screen.

The committee meeting ended and we were told that they would evaluate the matter and give us their decision in due course. A day or two later they came to our home to tell us that they had decided to disfellowshiped Mavis and I was to be publicly reproved. For some reason, which I've never understood, the committee took a harder view of Mavis than myself. Perhaps it was because of her emotional illness and her inability to function on any level for so many years. The Mavis they knew was far different from the one who had labored so faithfully and so hard in the ministry for so many years. Also, a few months earlier, we had been visited by a circuit servant and one of the elders now serving on the judicial committee. This visit was for the purpose of encouraging us to begin attending meetings again. At one point in our conversation, Mavis said, "The Witnesses are brainwashed." Her remark was prompted by a television documentary she had recently viewed about the mind-controlling tactics used by certain religious cults in America. The program specified 7 or 8 characteristics such "cults" had in common, she realized that Jehovah's Witnesses used almost all of the same tactics. Because the program was defining such controlled indoctrination as "brain washing," she concluded that the Witnesses were also brainwashed. Perhaps it was this remark that convinced the circuit servant and the elder that Mavis was beyond recall. Whatever the reason, they judged her more harshly than they did myself.

Their decision to disfellowship only Mavis came as a shock to me. That Mavis should be considered more reprehensible than me, made no sense at all. I encouraged her to appeal their decision, which Society policy allowed her to do. She did appeal and in due course an appeal committee of three elders outside of the Owatonna area was appointed to hear her appeal. They met with her together with the initial committee to review the facts. We knew two of those men from our earlier ministry in the Twin City area. Our daughter also attended this hearing. When it was over, and we were asked to leave the building temporarily while they made their decision, our daughter confided to her mother that she thought they would overturn the decision of the first committee. They did not. The initial decision remained in force.

As winter reluctantly gave way to spring, I had time to reflect on the turbulent decade just past. So much had happened and so many things were irrevocably changed, it was difficult to emotionally orient myself. At this time we were still having contact with our daughter and her family as well as my mother and aunt LuCretia and Mavis' sister Laverne. Those family members living close (everyone above except Laverne) continued to visit us, and we were welcome in their home even though Mavis was disfellowshiped. What made this possible was a recent change the Society had made regarding *family ties* and a disfellowshiped member of a family. This new policy was spelled out in *The Watchtower* of August 1, 1974:

> Since blood and marital relationships are *not dissolved* by a congregational disfellowshiping action, the situation within the family circle requires special consideration. A woman whose husband is disfellowshiped is not released from the Scriptural requirement to respect his husbandly headship over her; only death or Scriptural divorce from a husband results in such a release. . . Parents similarly remain under the injunction to "go on bringing up their children in the disciple and mental-regulating of Jehovah" even though a baptized son or a daughter yet a minor is disfellowshiped. (Eph. 6: 4) And sons and daughters, of whatever age, remain under the obligation to "honor their father and mother" although one or both of these may be disfellowshiped (Mat.15: 4; Eph. 6: 2) This is not difficult to understand when we consider that, according to the Scriptures, even political officials of this world are to be shown due honor by Christians —Rom. 13: 1,7. —Page 470. (Italics not in original)

As to disfellowshiped family members (not minor sons or daughters) living outside the home, each family must decide to what extent they will have association with such ones. This is not something that the congregational elders can decide for them. What the elders are concerned with is that "leaven" is not reintroduced into the congregation through *spiritual fellowshiping* with those who had to be removed as such "leaven." Thus, if a disfellowshiped parent goes to visit a son or daughter or to see grand-children and is allowed to enter the Christian home, this is not the con-cern of the elders. Such a one has *a natural right* to visit his blood rela-tives and his offspring. Similarly, when sons or daughters render honor to a parent, though disfellowshiped, by calling to see how such one's physi-cal health is or what needs he or she may have, this act in itself is not a spiritual fellowshiping. —Page 471. (italics not in original)

This policy represented a more humane and scripturally balanced view of disfellowshiped persons than had been in place before. I remem-ber how well this material was received by Witnesses who often had to repress their own compassionate feelings in order to comply with the more stringent policy that preceded it. My mother had a sister, my aunt Vera, who had been disfellowshiped in the 1950s, and she and my aunt LuCretia cut her off completely—having no contact whatsoever with her for many years. But when this article was studied in the congrega-tions they felt free to telephone her. I was in my mother's home when this call was placed and remember how happy Mom and aunt LuCretia were to speak with their sister once more. They could do this in good conscience because *The Watchtower* allowed their conscience to do it. But in a short time this policy would change.

The more I reflected on the judgment Mavis and I received, the more I resented it. What had we done that warranted the label: "apostate?" Had we lied? Had we misrepresented the facts? Had we taught some unscriptural doctrine? Did we underhandedly or capriciously seek to subvert the faith of others? The answer to all of those questions was no. We had spoken to a few family members and friends about facts we had learned that seriously affected our religious equilibrium—things that begged to be addressed—*needed* to be addressed, but we never renounced being Witnesses or argued that the Watchtower Society did not represent the "faithful and discreet slave" of Matthew 24:45-47. Still, Mavis had been disfellowshiped and I had been publicly reproved "for conduct un-becoming a Christian."

As we assessed our situation following the committee hearings, we concluded that everything hinged on the Society's claim of representing the "faithful and discreet slave" mentioned in Matthew 24:45-47. If they had this authority, we would be obliged to submit to that authority in faithfulness to God and the Lord Jesus. The question was: does the Society's history support that claim? I determined that I would research this cardinal tenet of our faith. I spent months gleaning information from official Watchtower sources in order to understand specifically what was taught about this doctrine. The final product of that research was a 21-page treatise I titled: "The Faithful and Discreet Slave."

That thesis proved to be the final "nail in the coffin." Because of its importance I have decided to include it in the Appendix of this book. Some of the material contained in it has already been presented in the book, but the treatise arranges the material in a different format which will help the reader better understand its significance. The doctrine, as taught by the Society, rests on two pillars: (1) Jesus is said to have installed a composite slave organization with an attending governing body on Pentecost Day in A.D. 33. This composite slave organization, according to their view, was to have a continuous, uninterrupted existence down to the end of the present world. (2) Jesus returned invisibly in 1914 and began an inspection of all religions claiming to serve him. Out of all those inspected, only one group proved faithful and worthy of his approval: the WBTS. In the spring of 1919, Jesus gave them the exclusive right and authority to represent him as his exclusive channel of communication. What do the historical and biblical facts show in this regard? Do they substantiate that claim? No!

"The Faithful and Discreet Slave" treatise is reproduced in the Appendix to help break the grip of fear that prevents rational examination and evaluation of the Scriptures and the historical facts. As long as a person is intimidated by the WBTS' posturing itself as having authority over his or her life, they will never experience the joy of freedom in Christ. "For such freedom Christ set us free. Therefore, stand fast, and do not let yourselves be confined again in a yoke of slavery." (Gal. 5: 1 *NWT*)

Chapter 16

Disfellowshipped For Apostasy

N ow fully convinced that God and Christ were not asking me to submit to the religious authority the Watchtower Society claimed for itself and having lost confidence in their spiritual insight and veracity, I decided the time had come to officially sever my relationship with them. It wasn't that I knew of anything better. I did not. But I could no longer give them what they demanded of me: unquestioned loyalty and subjection. There was no middle ground, no comfort zone in which I could harbor certain reservations and still function in a whole-hearted way. To have continued to submit to that degree of control, given what I knew, would have destroyed me; I would have had to sell myself in order to remain a Witness.

On September 14, 1981, I wrote a brief note to the elders of the Owatonna, Minnesota congregation of Jehovah's Witnesses, in which I said: "I have decided that I no longer want to be identified with a religious organization that brands me an apostate for questioning some of its teachings." In a letter dated September 21, the elders responded:

> The Owatonna Body of Elders has received and read your letter regarding your desire to disassociate yourself. Please realize, Ron, that it is of the utmost necessity, because of the circumstances and past judicial action, to meet with you again.
>
> A meeting has been arranged for Saturday, September 26 at 2:00 P.M. If you do not wish to attend please inform us by letter and we will follow recommended procedure. The meeting will be at the Owatonna Kingdom Hall.

The "past judicial action" was in reference to their having placed me on "public reproof" in February 1981. Organizational policy now insisted that I meet with them again. I responded by writing the following:

As I explained in my note sent to you on September 14, 1981, I can no longer identify myself with a religious organization that labels me an apostate for questioning some of its teachings. That being the situation it would be inconsistent of me to respond to its organizational procedure. Therefore, I will not be in attendance at the meeting on the 26th.

I harbor no ill will toward you as individuals. I know that you are acting out of loyalty to the organization and to Jehovah God as you perceive His will. I respect that even though I do not agree with your perception of things. I, too, must act consistent with my faith and understanding of what I perceive God's will to be for me. One day we will all stand before the judgment seat of the Lord Jesus Christ, and we will be judged not only on our deeds but our judgment of others. The measure we measure out to others will be the measure measured out to us. I do not stand in judgment of you. Rather, I pray for you that Jehovah God, through His Son, Jesus Christ, will extend mercy to you as I desire mercy for myself.

Though I had voluntarily separated myself from the organization it was now necessary for the elders to follow through with the Society's current directives in such matters. In a brief letter sent by them dated October 5, 1981 they said:

The Owatonna Congregation Body of Elders have found it necessary to disfellowship you. This action is effective as of Sept. 27, 1981.

The letter was not signed but bore the names of David Skusa, Lorice Wilkie and Jerry Ronan, all elders of the Owatonna Congregation.

Relations within my extended family had been severely strained for some time prior to this, but when it was learned that I had disassociated myself and was subsequently disfellowshiped, family relationships became even more difficult. There was no question but that our family would abide by whatever policy was in place regarding the treatment of and association with family members who were disfellowshiped. The dividing line in this matter was determining what were viewed as natural family ties and what were religious ties. The policy in place at the start of 1981 was clear in making a distinction between the two. What was to be avoided, the Society had said, were religious ties with disfellowshiped family members. A disfellowshiping action did not break family ties or annul familial affection or responsibilities. The congregational elders were instructed not to attempt to police the interaction of family members which were the product of natural relationships.

While our family members were obviously distressed and deeply disappointed in us, they did not avoid seeing us. We visited one another, ate meals together and in various ways continued some semblance of

family. Although Mavis had been disfellowshiped in February, our daughter arranged for a beautician, also a Witness, to come to our home with
Jamie, my mother and aunt to give Mavis a permanent. About this time,
Frank and Jamie moved into a new home and, together with several Witnesses, we helped with the moving. When Mavis phoned her sister
Laverne in Idaho and informed her that she had been disfellowshiped
she asked her if she would continue to speak to her and write her. Laverne
unhesitatingly assured Mavis that she would do both and seemed surprised that Mavis would think differently. Another couple, also Witnesses,
took us out to dinner during this time. And in the previous chapter I
mentioned how the material in *The Watchtower* of August 1, 1974
prompted my mother and aunt to phone their disfellowshiped sister they
hadn't spoken to in years. I believe that over time we could have worked
out a reasonable and mutually comfortable family arrangement without
destroying family relationships. However, that was not going to happen.

A new policy towards disfellowshiped Witnesses appeared in the
September 15, 1981 issue of *The Watchtower*. This new policy elimi-
nated virtually all contact of any sort with those disfellowshiped or disassociated from the congregation. (For those unacquainted with Watchtower policy it should be explained that a disfellowshiped person is one
that *the organization* has taken action against, while a disassociated person is one who *voluntarily* severs relationship with the organization.) In
a section of the magazine that dealt with disfellowshiped relatives not
living at home it said:

> The second situation that we need to consider is that involving a
> disfellowshiped or disassociated relative who is *not* in the immediate fam-
> ily circle or living at one's home. Such a person is still related by blood or
> marriage, and so there may be some limited need to care for necessary
> family matters. Nonetheless, it is not as if he were living in the same
> home where contact and conversation could not be avoided. We should
> keep clearly in mind the Bible's inspired direction: "Quit mixing in com-
> pany with *anyone* called a brother that is a fornicator or a greedy person .
> . . not even eating with such a man." —1 Cor. 5: 11
>
> Consequently, Christians related to such a disfellowshiped person liv-
> ing outside the home should strive to avoid needless association, even
> keeping business dealings to a minimum.—*The Watchtower*, September
> 15, 1981, page 29. (Italics in original)

The Scripture text (1 Cor. 5: 11) given in the above was in relation to
a man who was practicing incest—living with his father's wife. He apparently saw nothing wrong in this and continued to associate with the

Corinthian brothers and was accepted by them even though they knew his situation. The apostle Paul pointed out how seriously wrong this was and that the man should be expelled from the Christian community. The Society was now taking this specific case and making it an indiscriminate *blanket policy*—covering every case of disfellowshiping and disassociation. At this moment in time there were thousands of long-standing and loyal Witnesses being judicially condemned for voicing criticism of the Society for calling attention to its history of failed predictions. Some, who simply decided they could no longer support the organization because of their repeated errors simply removed themselves from association. These too, would now be treated as murderers and fornicators. In other words, there was no honorable way a person could walk away from the organization. Some simply packed up and moved to other locations where they were not known.

In most cases, it was not a matter of people wanting the freedom to live debauched lives. Nor was it a matter of questioning the Bible and its inspiration. Nor was it a matter of questioning the moral teachings of the Bible or its hope for the future. It was a matter of historical facts being voiced by honorable people who challenged the Society's spiritual authority. The Society would silence all such talk by making it a capital crime. People *not* guilty of immorality would now be treated *exactly* as those who were guilty of practicing things specifically condemned in the Bible. But where in the Bible is it shown that questioning or doubting imperfect, *uninspired* men is a disfellowshiping offense? Where in the Bible does it say it is a sin to expose error? If a religious system declares questioning and openly discussing errors in their religion a sin worthy of excommunication, they have the right to do that. But they do not have the right to misuse the Scriptures in the process, which was what the Society was now doing—coating their arbitrary policy with a scriptural veneer.

The new policy virtually destroyed family ties. There was no longer any suggestion that "sons and daughters of whatever age" remained under the obligation to "honor their father and mother;" there was no more talk about the "natural right" of disfellowshiped persons to visit their children or grandchildren as they had argued just a few years earlier. Note the following in this regard:

> Normally, relatives are often together at meals, picnics, family reunions or other social gatherings. But when someone has unrepentantly pursued sin and has had to be disfellowshiped, he may cause difficulty for his Christian relatives in regard to such gatherings. While they realize that

they are still related to him, they do not want to ignore Paul's advice that faithful Christians should "quit mixing in company" with an expelled sinner.—*Ibid*. page 30, par. 22.

Concerning social gatherings they added:

For example, a Christian couple might be getting married at a Kingdom Hall. If a disfellowshiped relative comes to the Kingdom Hall for the wedding, obviously he could not be in the bridal party there or "give away" the bride. What, though, if there is a wedding feast or reception? This can be a happy social occasion, as it was in Cana when Jesus attended. (John 2:1,2) But will the disfellowshiped relative be allowed to come or even be invited? If he is going to attend, many Christians, relatives or not, might conclude that they should not be there, to eat and associate with him, in view of Paul's directions at 1 Corinthians 5: 11.

Thus, sometimes Christians may not feel able to have a disfellowshiped or disassociated relative present for a gathering that normally would include family members.—*Ibid*. page 30, par. 23,24.

Within a few short weeks after the above was presented in *The Watchtower* we received a letter from our daughter, sadly informing us that she and the family could no longer have *any* association with us. In part, she wrote:

Although much of what you say is based in fact, I feel you've blown it all out of proportion. You're not willing to wait on Jehovah and in the process have thrown away so much good. I feel as tho you've turned your back on Jehovah.

She mentioned having stayed close to us even when her mother was disfellowshiped but doing this, she went on to explain, had caused her to take what she called "detours" (translation: "compromises") in the process and she could no longer do that. She said:

I found myself troubled and shaken in my own faith. I've had to search my heart and the scriptures to reestablish that faith in Jehovah and the organization I feel he is using to feed his sheep.

She went on to cite the text from 1 Corinthians 5: 11-13 used in *The Watchtower* article discussed above. Commenting on that in relation to us, she wrote:

In Israel, when someone turned their back on Jehovah they were stoned to death. (Deut. 17: 2-7) In early Christian times Paul said to "remove that one from your midst" (1 Cor. 5: 11-13) actually quoting from the law of Israel regarding stoning. Such ones were considered spiritually dead.

Christians had no association with such ones, only in providing the necessities of life if need be.

The text from Deuteronomy she cited was addressing the worship of false gods and the one from Corinthians as explained earlier, had to do with incest. Our daughter now was seeing her parents through the prism of these texts— persons guilty of the most despicable of sins. She made it clear that she could not, in good conscience, continue to associate with us or communicate with us unless it was absolutely necessary:

> You've turned another direction and you have to go that way without me, without us . . . I'm letting go, Momma, Daddy and I'm asking that you let go of me and us. Please don't call or write unless it's absolutely necessary.

The near overwhelming pain she had experienced in making that decision and putting it in writing was palatable. Receiving that letter was equally painful. So it was in the autumn of 1981 that our shunning by the family began. Our three grandchildren, Francesca, Andrew and Matthew , ages 13, 11 and 2 respectively, would not be seen by us again. The only exception was my visit to Tucson, Arizona, when I attended my mother's memorial service. Mavis did not go with me on that flight to Tucson, so she has never seen them again.

Those children are now married, and at least two of them that we know about have children of their own. When Francesca was to be married, Jamie wrote to inform us of that but said it would be best if we did not attend the wedding. It wasn't until I looked over my mother's things in 1996 that I saw Francesca's wedding picture. As for my mother, I never saw her after 1981. In the early nineties I impulsively phoned her and asked if I could come for a short visit of an hour or two. I caught her by surprise and she hesitatingly agreed that I could do that. We set a day and time. Several hours later that day, she phoned back and tearfully said that she could not go through with her permission for me to visit. I felt terribly sad for her and assured her that it was okay, that I understood. I took the opportunity to confirm my love for her and to tell her that she had done the very best she knew how as a mother. She continued to weep during most of the few minutes we talked. It would be the last time I would hear her voice.

After 1981, I made several attempts in letters to the family taking issue with their decision to cut us off totally, but that proved futile and only served to hardened them further. What little contact we have had with the family has been in the form of a few phone calls and a few letters which usually informed us of some family member's serious illness or death. Last year (2005), we heard from Jamie in relation to our 60th wedding anniversary, and we were pleased by the kind way she expressed her affection for us. She has expressed her willingness to care for us if such a need arose. While we appreciate that, we are hopeful that there will not be a need. After 25 years of separation none of us is the person he or she once was. There have been no shared experiences to weld us together as a family unit. That is the reality. Mavis was able to accept the separation better than I was. It took me many years to finally accept that there would never be a reconciliation. But when that acceptance finally came, it brought with it a measure of peace, and for that I am very grateful.

We lost family, friends and a worldwide religious/social structure that constituted our world. But the pain of loss and hurt inflicted has not been one-sided. Those of our family who have remained loyal Jehovah's Witnesses these many years have also suffered the pain of loss. A mother lost her only son, a daughter lost her parents. Children lost their grandparents. And those losses are exacerbated by the conviction that we have turned our backs on Jehovah God and are unworthy of life. For a believing mother and daughter to bear that burden has to be the greatest pain and suffering of all.

Chapter 17

"Don't Lose Your Inheritance"

The decade I spent reevaluating the Watchtower Society and its role in the outworking of God's revealed will in the twentieth century, focused on its history of failed expectations—these expectations were heralded as revealed truth in many millions of pieces of literature in many languages and systematically taught by enthusiastic devotees. What was not clearly discerned by me, even as late as 1981, was the destructive effect this system of date-setting and corollary doctrines had on the gospel of the kingdom of God, as preached by Jesus and his apostles.

It was only after having separated myself from the Watchtower system that my relationship with God came into sharper focus. The hope of future life I had nurtured all my life was a hope premised on the accuracy of the Watchtower's perception of what God was doing, when he was doing it, and through whom he was doing it—a premise I now concluded was a false premise. The Watchtower doctrine regarding two classes of Christians: one having a heavenly hope which is limited to 144,000 persons and a second class having an earthly hope of life. As a youth I was told that this second hope was the only one available to me, because the heavenly hope essentially ended in 1935—10 years before I was born. Because the Watchtower Society makes itself essential to realizing this hope, they are, for all practical purposes, God's broker. If you want everlasting life on a paradise earth, you must submit to the spiritual authority invested by Christ Jesus in the WBTS; those are the terms.

It was this belief that raised much fear in my mother's heart when she learned that I had separated myself from the organization. In her mind, I was cutting off my life-support. In one of our last conversations in 1981 she cautioned: "Don't lose your inheritance." From her point of view that was exactly what I was doing. No amount of argument in refutation of that viewpoint penetrated her mindset. At one point she said, "If I lived a thousands years I would never understand what you are doing." Spiritual life outside of the organization was unthinkable to her.

It is not uncommon for Witnesses to ask someone who leaves the Witnesses to ask: "Where will you go?" What they mean is what other religious denomination or sect will you go to? Sometimes the words of the apostle Peter are heard in this context. When Jesus asked if his most intimate followers were going to desert him as some others were doing, Peter responded: "Lord, to *whom* shall we go? You have the words of eternal life. We believe and know that you are the Holy One of God." (John 6: 68,69 *NIV*) The Witnesses interpret Peter's confession to mean: "To what other religion can we go? The organization has the words of everlasting life, and we believe and know this organization is of God." But that interpretation of Peter's words is skewed by their highly sectarian approach to the Bible. The apostle Peter focused on the *person* of Christ: *he* was the anointed one of God, not an organized system of religion. (Matt. 16: 13-17) The passing of nearly two thousand years has not changed this basic truth. Jesus remains the one who has the words of eternal life, and we must listen to his words and obey his words if we hope for his approval and the approval of his Father. (John 12: 44-50) That became my new belief.

I also let go of the idea of a quota system as regards being put right with God. The idea that only a certain number (144,000) could be justified or declared righteous through faith in Jesus Christ, no longer made sense to me. We are told that the Father's will is for "all men to be saved," and Jesus said: "whoever comes to me I will never drive away." (1 Tim. 2: 3; John 6: 37) Jesus then summarized the matter for us by declaring: "For my Father's will is that *everyone* who looks to the Son and believes in him shall have eternal life, and I will raise him up at the last day." (John 6: 40 *NIV*) Those who were to become Abraham's children were said to be an unnumbered multitude: "I will indeed bless you, and I will multiply your descendants as the stars of heaven and as the sand which is on the seashore." (Gen. 22: 17 *RSV*) Those descendants would prove to be people from all nations who had a faith like his. Whether the figure of 144,000 found in Revelation is a literal number or a symbolic number I do not know. But I decided that no interpretation of that number should be allowed to enforce a numerical limit as to how many God would draw to his son during the "day of salvation." (2 Cor. 6: 2)

To its credit, the Society taught me that the Bible was the inspired word of God. I never doubted that what the apostle Paul said was true:

"All Scripture is God-breathed and is useful for teaching, rebuking, correcting and training in righteousness, so that the man of God may be thoroughly equipped for every good work." (2 Tim. 3:16,17 *NIV*) Moreover, they taught me that God remained true even though the teaching of some men may prove untrue and misleading. So I came to my religious crossroad with a measure of confidence that the Scriptures contained all that I needed to move on.

I am not suggesting that I came away filled with enthusiasm for my new religious "freedom." Far from it! I was greatly disoriented and upset. While I had broken away *intellectually*, I remained in many respects *psychologically* bound. I had been a loyal and zealous Witness for many years and had accepted completely all they had taught me about the organization in relation to its sacred status and the need to stay close to it for salvation. I grew to have a deep respect—a reverence—for the organization. It would take time for my emotional acceptance to catch up to my intellectual acceptance that what I had believed was deeply flawed. In addition to that was the recent loss of my family and social structure. This too, had a negative impact on my state of mind.

I never blamed God for my having invested so much of my life in a movement that proved unworthy of the commitment I brought to it. The blame rested with men: myself and those who taught me. For my part, I made the mistake of putting too much faith in men, something the Scriptures tell us not to do. "Do not put your trust in nobles, Nor in the son of earthling man, to whom no salvation belongs." is the way Psalm 146:3 reads in the Witnesses *New World Translation*. My mentors had fallen into the trap of teaching things that were not sound doctrine and I fell into the trap of sitting at their feet. Paul had warned certain teachers in his day about building our faith structure with combustible materials:

> According to the undeserved kindness of God that was given to me, as a wise director of works I laid a foundation, but someone else is building on it. But let each one keep watching how he is building on it. For no man can lay any other foundation than what is laid, which is Jesus Christ. Now if anyone builds on the foundation gold, silver, precious stones, wood materials, hay, stubble, each one's work will become manifest, for the day will show it up, because it will be revealed by means of fire; and the fire itself will prove what sort of work each one's is. (1 Cor. 3: 10-13 *NWT*)

Much of what I had been taught could not endure the fiery heat of sound doctrine. Much of it was burnable stuff, not the least of which was that there was a new gospel to be preached, a gospel different from the one preached for nearly two thousand years. While Jesus Christ is featured in this new gospel or good news, the materials built on him as a foundation was mostly "wood, hay and stubble." Combustible! And in addition to changing the historic good news they inserted themselves as an essential component in the administration of the salvation process this new gospel created:

> No doubt, before the "great tribulation" is finished, we will see the greatest witness to God's name and kingdom in the history of this world. And while now the witness yet includes the invitation to *come to Jehovah's organization for salvation*, the time no doubt will come when the message takes on a harder tone, like a "great war cry."—*The Watchtower*, November 15, 1981, page 21. (Italics not in original)

> No matter where we may live on earth, God's Word continues to serve as a light to our path and a lamp to our roadway as to our conduct and beliefs. (Ps. 119: 105) But Jehovah God has also provided his visible organization, his "faithful and discreet slave," made up of spirit-anointed ones, to help Christians of all nations to understand and apply properly the Bible in their lives. Unless we are in touch with this channel of communication that God is using, we will not progress along the road to life, no matter how much Bible reading we do.—Compare Acts 8: 30-40.— *The Watchtower*, December 1, 1981, page 27.

The exalted level on which the publishers of *The Watchtower* place their worldwide organization is of their creation alone. The Scriptures cannot be used properly to demonstrate the truthfulness of their presumptuous claim. They teach that the "faithful and discreet slave" organization has been in place since 33 A.D. If that was so then it had to always be true that one had to come to it for salvation. But where in the Scriptures do we see the teaching of this concept by Jesus or the apostles? Do we have any indication that one must have faith in an earthly organization as well as faith in God and Christ? Jesus said, "Do not let your hearts be troubled. You have faith in God; have faith also in me." (John 14: 1, *NAB*)

Believers are not commanded to put faith in the apostles or the collected body of believers—the body of Christ. We are called to love one another and seek the well-being of one another, even die for one another, but we are not told to put faith in one another individually or collectively. The apostle Paul would have corresponded in his day to what the Watchtower would now call a member of the Christian "Governing Body." Yet, when writing to the congregation in Corinth about his delay in visiting them, he said, "But I call on God as witness against me: it was to spare you that I did not come again to Corinth. I do not mean to imply that we lord it over your faith; rather, we are workers with you for your joy, because you stand firm in faith." (2 Cor. 1: 23,24, *NRSV*) The apostle Paul viewed himself and other teachers of his day as "only servants, through whom you came to believe—as the Lord has assigned to each his task." (1 Cor. 3: 5 *NIV*)

Jesus cautioned against seeking places of honor or authority over others in the Christian fellowship. When the mother of John and James Zebedee requested that her sons be given places of honor in Jesus' kingdom, he said, "You know that the rulers of the Gentiles lord it over them, and their high officials exercise authority over them. Not so with you. Instead, whoever wants to become great among you must be your servant, and whoever wants to be first must be your slave—just as the Son of Man did not come to be served, but to serve, and to give his life as a ransom for many." (Matt. 20: 25-28 *NIV*)

The early church was not under the authority of a human governing body. It was under the authority of the Holy Spirit, the counselor or advocate that Jesus had promised to send in his absence. (John 14: 15-15, 25,26; 16:5-15) The Scriptural record shows that the Holy Spirit operated on and through *individuals*, not through a religious hierarchy. The council that met in Jerusalem to consider the matter of Gentile observance of the Law was not what the Watchtower Society would have us believe was an early example of a governing body, in session, functioning for the worldwide community of believers. The counsel was convened due to events beyond their control.

A careful reading of the circumstances that led to that assembly clearly shows that their collective decision was forced upon them by the strong evidence presented *to* them—not *from* them! God was drawing people of the nations—Gentiles, apart from the demands of the Law—and the function of the Holy Spirit was making this plain. God did not reveal his will in this matter to a "governing body" which, in turn, made some authoritative proclamation that became "new light" to the community of faith. What the counsel decided was really after the fact. Paul and Barnabas as well as the apostle Peter had already had the truth revealed to them in this matter by the work of the Holy Spirit before the assembly in Jerusalem. (Compare Acts 10: 1-48; Galatians chapters 1,2) The same was true regarding Paul and Barnabas' missionary work. They were not sent out by any central governing body but by the local congregation in Antioch. Again, this was all under the authority and direction of the Holy Spirit. (Compare Acts 13: 1-3)

It is interesting to note that in the Watchtower Society's two-volume Bible dictionary, *Insight on the Scriptures*, you will not find a topical listing for either ORGANIZATION or JEHOVAH'S ORGANIZATION. Why? Because *organization* is not a biblical concept. It is not simply that the word is missing in the Bible; the concept is missing! In volume one of the dictionary you will find considerable information under the word COVENANT. Why? Because Yahweh God is a covenant God, not a God of organization. The Watchtower Society places great emphasis on "Jehovah's organization" and the need to come to it for salvation, which bypasses the need for a covenant relationship between the believer and God. I decided that the safest thing for me to now do was to read the Scriptures and accept what those Scriptures had to say about how salvation is offered in Christ Jesus. I would no longer approach those Scriptures with a sectarian template that interpreted the Bible's meaning for me and told me in advance what I would find there. If the Bible represented the *revealed* Word of God, and I believed that it did, then I reasoned that it should not be necessary to have someone reveal to me what had already been revealed thousands of years earlier.

This determination has served me well in the decades that have followed. Moreover, having had considerable experience with the pitfalls presented in a sectarian approach to the Bible, I made a pledge to myself that I would hold as much as possible to the language of Scripture and be aware of the danger of bringing presuppositions to it. Also, my years of experience taught me how to more readily recognize when the Bible was being manipulated by others to have it say something it did not say. By God's grace, I have progressively come to understand something of the depth, height, width and breadth of God's love manifested in Christ. (Eph. 3: 14-19)

What follows in the remaining chapters of this book summarizes what I consider fundamental in determining one's relationship with God and Christ. In addition, I will also explain how I found local fellowship with a community of believers that has provided many opportunities for personal growth and ministry.

Chapter 18

The Immutable Good News

The good news or gospel of the kingdom of God began to be preached nearly two thousand years ago, when John the Baptist appealed to his fellow Israelites to "repent, for the kingdom of heaven is near." (Matt. 3: 2) John's ministry served to prepare the hearts and minds of people for the promised kingdom of God and introduce them to their promised messiah, Jesus Christ. Later, when Jesus learned that John had been imprisoned, he went north to the territory of Galilee and echoed John's plea to the nation: "Repent for the kingdom of heaven is near." (Matt. 4: 17) Jesus' itinerant ministry featured the kingdom theme: "Jesus went throughout Galilee, teaching in their synagogues, preaching the good news of the kingdom, and healing every disease and sickness among the people." (Matt. 4: 23) The kingdom of God was the central theme of Jesus' teaching:

> According to all three Synoptics, the kingdom of God was the central theme of the preaching and teaching of Jesus. The phrase occurs fourteen times in Mark, thirty-two times in Luke, but only four times in Matthew (12: 28; 19: 24; 21: 31,43). In its place, Matthew substitutes "the kingdom of heaven." (Lit. "The kingdom of the heavens,") Although dispensational theology has customarily made a theological distinction between these two terms, the simple fact is that they are quite interchangeable (cf. Mt. 19: 23 with v. 24; Mk. 10: 23). In Jewish rabbinic literature, the common phrase is "the kingdom of the heavens." In Jewish idiom, "heaven" or similar term was often used in place of the holy name. (See Lk.15: 18; Mk. 14: 61)—*International Standard Bible Encyclopedia*. Vol. 3, p.24.

In regard to that kingdom, it should be noted that the correct phrase is "the kingdom *of* heaven," not "the kingdom *in* heaven." In other words, there is a kingdom of God—a kingdom that functions under his auspices and control, that will ultimately triumphant over all of God's enemies and restore his sovereignty over the earth. The ruling monarch of that kingdom is the Lord Jesus Christ. Concerning his rule we are told, "He must reign until he has put all his enemies under his feet. The last enemy to be destroyed is death." (1 Cor. 15: 25,26) However, this ultimate, far-reaching effect of the kingdom of God was not fully appreciated by its initial hearers.

The preaching about that kingdom began in God's covenant nation of Israel, chaffing under the yoke of Roman rule. The nation had not known freedom from foreign rule from the time of their overthrow by the nation of Babylon in 586 B.C. Successive world powers—Babylon, Medo-Persia, Greece and now Rome—had dominated the nation for more than six hundred years. While God had enforced the consequences for Israel's rebellious and idolatrous behavior by having them taken off their land and carried into bondage, he also gave them the hope of a future restoration. So when Jesus incorporated the language of restoration hope as part of the kingdom message, it ignited the flame of expectancy in the hearts of many.

In his hometown of Nazareth, Jesus entered the synagogue one Sabbath day and read the following text from the prophet Isaiah to those assembled there: "The Spirit of the Lord is on me, because he has anointed me to preach good news to the poor. He has sent me to proclaim freedom for the prisoners and the recovery of sight for the blind, to release the oppressed, to proclaim the year of the Lord's favor." After saying these things, he added: "Today this scripture is fulfilled in your hearing." (Luke 4: 18,19,21 *NIV*).

Of course, Those drawn to Jesus and his kingdom message assumed that he would reestablish Israel's monarchy at that time. He was a son of David's house, to whom God had promised a dynasty of kings that would never end. (2 Samuel 7:11-16) When the last monarch of David's line, king Zedekiah, was removed from the throne, God, speaking through the prophet Ezekiel, declared: "A ruin! A ruin! I will make it a ruin! It will not be restored until he comes to whom it rightfully belongs; to him I will give it.'" (Ezekiel 21: 27 *NIV*) Many believed the time had now arrived for that restoration and that Jesus would sit on David's throne in Jerusalem. In fact, his mother Mary had been told by the angel Gabriel that her son would be great and that "God will give him the throne of his father David." (Luke 1: 32)

It was not understood that before Jesus could be enthroned as king it would be necessary for him to first die as the "Lamb of God." (John 1:

36) As the apostle Paul would later explain in considerable detail in Romans chapter five, it was necessary that Jesus give his life as a ransom to redeem fallen humanity from the consequences of sin caused by Adam's fall. (Mark 10: 45) The death of Jesus was a crushing blow to the kingdom hopes of his disciples. But their hope was restored when they became convinced of his resurrection. He made a number of appearances to them in the short time before he was taken up to heaven to sit at his Father's right hand. The disciple Luke makes mention of these post-resurrection experiences and says, "He appeared to them over a period of forty days and spoke about the kingdom of God." (Acts 1: 3) So we learn that the kingdom theme continued to be on the lips of Jesus after his resurrection. On one such occasion he was asked: "Lord, are you at this time going to restore the kingdom to Israel?" In answer Jesus said, "It is not for you to know the times or dates the Father has set by his own authority. But you will receive power when the Holy Spirit comes on you; and you will be my witnesses in Jerusalem, and in all Judea and Samaria, and to the ends of the earth." (Acts 1: 6-8 *NIV*)

Despite this clear directive, many have ventured into this forbidden area and have presumptuously and triumphantly preached their "times and dates," regarding the kingdom of God. Unfortunately, many innocent people have been duped into believing such things to their ultimate disappointment and sense of betrayal. All of this could have been avoided if people had simply listened to what Jesus had to say about the matter. Despite what the Lord said, many have attempted to decipher certain signs as indicating the nearness of his return and kingdom rule. Part of the problem is how the contents of Matthew, chapter 24 have been misinterpreted, not just by Jehovah's Witnesses, but by evangelicals as well. Jesus had just told his disciples that the temple in Jerusalem being elaborately renovated by king Herod would be destroyed completely. Shocked by such a prospect the disciples inquired as to when this would happen. However, in phrasing their question they asked other questions: "'Tell us,' they said, (1) 'when will this happen, and (2) what will be the sign of your coming and (3) the end of the age?'" (Matt. 24: 3) Apparently, the disciples lumped the three questions together because they assumed they would all take place simultaneously.

Jesus answered their questions in the remaining verses of Matthew, chapter 24. The problem in understanding his answer rests in properly separating his words and applying them to the right question. As regards the first question relating to the destruction of the temple, Jesus gave a detailed answer as to what to expect in the years leading up to that destruction, which occurred in A.D. 70 by the Roman legions. When we compare Matthew 24 with Luke 21, we find a number of specifics that enabled the disciples to discern the time and flee from danger. But when we come to the other questions about his return and the end of the age, we see something different. He said that the common events of history (wars, famines, earthquakes, etc.), would continue to the end of the age. These things were *non-signs* as regards the pinpointing of his return and the end of the age. None of those things would provide a clue as to the nearness of Christ's coming or the end of the age because they would be a common phenomena in every period of time. The disciples were warned not to respond to such *non-signs,* or get excited by some false prophet in regard to these things. To be sure, by the way these things are worded in Matthew and Luke it is not easy to determine what is being applied to each The wording presents certain knots that need to be untangled, so to speak. But those knots are untangled by what we are told regarding Jesus' return and the end of the age.

The coming of the kingdom is associated in Scripture with the second coming of the Son of Man. These events come under the cloak of secrecy because they happen simultaneously. Concerning his return Jesus himself said, "No one knows about that day or hour, not even the angels in heaven, nor the Son, but only the Father." (Mark 13: 32,33-37) The apostle Paul reinforced the sudden, unexpected nature of that event when he wrote: "Now, brothers, about times and dates we do not need to write to you, for you know very well that the day of the Lord will come like a thief in the night." (1 Thess. 5: 2) So when Jesus said, "And this gospel of the kingdom will be preached in the whole world as a testimony to all nations, and then the end will come," (Matt. 24: 14) he was not saying a *new gospel* of the kingdom was going to be preached—one that identified the very generation that would witness its coming. No, he was merely saying that *in addition* to all the other factors he spoke of, his disciples would continue to preach the immutable good news or gospel of the kingdom. That was the thrust of Jesus' remarks in Acts 1: 8, "you will be my witnesses . . to the ends of the earth." Jesus' faithful disciples were to be found faithfully preaching the good news of the kingdom. They were not to be found trying to uncover divine secrets regarding the times and dates God has reserved for himself.

After receiving power on Pentecost day, the fellowship of believers underwent a profound change in understanding regarding the coming kingdom of God. The new covenant arrangement was now in effect and a new creation appeared. The kingdom hope was dramatically enriched by such things. The kingdom had both a here and now aspect as well as a then and there aspect. Already, Christians were to think of themselves as glorified with the enthroned Christ at God's right hand. (Eph. 2: 6) This new, exalted relationship is thoroughly presented in the early chapters of Paul's letter to the Ephesians. He summarizes that wonderful gospel in chapter 4: "There is one body and one spirit—just as you were called to one hope when you were called—one Lord, one faith, one baptism; one God and Father of all, who is over all and through all and in all." (Eph. 4: 4-6)

In the above words the apostle Paul outlined the gospel that was to be preached until the end of the present age. Concerning this wonderful reconciliation with God through Jesus Christ and the "one hope" it offers, Jude wrote: "Dear friends, although I was very eager to write to you about the salvation we share, I felt I had to write and urge you to contend for the faith that was once for all entrusted to the saints." (Jude 1: 3) The *New World Translation* reads, "I found it necessary to write you to exhort you to put up a hard fight for the faith that was *once for all time* delivered to the holy ones." All that was delivered to the holy ones in the first century constituted the good news that was to be joyfully preached and lived until the end of the present age.

That gospel cannot be added to or subtracted from, although efforts were made from the beginning to do so. Early on, certain Jewish adherents of the Law, who accepted Jesus as the messiah, would have Gentile believers be circumcised as necessary for salvation in Christ. When the apostle Paul learned of this he was furious. He wrote: "I am astonished that you are so quickly deserting the one who called you by the grace of Christ and are turning to a different gospel—which is really no gospel at all." (Gal.. 1: 6,7) This "different gospel" did not deny Christ, it only *added* the need of circumcision. Yet, Paul said it was "no gospel at all." Abraham had received circumcision as a sign of the covenant between himself and Yahweh God. (Gen. 17: 9-14) Moreover, every male descendant of Abraham was to have this ritual performed. It was styled as an "everlasting covenant," and had been faithfully practiced for two thousand years. Circumcision was commanded in the Law of Moses, but Paul says to add it to the gospel of Jesus Christ was deadly. (Lev. 12: 1-3) He went so far as to say, "Mark my words! I, Paul, tell you that if you let yourselves be circumcised, Christ will be of no value to you at all." (Gal. 5: 2) Strong words, these, but they underscore the danger of adding to the gospel. In the strongest possible terms Paul declared: "But even if we or an angel from heaven should preach a gospel other than the one we preached to you, let him be eternally condemned! As we have already said, so now I say again: if anybody is preaching to you a gospel other than what you accepted, let him be eternally condemned." (Gal. 1: 8, 9)

Against this inspired testimony what are we to say to someone who introduces a new hope wrapped up in a new gospel? Based on what we read in the Scriptures it must be rejected out of hand as a false gospel— no gospel at all. The biblical good news is an immutable gospel; it cannot be changed. To add to it or subtract from it is to destroy it. As for the two flocks of sheep Jesus alludes to in John, chapter 10, these clearly represent the Jewish flock which was penned within the Mosaic Law Covenant and later joined by "other sheep" which represented non-Jewish, or Gentile believers who were never in the Jewish sheepfold. The function of the Holy Spirit led to the breaking down of the wall that separated these two ethnic societies. (Eph. 2: 11-18) In this way believing Jew and believing Gentile became one flock, one shepherd, just as Jesus had foretold. (John 10: 16) They came to share in the "one body, one Spirit, one hope (not two), one Lord, one faith, one baptism, one God and Father of all." (Eph. 4: 4-6) It is *this* good news of the kingdom that would continue to be preached until the end of the present age. It is *this* good news that I have received in faith and share with others. There simply is no other.

Chapter 19

My
True
Inheritance

It wasn't first after leaving the Watchtower system that I began to look at the Scriptures more seriously. The Bible had always been central to my faith and reading it was a constant source of instruction, comfort and encouragement. My wife and I made an effort to read through the entire Bible once each year. I read with enthusiasm the Society's *New World Translation of the Christian Greek Scriptures,* published in 1950. In time I came to realize that the Society's translation was not free of bias. I now realize that all translations have certain biases. Translators are not free of scholarly bias and their predispositions have an effect on what they see in the manuscript evidence and how they translate that evidence. For this reason I have found it best not to select one translation to the exclusion of all others in personal Bible study. By comparing translations one is able to get a broader perspective of the nuances present in the original Hebrew and Greek text.

Early on, in the 1940s, I primarily used the *King James Version* and *The American Standard Version* in Bible reading and study. In my public ministry I invariably used the *King James Version,* because that was the one most people viewed as the "true" Bible. In using the *King James Version,* I had no difficulty in making a case for my doctrinal structure. When we approach the Scriptures with a firm doctrinal system in place we will find the evidence we seek to substantiate that system of belief. That predisposition is a greater hindrance to finding the true message of Scripture than the particular translation we use. If we are not careful, we will read *into* the Scriptures concepts we have picked up along the way, rather than reading *out of* the Bible what it really says. In my case, I read the Bible with Watchtower theology in mind. I had full confidence that the translators of *The New World Translation* would not allow their prejudices to bias their translation. More than that, I rejected even the thought that they might *have* prejudices that would influence their choice of words in the first place.

In retrospect, I realize that I was naive and unrealistic in my approach to Bible study. The major problem for me was that virtually all of the New Testament was read by me as a *third party*. I knew the Christian Greek Scriptures were written by and for those disciples in the new covenant arrangement—spirit-begotten Christians (limited in number to 144,000). This meant that what was said in those Scripture did not have a *direct* application to me. It was only by *extension* that those writings involved me and to all those not in the new covenant—the so-called "other sheep" who were outside of that covenant according to Watchtower doctrine.

That unscriptural view of matters prevented me from hearing what God had to say to me in a personal way. For example, in the apostle Paul's letter to the Roman church he sets forth the truth that both Jew and Gentile are reconciled to God through Jesus Christ by means of faith. "But now a righteousness from God, apart from law, has been made known, to which the Law and the Prophets testify. This righteousness from God comes through faith in Jesus Christ to all who believe. There is no difference, for all have sinned and fall short of the glory of God." (Rom. 3: 21-23 *NIV*) The righteousness due to faith of which the apostle speaks is one of the benefits that flow to those in the new covenant.

In the following chapter Paul uses the patriarch Abraham as the prime example of how God justifies someone due to faith. He points out that Abraham was justified prior to his being circumcised and that circumcision, which came years later, merely confirmed the righteousness he had already obtained from God by faith. (Rom. 4: 1-10) He then argues that, in this way, Abraham became the "father" of both Jew and Gentile believer. "And he received the sign of circumcision, a seal of the righteousness that he had by faith while he was still uncircumcised. So then, he is the father of *all* who believe but have not been circumcised, in order that righteousness might be credited to them. And he is also father of the circumcised who not only are circumcised but who also walk in the footsteps of the faith that our father Abraham had before he was circumcised." (Rom. 4: 11,12 *NIV*) That Abraham was the "father" of all who are put right with God by means of faith—Jew and Gentile—means that all believers are sons of Abraham!

But, as a Jehovah's Witness, I could never apply what Paul said about Abraham being the father of us *all* to include me. Why? Because Paul was writing to those disciples in Rome who had been brought into the new covenant—the saints or holy ones. (Rom. 1: 7) I had been told that the door of opportunity to become a holy one in the new covenant had been closed in A.D.1935. In this way I was prevented from realizing that all persons who put faith in Jesus Christ are reconciled to God and are justified. (Rom. 5: 1) In effect, I was reading a letter written to someone else. Reading Romans and the other letters that made up the New Testament was like reading letters from a loving father to his children in which the father expresses his love for his children and explains what he has done and what he will yet do on their behalf. I could not think of myself as one of them, because I was not one of his sons. It was through this doctrinal paradigm that I read about new covenant Christianity.

Where, then, did my sense of religious security rest? My standing with God was premised on the teaching that my active association with "God's Organization" established my good standing with God. But there was no *relationship* to God in that standing. An experience I had a few years ago illustrates this matter. We were called on by a Witness who obviously did not know we were former Witnesses. He seemed quite knowledgeable and he proceeded to talk to me about world conditions and the need for a sure hope for a better world. I allowed him to continue for a few minutes and then I asked if I could ask him a question. He said, "Yes."

I asked: "What is your relationship with God?"

He answered by reading extensively from Romans chapter 8 down to verses 20-22 which, according to the *New World Translation*, he was using, reads: "For the creation was subjected to futility, not by its own will but through him that subjected it, on the basis of hope that the creation itself also will be set free from enslavement to corruption and have the glorious freedom of the children of God. For we know that all creation keeps on groaning together and being in pain until now." (Rom. 8: 20-22 *NWT*) These verses speak of "creation" ultimately being rescued from its futile condition and coming to have the freedom enjoyed by the "children of God." He identified himself, not with the "children of God" but with "the creation" yet to be set free. This was his answer to my question: "What is your relationship to God?"

"Your answer," I said, "seems nebulous to me."

He said it wasn't nebulous, but he didn't try to clarify the matter further.

I then asked: "Do you believe you are led by God's Spirit?"

To this he said, "Yes."

I pointed out that in his reading from his own Bible he read a verse that said, "For *all* who are led by God's spirit, these are God's sons." (Rom. 8: 14)

His reply was, "It leads me in a different way."

In saying this he had to deny to himself what the verse specifically said in his own Bible: that *"all* who are led by God's Spirit are sons of God." Why the denial? Because he was conditioned to believe, as I once was, that he was not a son of God.

The context in which the apostle says that all of God's sons are led by his Spirit contrasts those being led by the fleshly spirit. These two spirits are opposed to each other. Either one is directed by God's Spirit or he is controlled and directed by his fallen human spirit. There is no "different way" in which God's Spirit functions in the heart and mind of believers. But this Witness came up with this rationalization because he couldn't accept what Paul said. The truth was he had no personal relationship with God. Those identified as "the creation" in Romans 8: 19-22 represent future beneficiaries of God's kingdom under Christ—not disciples of Jesus Christ. That he identified himself with those future beneficiaries told me he had no *present* relationship with God—only a *prospective* one. That was his hope.

To have been delivered from that destructive gospel was the greatest of deliverances. It is true that our Lord said that the road to life was narrow and few would find it, but at the same time he made it clear that he would never turn anyone away who came to him.(cf. Matt.7: 13,14; John 6: 35-37) The wonderful invitation of becoming a disciple extended by the Lord himself, offers encouragement that all who earnestly seek him will be welcomed by him. (Matt.11: 28-30) Jesus' expansive invitation to come to him echoes his Father's desire to see all people saved. When the apostle Paul encouraged prayers for kings and others in authority he buttressed the correctness of this by declaring: "This is good, and pleases God our Savior, who wants *all men* to be saved and to come to a knowledge of the truth." (1 Tim. 2: 3,4 *NIV*) And immediately after saying that, he added: "For there is one God and one mediator between God and men, the man Christ Jesus, who gave himself as a ransom for *all men*—the testimony given in its proper time " (1 Tim. 2: 5,6 *NIV*)

How are we to understand what the apostle says about *all men*? Is there any suggestion that *all* in this context is restrictive, or does the context convey an all-inclusive sense? Paul says that prayers where to be offered for *all* in positions of authority. (vs. 2) This would include all such ones. He says God wants *all men* to be saved. (vs. 4) Do we conclude from that that God only wants certain ones to be saved or do we accept the obvious meaning that he wants everyone to be saved? To this desired end, God has made provision for all by providing a mediator for all. (vs. 5) This required that a ransom be paid by the man Christ Jesus for all men. (vs. 6) And the apostle John reminds us "He [Jesus] is the atoning sacrifice for our sins, and not only for ours but also for the sins of the whole world." (1 John 2: 2 *NIV*)

We find similar language being used by the apostle in his letter to Roman Christians. In contrasting the effects of Adam's sin and Christ's sacrifice, he says, "Consequently, just as the result of one trespass was condemnation for *all men*, so also the result of one act of righteousness was justification that brings life for *all men*." (Rom. 5: 18 *NIV*) And while God makes provision for all in the sacrifice of his only begotten Son, not everyone takes advantage of that provision. The provision for having Jesus serve as our mediator between us and God is acquired by faith. Faith is manifested when one understands and accepts the offer of forgiveness and reconciliation God offers through his Son as explained in Scripture. And for anyone reading this book who is still held captive by a teaching that denies them that reconciliation, I strongly urge them to read the book of Romans and accept at face value all that the apostle has to say about reconciliation. All humanity is represented in Paul's presentation.(cf. Rom. 4: 18-5:19) Don't allow anyone to short-change your spiritual inheritance.

Paul encourages us by saying:

> Salvation that comes from trusting Christ—which is the message we preach—is already within easy reach. In fact, the Scriptures say, "The message is close at hand; it is on your lips and in your heart." For if you confess with your mouth that Jesus is Lord and believe in your heart that God raised him from the dead, you will be saved. For it is by believing in your heart that you are made right with God, and it is by confessing with your mouth that you are saved. As the Scriptures tell us, "Anyone who believes in him will not be disappointed." Jew and Gentile are the same in this respect. They all have the same Lord, who generously gives his riches to all who ask for them." (Rom. 10 : 8-12 *NLT*)

It has been into the new covenant arrangement that all believing ones have been and are being gathered. There is no quota given in Scripture as to how many this covenant will ultimately contain. The promise of a new covenant was given to the nation of Israel at a critical time in its history. Israelites were about to go into exile and their sacred temple, which was the focal point of the law covenant, was about to be destroyed by the Babylonian army. No doubt the wording of that promise gave them hope during the ensuing centuries they would suffer under the control of succeeding world powers. Jeremiah was inspired to prophesy:

> Look, the days are coming, Yahweh declares, when I shall make a new covenant with the House of Israel (and the House of Judah), but not like the covenant I made with their ancestors the day I took them by the hand to bring them out of Egypt, a covenant which they broke, even though I was their Master, Yahweh declares. No, this is the covenant I shall make with the House of Israel when those days have come, Yahweh declares. Within them I shall plant my Law, writing it on their hearts. Then I shall be their God and they will be my people. There will be no further need for everyone to teach neighbour or brother, saying, "Learn to know Yahweh!" No, they will all know me, from the least to the greatest, Yahweh declares, since I shall forgive their guilt and never more call their sin to mind. —Jeremiah 31: 31-34 *NJB*.

The covenant that Yahweh God promised to make with Israel went into effect with the death, resurrection and glorification of Jesus Christ. On the eve of his death he took a wine cup and said, "This cup is the new covenant in my blood, which is poured out for you." (Luke 22: 20 *NIV*) At Pentecost, less than two months later, that covenant went into effect because the resurrected Son of Man had appeared in God's presence in heaven to present the value of his sacrifice. The writer of Hebrews testifies:

> He did not enter by means of the blood of goats and calves; but he entered the Most Holy Place once for all by his own blood, having obtained eternal redemption. . .For this reason Christ is the mediator of a new covenant, that those who are called may receive the promised eternal inheritance—now that he has died as a ransom to set them free from the sins committed under the first covenant. (Heb. 9: 12,15 *NIV*)

Soon, under the direction of the Holy Spirit, non-Jews or Gentiles were welcomed into that new covenant arrangement. Writing to these Gentile Christians the apostle Paul said:

> Therefore, remember that formerly you who are Gentiles by birth and called "uncircumcised" by those who call themselves "the circumcision" (that done in the body by the hands of men)—remember that at that time you were separate from Christ, excluded from citizenship in Israel and foreigners to the covenants of the promise, without hope and without God in the world. But now in Christ Jesus you who once were far away have been brought near through the blood of Christ. (Eph. 2: 11-13 *NIV*)

The word covenant is plural here, indicating that more than one covenant was involved. The new covenant first spoken of by the prophet

Jeremiah, was one of those covenants and the second one was the one made with Abraham which promised that he would become the father of many nations and through whom many would be blessed. (Gen. 17: 5; 22: 17,18; Jer. 31: 31-34) Both covenants find their fulfillment in the Christian church. When Paul was explaining how Abraham became the father of all those having faith, he indicated that this was pointed to in the promises God gave Abraham. "Therefore, the promise comes by faith, so that it may be by grace and may be guaranteed to all Abraham's off-spring—not only to those who are of the law but also to those who are of the faith of Abraham. He is the father of us all. As it is written: 'I have made you a father of many nations.'" (Rom. 4: 16,17 *NIV*)

The last sentence in the above quotation is taken from Genesis 17: 5. Paul makes it clear that the prophecy was beginning to undergo a fulfillment in the first century as Gentile believers were being brought into the Christian fold. This also fulfilled Jesus' words recorded in John 10: 16: "And I have other sheep, that are not of this fold; I must bring them also, and they will heed my voice. So there shall be one flock, one shepherd." (*RSV*) Paul reflects the same thought when speaking of Jew and Gentile believers:

> For he himself is our peace, who has made the two one and has de-stroyed the barrier, the dividing wall of hostility, by abolishing in his flesh the law with its commandments and regulations. His purpose was to cre-ate in himself one new man out of the two thus making peace, and in this one body to reconcile both of them to God through the cross, by which he put to death their hostility." (Eph. 2: 14-16 *NIV*)

It began to be obvious to me that Jesus had the new covenant arrangement in mind when he initially spoke to his Jewish disciples about having "other sheep" that he would gather in addition to the Jewish sheep held within the confines of the Mosaic law covenant and join the two (Jew and Gentile) together into one flock under one shepherd. Without a forced application, his words fit perfectly with how events unfolded and how the apostle Paul later explained matters. God's promise to Abraham was that through him and his seed or offspring, all families of the earth were to be blessed. (Gen. 12: 3) The apostle Paul, in his letter to the Galatian churches, makes an application of that promise of blessing to those Gentiles who had now become disciples of Jesus Christ. He wrote:

> Consider Abraham: "He believed God, and it was credited to him as righteousness." Understand, then, that those who believe are children of Abraham. The Scripture foresaw that God would justify the Gentiles by faith, and announced the gospel in advance to Abraham: "All nations will

be blessed through you." So those who have faith are blessed along with Abraham, the man of faith." (Gal. 3: 7-9 *NIV*)

These Gentile believers were among the first to be blessed by Abraham's seed, Jesus Christ. Because their being blessed was premised on their faith in Jesus Christ as the promised seed, they also became Abraham's sons. As Abraham was the father of all (Jew and Gentile) having a faith like his, Paul identified them as both children of Abraham as well as people of the nations who were being blessed. Speaking of them as children of Abraham, underscores the fact that those who demonstrate faith are put right with God just as Abraham had been put right with God by his faith. As Paul would later say in the same letter, "If you belong to Christ, then you are Abraham's seed, and heirs according to the promise." (Gal. 3: 29 *NIV*)

Becoming Abraham's seed or children did not make them a part of the *promised seed*, through whom the blessing was to flow to them. No, they were beneficiaries of the blessings that came from that seed—Jesus Christ. The seed or offspring through whom all blessings were to come was singular—not plural: "The Scripture does not say 'and to seeds,' meaning many people, but 'to your seed,' meaning *one person*, who is Christ." (Gal. 3: 16 *NIV*) The word translated Christ here is the Greek word *Christos*, and corresponds to the Hebrew word *mashiah* (Eng. messiah) which means anointed. There is but one Messiah, not many. There is but one seed of promise, not many. And through this one seed of Abraham, the Gentile believers were receiving the promised blessing. Not only were people of the nations now being blessed, but the natural descendants of Abraham, who had the faith of Abraham, were also being blessed. In talking to his Jewish compatriots who shared culpability in the unjust execution of Jesus, the apostle Peter said:

> And now, friends, I know that you acted in ignorance, as did also your rulers. In this way God fulfilled what he had foretold through all the prophets, that his Messiah would suffer. Repent therefore, and turn to God so that your sins may be wiped out, so that times of refreshing may come from the presence of the Lord, and that he may send the Messiah appointed for you, that is, Jesus, who must remain in heaven until the time of universal restoration that God announced long ago through his holy prophets. . . You are the descendants of the prophets and of the covenant that God gave to your ancestors, saying to Abraham, "And in your descendants all the families of the earth shall be blessed." When God raised up his servant, he sent him first to you, *to bless you* by turning each of you from your wicked ways." (Acts 3: 17-21,25,26 *NRSV*).

The matter can be summarized as follows: Jesus Christ became the seed through whom all nations of the earth were to be blessed. The first nation to be blessed were those natural descendants of Abraham who repented of their sins and accepted the forgiveness offered through Jesus Christ in the new covenant arrangement. When the gospel or good news was later taken to the Gentiles they received the same blessing through their faith in God's provision through Christ. All such ones, Jew and Gentile alike, were recipients of the promised blessing that was to flow to all nations through Abraham's seed, Jesus Christ. Now that both Jew and Gentile were one body of believers due to their faith in Jesus Christ, they were unitedly reconciled to God and adopted as sons. To the Galatians Paul wrote:

> You are all sons of God through faith in Christ Jesus, for all of you who were baptized into Christ have clothed yourselves with Christ. There is neither Jew nor Greek, slave nor free, male nor female, for you are all one in Christ Jesus. If you belong to Christ, then you are Abraham's seed, and heirs according to the promise." (Gal. 3: 26-29 *NIV*)

Understanding this clear, scriptural explanation of how the new covenant and the Abrahamic covenant work together through Jesus Christ, enabled me to accept the promises resident in those covenants. I could now think of myself as both a son of Abraham and a son of God by means of my faith in Jesus Christ. My mind and conscience were set free because my sins were forgiven and forgotten by God. I began to experience that unique peace that Paul writes about, "Therefore, since we have been justified through faith, we have peace with God through our Lord Jesus Christ, through whom we have gained access by faith into this grace in which we now stand. And we rejoice in the hope of the glory of God." (Rom. 5: 1,2 *NIV*) I now understood and accepted the true inheritance: heirs of God and co-heirs with Christ. (Rom. 8:17)

While the Watchtower Society acknowledges that Jesus is the Seed of Abraham, it speaks of him in this regard as only a the *primary* seed. In saying this, they lay the groundwork for arguing that there are others who share with him as the *secondary* seed that people must acknowledge, together with the *primary* seed, if they are to be blessed. It comes as no surprise that the Watchtower Society claims to represent that *secondary* seed that everyone must acknowledge if they are to receive the Abrahamic blessing. Their official teaching is summarized below:

> Who *primarily*, was the seed of Abraham, by means of whom all nations of the earth would eventually bless themselves? The apostle Paul identifies this primary Seed as being Christ —Galatians 3: 16.

Further, since Jehovah promised Abraham that he would multiply his seed, what persons would make up the *secondary* part of Abraham's seed? Who would be the "heirs with reference to a promise," "joint heirs" with the *primary* Seed, Christ? (Galatians 3 : 29; Romans 8: 17) For some 2,000 years even the number of those who would make up the *secondary* "seed of Abraham" remained unknown to humans, like "the stars of the heavens" or "the grains of sand that are on the seashore." Then, toward the end of the first century C.E., the apostle John heard '"the number of those who were sealed, a hundred and forty-four thousand, sealed out of every tribe of the sons of Israel.—Genesis 22: 17; Rev.7: 4. —*The Watchtower*, August 15, 1983, page 15 (italics not in original).

By putting matters as they do, the Society would have you believe (and millions of Jehovah's Witnesses do believe), that in order to receive blessings from God through Jesus Christ, you must accept them as a part of Abraham's seed. In other words, you cannot approach the *primary* seed (Jesus) unless you recognize the *secondary* seed—the Watchtower system of religion. By putting a limit of 144,000 on who can be in the new covenant and deciding that only their organization could have any of that number and that the opportunity to be included in that number effectively ended in A.D.1935, means that less than 1% of the millions of Witnesses claim to be in the new covenant and Abraham's children. Addressing those who are told they are excluded from the new covenant as well as God's covenant with Abraham, they offer the following:

Although they are not a part of the spiritual seed produced by the Abrahamic covenant and therefore are "not of this fold," these "other sheep" are definitely a part of the "nations of the earth" who can bless themselves by means of the seed. (John 10: 16a; Genesis 22: 18) It follows that they must have faith like Abraham, whose life prospects also are earthly, and "walk orderly in the footsteps of that faith." (Rom.4: 11,12,16) They must show their subjection to the Fine Shepherd, Christ, the *primary* Seed of Abraham. They *must also cooperate* with the remnant of the *secondary* seed of Abraham, becoming "one flock' under 'one shepherd." (John 10: 14,16b)"—*The Watchtower*, August 15, 1983 page 21. (italics not in original)

The above ignores the fact that the apostle Paul emphasized that the promised seed was not plural but singular. (cf. Gal. 3: 16) As THE SEED, Christ cannot be rightly spoken of as only the *primary* seed. He was the promised seed—period! It also ignores the fact that Paul taught that Abraham is the father of us all. (Rom. 4: 16,17) Telling people "they must have a faith like Abraham," but denying that such faith makes them children of Abraham as well as sons of God, is unconscionable. And by saying people *must* cooperate with the remnant of the *secondary* seed, is just another way of saying people must be in subjection to them in order to prove their subjection to Christ. This is the "good news" they preach.

On that historic day of Pentecost, nearly two thousand years ago, God inaugurated a new covenant through his Son, and from that day forward the invitation to become reconciled to God through his Son has been the clarion call of ministers of the new covenant. As such a minister the apostle Paul declared:

> All this is from God, who reconciled us to himself through Christ and gave us the ministry of reconciliation: that God was reconciling *the world* to himself in Christ, not counting men's sins against them. And he has committed to us the message of reconciliation. We are therefore Christ's ambassadors, as though God were making his appeal through us. We implore you on Christ's behalf: Be reconciled to God. God made him who had no sin to be sin for us, so that in him we might become the righteousness of God. (2 Cor. 5: 18-21 *NIV*)

It was not the prerogative of the apostles or other evangelists of the good news to decide when the invitation to become reconciled to God by having one's sins forgiven should come to a close. Their obligation was to faithfully herald that divine invitation. For this reason I could only conclude that it is the only means of reconciliation with God—the only means of having a relationship with God. As I grasped this reality my view of myself in relation to Jesus Christ changed everything. My mother's fear that I would "lose my inheritance," by leaving the Watchtower organization, was scripturally unsound. The invitation to be part of those "nations to be blessed" and become a part of God's family is unlimited and has continued down through the intervening centuries which time period is spoken of as the "day of salvation." This is the gospel. There is no other.

NOTE: Because God is first and foremost a covenant God and not a God of organization, I have included a discussion of this matter in the Appendix.

Chapter 20

Life Outside of "Paradise"

After having been officially disfellowshiped in September of 1981, I found myself in a strange new world. While it is true that I stopped associating in the spring of 1980, after a decade of declining zeal, there was something final about 1981. In some ways nothing had changed: I was the same person who awoke each day to move through a pattern of activity I had known for years. The sights, sounds, and rhythms of the day were much as they had been. Yet, there was a certain strangeness that infiltrated each moment—each conversation. One life had ended and another had begun. What that life would prove to be was wrapped in uncertainty. As Witnesses we had been told that we lived in a spiritual paradise. Only within the confines of the Watchtower religious system did true Christian faith, hope and love exist. Everything outside, including all other religions, was Satan's domain. I was now outside of that organizationally-defined "paradise" and the only reality at the moment was that nothing would ever be the same.

My life's objectives and identity as a person had been so interwoven with the Watchtower movement and its world view that leaving it created a vacuum in my life. I felt like I had been separated from a part of myself. To be disconnected from a way of life that dominated every aspect of your being is a very strange and disorienting experience. It would be years before I would completely adjust to this new reality. During that emotional and intellectual transition I replaced trust in an organized system of religion with the more personal trust God provides in trust in Christ Jesus. This trust provides a sure foundation for the hope we are called to have. That hope, as defined in Hebrews 6:19, "is like an anchor for our lives, an anchor safe and sure." But to find that safe anchor of hope it was necessary to experience the free fall from what I had anchored my life to for so many years.

I remember a moment when I was reflecting on these matters and searching my mind as to what I would have wanted to do with my life had I not been a Witness. I concluded that I would have wanted to be a minister. It was a self-discovery that told me I wasn't a believer because I was a Witness, but a Witness because I was a believer. I found comfort in that knowledge. As a believer I had to move on even though I was uncertain as to what that would mean. Another matter that I pondered at this critical moment of truth was who or what I was. My former guides told me I was a wicked, unfaithful, ungrateful and presumptuous apostate—someone who had turned away from the light of truth. Jesus had said:

> No one who puts his faith in him comes under judgement; but the unbeliever has already been judged because he has not put his trust in God's only Son. This is the judgement: the light has come into the world, but people preferred darkness to light because their deeds were evil. Wrongdoers hate the light and avoid it, for fear their misdeeds should be exposed. Those who live by the truth come to the light so that it may be clearly seen that God is in all that they do. (John 3:18-21 *REB*)

If I was as evil as they said I was, why was I drawn to the light? Why did I have this unquenchable thirst for what was true and righteous? While I didn't feel capable of passing judgment on myself, I did find encouragement in Jesus' words. I still wanted to see God proven true and was willing to reevaluate everything I had once believed in order to put myself right with him. I had experienced something akin to what the apostle Paul had said when writing to the congregation in Corinth, counseling them to be careful how they built on the foundation of faith in Christ he had laid. He had heard reports of factions in the Corinthian fellowship and he was concerned that this could prove most harmful. In part, he said:

> According to the grace of God given to me, like a skilled master builder I laid a foundation, and someone else is building on it. Each builder most choose with care how to builds on it. For no one can lay any foundation other than the one that has been laid; that foundation is Jesus Christ. Now if anyone builds on the foundation with gold, silver, precious stones, wood, hay, straw—the work of each builder will become visible, for the Day will disclose it, because it will be revealed with fire, and the fire will test what sort of work each has done. If what has been built on the foundation survives, the builder will receive a reward. If the work is burned up, the

builder will suffer loss; the builder will be saved, but only as through fire.
—1 Cor. 3: 10-15 *NRSV*)

The "builders" I had looked to had built on the foundation of Jesus Christ with a great deal of combustible material—wood, hay and straw. Discoveries had provided the match that ignited those materials. Nearly all of my belief structure had burned up. The only thing that remained was a basic belief in God and Jesus Christ and the conviction that the Scriptures which revealed them were inspired. I needed to rebuild on the foundation of Jesus Christ and avoid, to the best of my ability, those teachings that could not endure the searing heat of truth. Also, I would try to forge a ministry to fulfill that deep desire I had to share God's grand cause in Christ Jesus and be of some help to others.

I had no indication of what was happening at the very heart of the organization in the spring of 1980. I had arrived at my own crisis of conscience apart from the influence of others. It soon became apparent, however, that my experience and that of my wife was not unique. Unknown to us at the time, tens of thousands of Witnesses around the world were leaving the organization and being labeled as apostates. This phenomenon was a grass roots reaction to the decade-long speculations leading up to 1975. Expectations regarding the significance of that year, so carefully cultivated by the Society, had fallen to the ground unfulfilled. For many it was the last straw. There had been so many failed predictions in their 100-year history, the 1975 speculation, while not as specific as some of the earlier ones, was like the "straw that broke the camel's back."

The speculation regarding the coming of the kingdom of God in 1975 had made sense to the Witnesses because by that year the 1914 generation was, for all practical purposes, passing away. It was for this reason that the Witnesses were willing to accept the organization's speculations about 1975. It's failure simply exhausted the last ounce of credibility many had that the Society had been directed by God's Spirit in these matters. This, in turn, undermined their basic claim for being: namely, that the last days began in 1914 and God had chosen this organization to proclaim this truth. The whole house of cards was now in danger of collapse. It was that fear that caused the leadership to lash out at any and all who questioned them in any way. This siege mentality prompted the cruel harshness embedded in the revised disfellowshiping/disassociating policy. The strength of a dictatorial religion rests on the total control of thought. If thought control is lost, the whole enterprise is lost. In other words, the strength of such an organization is also its weakness. The

Watchtower Society would now feel justified in "stoning to death" any and all who voiced criticism of them

Because there were more and more casualties resulting from this harsh treatment, I felt a moral obligation to share with others the research I had assembled on the matter of the "Faithful and Discreet Slave" doctrine. This teaching was the very foundation of the Society's claim to spiritual authority. Once a person accepted this doctrine, the Society owned that person. Only by freeing people from this unscriptural grip of fear, would it be possible for them to give a fair consideration of the historical and biblical evidence that clearly undermined their claim. While I made no effort to force it on anyone who didn't want it, I did make it available to those who showed an interest in reading it. In this way I gradually came in contact with hundreds of people who were going through what we had experienced. My fear was that losing faith in the organization would also translate into loss of faith in God. Sharing my research now proved to be the beginning of a ministry that would, in time, touch the lives of thousands of people.

A group of former Witnesses in British Columbia, Canada obtained a copy of my treatise and requested permission to publish it in a periodical named *The Bible Examiner.* The editor was M. James Penton, a Professor of History and Religious Studies at Lethbridge, Alberta, Canada, and a fourth generation Witness who had been disfellowshiped in 1981, for speaking out against certain abuses and doctrinal errors he saw in the Watchtower system. I was pleased to have the treatise published and granted permission. It appeared in *The Bible Examiner* as a Special Issue, September-October 1982. Copies found their way to Europe and the British Isles and I received requests for permission to have it translated in other languages: Swedish, German, Spanish, etc.

It was through the distribution of *The Faithful and Discreet Slave* paper that I became acquainted with two men who had been targets of the Society's headquarter's inquisition in the spring of 1980: Raymond Franz and Edward Dunlap. Brother Franz had been a member of the Governing Body and had been asked to resign and leave Brooklyn headquarters. He was later disfellowshiped for having a meal with a dissasociated Witness, Peter Gregerson. In 1983 Franz wrote *Crisis of Conscience,* which set forth a candid and fully documented history of his lifelong association as a Witness and the Society's prophetic speculations. It has gone through several editions and been translated into a number of foreign languages. It is a *must* read for anyone who has a serious desire to understand the inner sanctum of Watchtower leadership. In 1991 Franz published another work, *In Search of Christian Freedom,* which provides an excellent guide for individual Christian growth and maturity. Both volumes are of the highest quality. They are available from Commentary Press, P.O. Box 43532, Atlanta, GA 30336.

The other man, Edward Dunlap, had been a prominent member of the headquarters staff in Brooklyn. He had served as Registrar of the Society's missionary school and also taught there. At the time he was disfellowshiped he was serving in the Writing Department as was Raymond Franz. Like Franz, Dunlap had spent his life in full time service. In February of 1983, I visited Ed and his wife Bette in Oklahoma City, spending a couple of days with them. Ed, who was in his mid-seventies at the time, was thoughtful, straight forward and unpretentious. He expressed no anger over his treatment by those who judged him an apostate. The only thing he had insisted upon was that he not be called and apostate Christian. He would accept being called an "apostate against the organization." And that was how he was labeled. He made a point of telling me the judicial committee that condemned him had treated him respectfully. That they would respect this man was understandable. He, together with Franz, was a principle contributor to the creation of one of the few books published by the Society that has had any extended value: the Watchtower Society's Bible dictionary, *Aid to Bible Understanding,* published in1971. (This was later republished in two volumes with a new title: *Insight on the Scriptures,* printed in 1988) He also wrote: *Commentary on the Letter of James* published by the Watchtower Society in1979. That he was one of the few men selected to work on such important projects testified to the high regard in which he was held for his intellectual and scriptural competence.

Returning home from Oklahoma, I reflected on my impressions of Ed and Bette and their treatment by members of the headquarters staff. Here was a man who had spent 50 years in association with the organization and had served in some of the highest places of responsibility and authority—a man they worked with day after day for years on end. Yet, in a matter of *days,* they could condemn and reject him. What chance, I thought, did lowly ones in the greater population of Jehovah's Witnesses have should they be viewed as a threat to the organization? They had no chance at all.

I thought about Ed and Bette and what a loss such people would be to any Christian fellowship. How many thousands of such people were now being branded as "apostates" by policies that condemned the open discussion of debatable beliefs and practices? I was in contact with hundreds of people who gave every evidence of having a deep love for God and an abiding confidence in the Scriptures. Many of them had been devoted servants and productive Witnesses for decades. What a waste. In its effort to "clean house," the Society was removing from its ranks some of the very best people they had. The greatest loser in all of this was the organization itself.

The toll of shattered lives caused by the dictatorial policies of the Watchtower Society is incalculable: families ripped apart; extreme emotional stress; the slandering of good names; and the shattering of hopes based on false premises. All of these things and more were being experienced by thousands of honorable people at this time. I recall a phone call from a woman who told me that she listened over and over again to some tape recordings I had sent her because she felt suicidal and listening to those tapes were all she had to keep from losing her mind. By the time she phoned she was beyond that moment of crisis, but she wanted me to know how much she appreciated having the information I provided on those tapes. She viewed them as saving her life. It wasn't that I personally gave her hope, but the views she heard on the themes of those tapes convinced her that she was neither crazy nor wicked; here was another former Witness articulating some of the very things she had concluded. This confirmation reassured her that she was not alone.

Realizing that this was the situation with many people, I decided to create a newsletter that would address many of the arcane doctrines of the Watchtower Society while providing a more scripturally sound viewpoint. I titled the newsletter, *The Christian Respondent,* and was intended to refute various propositions currently appearing in *The Watchtower.* The first issue was published in May 1984, on the topic: "The Generation That Will Not Pass Away." In all, I published 52 essays between 1984 and 1991. By that time I had exhausted the topics I wished to comment on. While I always tried to present something of a positive nature in regard to whatever topic was being critiqued, I felt the need to move away from this type of ministry. I did publish two additional copies in 1995 and 1997 which addressed certain changes the Society made in their doctrinal scheme which impacted on their "generation of 1914" concept.

While the number of subscribers to *The Christian Respondent* was never very high (487), it did benefit readers. After I ceased publication I received a number of letters thanking me for having published the material and expressing regret that I had decided to discontinue it. One reader, a former Witness elder who lived in Texas, wrote:

I read in the BRCI newsletter that you were having to discontinue regular publishing of The Christian Respondent. I know everyone will miss it. Although there are a lot of newsletters and magazines being published by ex-JWs, I heard far more favorable comments about yours than all the others put together. I wish I could have collected all the nice comments I heard about The Christian Respondent to pass on to you. It really ministered to a lot of people.

Another former elder living in Massachusetts wrote:

The announcement in <u>The Christian Respondent</u> that you would be ceasing publication truly saddened me. Your articles always struck me as something that a sincere J.W. could read without finding anything offensive, unless offended by truth itself. Your patience and gentleness in leading your readers to logical conclusions always impressed me. <u>TCR</u> will be missed.

Realizing that the value of something rests "in the eye of the beholder," tempered my pleasure from reading such letters of gratitude. Yet, I could only hope that my efforts over the years had proved to be of some value to a few. A close friend in Idaho, Rosalie Hughes, who had excellent computer skills, offered to convert the hard copies of *The Christian Respondent,* originally printed by mimeograph, to floppy disks. She spent many hours formatting the entire series which amounted to 259 pages of $8^{1}/_{2}$ x 11 copy. Thanks to her efforts I have been able to continue sending out the entire series in book form to interested persons. I still receive requests for it.

In 1984 the thought occurred to me that perhaps more people could be helped if a few of us got together and discussed what additional things could be done to facilitate the healing process of those exiting the organization. I discussed this with Peter Gregerson, and he agreed that it was worth a try and offered to host such a meeting. So it was that in the summer of 1985 about 35 former Witnesses attended this ad hoc meeting one weekend at Peter and Janet Gregerson's lodge on Lake Guntersville in Alabama. It was at this gathering that I met Ray Franz and his wife, Cynthia, for the first time. Ray brought his beloved dog, Lobo, along. Apart from the opportunity to fellowship in community (probably the first such opportunity for most), share experiences and enjoy one another's company, the most lasting result was the decision by the group to hold a conference the following year and invite as many former Witnesses as possible to attend. The idea behind this proposal was to provide people with an opportunity to ventilate their anger and hurt, and to offer healing and constructive suggestions to help them heal and move forward in more positive ways.

As a means to an end, we utilized an existing Alabama nonprofit organization to sponsor the conference. The name of the corporation was Biblical Research & Commentary International (BRCI). The conference became a reality the following year at Guntersville, Alabama, Friday, August 3 through Sunday, August 5. About a hundred former Witnesses attended. The program offered talks, workshops and discussions—all intended to minister to the needs of those struggling to put their lives together. I recall the pervasive mood of sadness, pain and frustration of many. One brother said that we were the "the wounded ministering to the wounded." That was true. Each of us was dealing with personal issues that were extremely difficult—isolation from family members who remained in the organization, confusion as to where to go religiously from this point onward, and the psychological damage that resulted from being labeled wicked and apostate. All of these things and much more were addressed during those several days. For me it was an opportunity to focus on the hurts of others and in the process to experience some healing in my own soul.

I would like to say that everything went swimmingly well and that we all came to a mutual agreement in these matters and were able to unite in a common objective, but that was not the case. Some suspected our motives, implying and even stating that we were trying to gain control over the minds of the brothers and sisters there and start a new religion. A few left the conference early because they were disappointed with the program. But there were others—the majority—who understood our real objective and were thankful for the opportunity to freely express themselves without fear of recrimination, something they could never do as Witnesses. What a blessing to feel safe enough to be honest about one's feelings and know that you were being listened to and validated as a person and a Christian. We were not trying to form a new organization to replace the one we had left. Nor were we trying to establish a doctrinal agenda for people to subscribe to. Our intent was to comfort and encourage those brutalized by a regimented form of religion and to lift their spirits to continue their walk of faith.

Despite the difficulties encountered during that first conference, we decided to have another meeting the following year and there has been one annually held ever since. A core of persons involved in that first conference have continued to support it until now. Not everyone who attends a BRCI conference continues to do so, which is fine with us. The purpose of BRCI has been to provide a sort of "Way Station" for those needing some rest and nourishment to move further on. If their stop at one or several of the conferences provided them with some insight and encouragement, then it had served its purpose, and we wished them God's speed. In this way, hundreds have been helped.

In 1988, BRCI established a telephone "Help-Line" (1-800-WHY-1914). People could call and receive information or simply talk with someone who could relate to their religious, spiritual or emotional problems after either leaving or being expelled by the Watchtower Society. This phone service enables people to call without surrendering their anonymity. This feature has emboldened those still associated with the organization to inquire about our ministry. Some Witnesses use fictitious names when calling the Help-Line, out of fear of discovery. Oftentimes, free literature must be sent to post office boxes because of fear of having material sent directly to their home. This is how pervasive and deep the paranoia created by a religious police state can be. Volunteers supply their phone numbers to be used as referrals around the United States and Canada. This enables the Help-Line Coordinator to refer people to one of these regional people who are geographically closer to them and able to be of greater personal assistance. People are encouraged to advertise the 1-800-WHY-1914 locally to let Witnesses know that such a service exists.

Marilyn Zweifel has served as the primary Help-Line Coordinator from the beginning and, despite failing health, continues to do so. Her caring, insightful and unassuming manner has comforted thousands who have called the Help-Line day and night these many years. While a few have assisted her at various times over the years, she has carried the heaviest load. She is often the target of hateful calls by local Witnesses who demonize her and everything BRCI is doing. It is not uncommon for such ones to be pleasantly surprised at her polite responses to such hateful remarks and apologize for their rudeness. The sacrifices made by Marilyn and her husband George, in this ministry have been substantial. They have mailed out many thousands of pieces of free literature to those requesting it. The Help-Line, like BRCI itself, is not dedicated to bad-mouthing the Witnesses. It is there to offer help to those who want it and to assure them that there is life beyond the Watchtower. A few years ago BRCI established a web site (www.brci.org) that is proving to be another fine way to inform people around the world of our activity.

BRCI is not a religion. It does not set forth a creed and has no local congregations. I consider the years I have been involved with BRCI as time well invested. Many who leave the highly organized Watchtower want nothing more to do with organized religion—not even a local, autonomous one. My wife, Mavis, falls into that category. When she learned of my helping to orchestrate an organization (BRCI) to further my ministry, she was beside herself with dismay. She felt that once we left the Witnesses, organized religion would no longer be a part of our life. We would now be free, she believed, to live a "normal" life. It created yet another crisis in our relationship. While her general health had greatly improved by this time she was not prepared for what I was now contemplating. I explained to her it was something I had to do. I told her I would not ask her to share with me in this ministry, but I needed the freedom to pursue it myself. It would be years before she would be able to fully accept this new activity. I am pleased to say that she has come not only to accept the BRCI ministry but also my various travels each year to a variety of Christian conferences around the United States. She realizes that such things are essential to my life—my reason for being.

Chapter 21

Rebuilding Spiritual Associations

Of the hundreds of conversations I've had with former Witnesses, the difficulty of finding satisfying Christian association is by far the most common problem. Few ex-Witnesses are psychologically prepared to walk out of the Kingdom Hall and into a church a few blocks away. Nothing in the Witness experience prepares them for the trappings, vocabulary or liturgy of the typical church. While I visited a few local churches shortly after severing my ties with the Witnesses, I failed to experience anything that attracted me enough to continue with any one of them. In retrospect, I realize that I was much too traumatized to rationally evaluate their respective worth. It would be nearly a decade before I would be able to seriously consider a committed association with a local body of believers.

Such reluctance and fearfulness may sound strange to many, but coming out of a highly structured and judgmental religious system does not prepare one for the mental and emotional adjustments that must be made to find a place within another believing community. When you have been systematically conditioned to believe that all other religious bodies are not only in error but demonic in nature, the process becomes extremely difficult. Because of this deep-seated fear, ex-Witnesses usually seek out former Witnesses like themselves to fill their need for religious community and worship. There is a certain comfort and security to be found with those who have shared a common experience and hold a basic understanding of Scripture.

The first ex-Witness that Mavis and I met with regularly was Emory DuPre, a Witness we had known for many years who had been disfellowshiped shortly after Mavis was, in early 1981. Emory's experience was quite unique. Through his personal study of Scripture he became convinced that he ought to partake of the emblematic bread and wine which commemorates the sacrificial death of our Lord, commonly called Communion in most churches. Jehovah's Witnesses observe what they call the Lord's Evening Meal or Memorial just once each year on the anniversary date that Jesus instituted the observance. In 1981 the anniversary date for the observance by the Witnesses was Sunday, April 19. Shortly before this date Emory made it known to his wife, Jean, also a Witness, that he intended to partake of the bread and wine at the Kingdom Hall that year. As previously explained, only those who claimed to be in the new covenant and a part of Christ's body, or Church, were authorized to do this. This body, according to Watchtower teaching, was limited to 144,000 and Emory did not claim to be of that number. It was taught that 1935 brought an end to this particular calling, so he identified himself as belonging to the different class of believers the Witnesses speak of as the Lord's "other sheep." (John 10: 16)

Like ourselves, Emory, became a Witness a full decade after the cut-off date of 1935. He was one of the 2.3 million Witnesses around the world at that time who were told they were excluded from the new covenant and not authorized to share in the symbolic meal commemorating the Lord's death. Despite this highly structured doctrinal scheme, Emory became convinced that as a Christian who put faith in Jesus' sacrifice for the forgiveness of sins he had both a right and as well as an obligation to observe the Lord's death by partaking of the bread and wine as the Lord had originally commanded. (Luke 22: 19) He discussed this with Jean, and she suggested that he discuss this with one of their congregational elders in the Blaine, Minnesota congregation, because it was unprecedented for one of the "other sheep" class to do this. He took her advice. He spoke with David Helstrom, an elder in his congregation about his decision on Tuesday, April 14. According to Emory's recollection of that meeting, Helstrom did not appear particularly disturbed about his decision. That evening, however, the DuPres received a phone call from the body of elders insisting that Emory met with them that very night. Jean informed them that Emory had gone out of town on business. The next day the DuPres received a registered letter which repeated the demand that Emory meet with them immediately. Jean conveyed these messages to Emory, who returned home on Friday, April 17. It was then that he learned that he had been disfellowshiped in absentia!

Emory had been a faithful Witness for thirty-three years. He was well known and respected in the Witness community. His life of service was free of reproach. Despite these things, within the space of *four days* his congregational elders excommunicated him for what he believed Jesus

Christ would have him do. He was not disfellowshiped for something he did, but for what he *intended* to do. Rather than wait until Emory returned home and spend the necessary time needed to carefully consider the matter with him they hastily excommunicated him. This not only destroyed his good name but cut him off from any further contact with his congregational elders, his Witness family and the worldwide community of Jehovah's Witnesses. Instead of counseling him and allow him to take responsibility before Jesus Christ for his action, they simply ended his life as a Witness without ever speaking with him. The matter was closed.

This swift execution came as a shock to both Emory and Jean. While Jean didn't agree with Emory, she was shocked by the haste and severity of the elders action. There was clearly an absence of brotherly love shown in the process. She later discussed this with the Society's visiting circuit overseer; his response to her was that the elders "knew what they were doing," thus concurring with their hasty action. Jean had been a life-long Witness. Her father, Harry Bullock had been a Church of Christ minister who had converted to the Watchtower religion many years earlier. He and his family had been prominent Witnesses in the Grand Rapids, Minnesota area. As a consequence, Jean and her brothers and sisters were raised in the Watchtower faith. Emory and Jean had two grown children, a son named Scott and a daughter named Korby. Both were still living at home. That their father, an honorable and dedicated Christian, could be treated as he was by a religious system that boasted of its love, was totally unacceptable by them and undermined their faith in it. They also felt the humiliation that comes when someone in the family is disfellowshiped. Scott moved out of the home.

Jean was angry with Emory and gave thought to divorcing him. Yet she felt compassion for him because she realized how devastated he was. In an effort to show him kindness, she mentioned that Mavis had also been disfellowshiped recently and perhaps he should talk to her. Emory phoned us and arranged to come down for a visit. In this way we learned of his experience, and Mavis shared her experience with him. While I hadn't been officially excommunicated yet (that came in September 1981), I had lost all confidence that God was using the Watchtower Society to deliver a final message to the world. My historical research together with the more recent failure of 1975 to usher in the kingdom of God had shattered all confidence that the organization was being used by Jesus Christ in a special way.

It was some time after this that Mavis and I began to met with Emory for Bible study and fellowship. The DuPres lived on the northern edge of Minneapolis near Blaine, Minnesota and we lived about 60 miles south of the Twin Cities, so we decided to meet about half way in the parking lot of a large shopping mall in Burnsville, Minnesota. Emory had a comfortable customized van and we would sit in it during our time together. Just being together for a couple of hours each week to socialize, share our faith, pray and read the Scriptures together meant a great deal to us in those early days of separation. It helped sooth the deep-seated pain and sense of loss we felt.

Jean continued to attend the Kingdom Hall and sarcastically referred to us as "The Van Set." Yet, she was greatly troubled by the way Emory had been treated and how quickly members of her own family were willing to believe the worst about him. A fair-minded person and having deep respect for the Bible, she began to read it privately in hopes of sorting out her own feelings and beliefs. She was criticized by her family for doing this, because in their mind to read the Scriptures apart from Watchtower literature was a dangerous thing. One member of her family telephoned the same elder that Emory had originally spoken to and told him that they should keep their eye on Jean because she was being influenced by her husband. This was not a call for compassion but rather alerting the elders to a potential apostate. Jean found these attitudes troubling and they did nothing to reinforce her confidence in the organization or its elders.

Gradually, Jean began to reevaluate her understanding of what was scripturally true and what God's will was for her. Little by little she allowed herself to socialize with us. This took considerable courage because just to be seen publicly with disfellowshiped people other than her husband, could lead to her own excommunication. I don't recall at what point it happened but the time came when Jean also sat in on our discussions and "The Van Set" came to an end. We began to meet in one another's home. Finally, about a year and a half after Emory had been disfellowshiped, she was asked to meet with the elders. When she inquired if it was a disfellowshiping hearing, she was told it was not; they only wanted to talk with her. Having lost confidence in them she saw no point in doing this so decided not to meet with them. Shortly after this phone call she learned that she, too, had been disfellowshiped. She was never informed by the elders of their decision but learned of it through gossip. Apparently someone had informed the elders that she was reading the Scriptures in the company of apostates, that was sufficient to condemn her.

About this time another couple, Bill and Alene Lufsky, who also had a Witness background and were friends of the DuPres, had joined our small group. Some time later their congregational elders paid the Lufskys a visit. While there they noticed a notation on Alene's kitchen calendar that had a scripture citation along with our name written on it. It wasn't long after this that she learned that she, too, had been disfellowshiped. For a number of years we met quite regularly. The difficulty of growing into something more substantial in the way of a Christian fellowship was hindered by the fact that we lived so far apart. We had to be content with meeting in one another's home and driving long distances to even do that. Yet it was immensely rewarding and filled a vital need in those early years of separation. We cultivated bonds of friendship during that time which remain solid to this day.

In July of 1982, the Minneapolis *Star Tribune* ran a story about the Witnesses and their severe disfellowshiping policy in which Emory was featured. Someone outside of the Twin City area had supplied the newspaper with the information that led to their interviewing Emory, Mavis and myself. The article was published in the July 22, 1982 issue of the Star Tribune together with a picture of Emory. The reporter, Kay Miller, caught something of the roller coaster of emotions Emory was still experiencing. She wrote:

> DuPre said "99 percent" of his friends and relatives completely shunned him. His wife, who as a spouse was exempted from the requirement that Witnesses shun the disfellowshiped, threatened divorce. His son moved away to avoid the stigma of a father who had been labeled an apostate. "For over a year, I was traveling alone," DuPre said. "It was hell on earth."

> DuPre is a tall, slender man of 54 who talks about his situation matter-of-factly, even when he ventures into an emotional area. But as he talks about the hardships of the past 15 months, his voice fades to a raspy whisper, until whole sentences get lost. But his frustration is given away by a persistent tapping of his foot on the bottom of the coffee table.

Miller phoned us and also included a couple of comments we made:

> "My wife and I were Witnesses for over 30 years and we began to question a few things," said Ronald Frye. Basically it came down to questioning some of the Watchtower Society time structure for the second coming of Christ and the arrival of the millennium. Their entire family, including their only daughter, refuses to see them or speak to them, Mavis Frye said. "We didn't have a permanent home life" while in the church, she said. "We moved around and served in the full-time ministry because the Watchtower encouraged that. Later I came to see the Watchtower as well-meaning, but imperfect, rather than God's exclusive channel of communication."

Miller also spoke with Forest Michaelson, who was serving as the Watchtower Society's city overseer in Minneapolis at the time. The Witnesses were in the midst of their annual district assembly being held at the St. Paul Civic Center. When questioned by Miller why so many people were being disfellowshiped for questioning certain beliefs, Michaelson said that such action was necessary in order to maintain a "clean organization." At the end of the article he is quoted as saying to Miller: "If you're one day away from the flood, would *you* be worrying about apostates or would you be talking about the day ahead?" Michaelson's analogy of being "one day away from the flood," was typical of the Witness mindset at the time. The failure of 1975 to see God's kingdom realized on earth could only mean that the end of the world was just ahead. Michaelson was a kind, intelligent and capable man, and I remember him with affection. But he had been taken captive by the delusional thinking generated by the Watchtower system of religion. He died a number of years later, still waiting for the end he implied was just "one day ahead."

In October of 1987 we came into contact with another couple recently separated from the Witnesses, Jeff and Debbie Luce, who also lived in the Minneapolis area. They had learned of the DuPres and had contacted them. In this way Luces came to read copies of *The Christian Respondent.* They expressed the desire to meet us and arranged to come down to our home together with the DuPres and Lufskys. Through the Luces we learned of a small Christian fellowship that regularly met at Fuller Park in Minneapolis. They had come into contact with this group which they referred to as a Bible Student Church.

The term Bible Student is a generic one which identifies a number of independent fellowships that grew out of the Watchtower movement in the early part of the twentieth century. These fellowships never grew in size as did the Watchtower Society with its organizational resources and aggressive proselytizing, but they drew many thousands away from the parent organization. These divisions began during Russell's lifetime and continued into the second presidency of Rutherford. These associations continue to exist and are quite active in America and Europe, but fall below the radar screen of contemporary religion due to their size. An excellent overview of their development and the doctrinal issues that generated their creation can be found in professor M. James Penton's excellent book, *Apocalypse Delayed: The Story of Jehovah's Witnesses,* published by University of Toronto Press, 33 E. Tupper St., Buffalo, NY 14203.

In various degrees these autonomous groups adhere to the theology of Charles T. Russell, whom they fondly refer to as Pastor Russell The most conservative of these associations continue to view his writings as essential to correctly interpreting the Bible, while others hold to some but not all that he taught. And there is what is referred to as Free Bible students who have, for the most part, moved beyond Russellite theology and seek a balanced approach to the Scriptures. The small, loosely knit Bible student body that met in Minneapolis would fall within the Free Bible student community of believers. This group was anchored by Wayne and Kathy Urbaniak. Wayne was from Illinois and had a Bible student background, while Kathy was a native Minnesotan who grew up in an equally strict religious sect. They met while in college. They had three children, twin girls D'Ann and Cheryl and a boy, David. I first met Wayne at Luces' home, and I was impressed by his gentle spirit and lack of dogmatism. He was a good listener.

I am thankful that Wayne wasn't a conservative Bible student with rigid views of Pastor Russell and his eschatological schemes, because that would have dissuaded me from looking into the fellowship further. But I saw in him a reasonableness and gentle spirit that appealed to me. Also, there were several other former Witnesses starting to attend the Fuller Park assembly, including Jeff and Debbie Luce. So I decided to attend their meetings. I found it helpful in broadening my religious perspectives and cultivating new friendships. We have grown very close to both the Luce and the Urbaniak families. Wayne and I have gotten together for lunch or dinner each month to discuss spiritual matters for many years now and that has proven to be very helpful to me. A couple of years ago the Fuller Park group disbanded and those associated with it have found their way into other Christian communities. But as I reflect on those years that I made the trip to Minneapolis to be in their midst, I realize how faith-strengthening that association was.

It was through the Urbaniaks that I learned of various conferences the Bible students held each year in the United States. The primary one they attended was the Berean Christian Conference held each July at the Grove City College in Grove City, Pennsylvania. Wayne encouraged me to attend one of the conferences which I did in 1989. I found it refreshingly different from what I had experienced at Watchtower conventions. There were constructive and faith-building activities for every age group. There were sermons, Bible studies and a menu of different group discussions covering a wide variety of interests one could choose from. The music was wonderfully inspiring and it often brought me to the brink of joyous tears. Here were whole families and several generations of families worshiping together in a week-long celebration of faith. Yet there was time set aside for relaxation and recreation. I had never experienced anything like it before. I felt sad for the many Witnesses I knew who would never experience anything like this in their life.

By the end of the 1980s, my circle of Christian associates had grown considerably. My initial association with only former Witnesses was now giving way to include believers from other strains of the Watchtower movement. Over time many of these Bible students had married people from different religious backgrounds and this contributed to a greater flexibility in their community. I came to realize that these people had everything they needed to work out their salvation. Moreover, they were doing all of this without a centralized organization dictating their every thought and action. There was an obvious bond of love that held these people together. As a Witness I had been told and strongly believed that we were the only ones who had the intense love for one another that Jesus spoke of that would identify his disciples. I now realized that that simply wasn't true. It was obvious that these people had such love. To be in their midst and be accepted at face value as a disciple of Jesus Christ, was most encouraging and deeply appreciated by me.

Within a year or two after attending my first conference, I was asked to lead a discussion group at Grove City. In subsequent years I have given a number of sermons and led study groups and Bible studies. While each conference has a theme, those who develop sermons and study material are on their own to prepare what they feel will be uplifting and educational. How different from what I had experienced as a Witness. Although I gave many talks as a Witness all of those talks were developed from detailed outlines provided by the Society. They decided what subjects would be developed and what would be said about those subjects. To have the freedom to develop material from the Scriptures alone and present it freely to an assembly of God's people was a wonderful and refreshing challenge. Here was true freedom in Christ!

In 1987, BRCI held its yearly conference in Arlington Heights, Illinois which is not far from Chicago where Wayne Urbaniak's family lives. He has a brother who lives in one of the suburbs there and he along with another man attended the BRCI meeting in Arlington Heights. It was in this way that I got to met Larry Urbaniak and Andy Jarmola, two brother's in Christ that I came to know and love. Larry and Andy were elders in the Berean Bible Students Church located in Cicero, Illinois (the church has since relocated to Lombard, Illinois). Some time later I was invited to speak there. I have visited this fellowship many times and have developed close friendships with many. What I especially like about the Berean Bible Student Church is that it is governed by a body of elders, serving without pay. Perhaps I am biased, but I see much to recommend unsalaried leadership in the church. These men appeared to be true elders in the biblical sense—mature in the faith and eager to serve others.

One year, while attending the Berean Christian Conference, I was approached by someone who asked if I would be willing to speak at other Bible Student conferences. I said yes, and as a result I was invited to attend and speak at the Christian Believers Conference held at Gordon College in Wenham, Massachusetts. I have served this conference a number of times in recent years and have added many new brothers and sisters to my believing family. Another conference held in California each year known as the Western Christian Believers Conference, has also invited me to speak and present workshops which I have done a number of times. These activities, together with my writing, my local ministry and ongoing involvement with BRCI, have given me an opportunity to serve the interests of others and advance God's cause in Christ to a degree I never imagined possible.

Now, twenty-five years removed from Jehovah's Witnesses, I have a family of brothers and sisters spread across the United States, England and Europe. From meeting in Emory DuPre's van as part of "The Van Set," my spiritual association has grown exponentially. Mavis has declined to join me in these activities and travels, but she has grown to accept them and realizes how important they are to me. That initial surge of enthusiasm and desire to serve in Christian ministry nearly sixty years ago has never diminished. There were years when my declining confidence in an organization of men sapped my spiritual energy and I lost the joy of service, but that dark night gave way to a renewed determination to keep seeking God's kingdom and his righteousness. In that process I have been given many opportunities to touch the lives of others, and my life has been greatly enriched in the process. But while my writing and conference ministry had been most rewarding, I felt the need for a local community in which I could fellowship and worship.

Chapter 22

The Need For A Local Community

When we moved to our present location in north-central Minnesota in 1991, I determined to make an effort to find a local community of believers with which I could fellowship. While my writing, correspondence and involvement with BRCI and the Bible student conferences gave me a sense of community and ministry, I felt the need for regular interaction with a local community of Christians. My reading of Scripture convinced me that Jesus' commands could be more fully lived out in this way. I believed he would want me to seek out such association.

We settled into our new home situated on 5 wooded acres, 9 miles south of Aitkin, Minnesota, a community of fewer than 2,000 people. I looked at the churches listed in the phone book and noted that one was identified as non-denominational. The fact that it was non-denominational suggested it might be less doctrinally rigid than the other churches listed. I telephoned the number given and spoke with the pastor, Markus Hill. I shared a little information about my religious background and told him of my interest in visiting the church. I made it clear that I wasn't interested in undergoing a doctrinal test. He assured me that there was no such test, and as matters turned out, there wasn't.

So it was that I came to visit Aitkin Community Church in May of 1991. They had no building of their own and were meeting each Sunday morning in the Seventh Day Adventist Church which held their services on Saturday. After pulling into the parking lot one Sunday morning, I sat there for a few moments collecting my thoughts and cranking up my resolve. I felt that certain uneasiness that comes from not knowing what to expect. I watched as a few people entered the church and then I, too, made my way inside. One person managed a passing greeting, but other than that I was ignored. I don't recall what the sermon was about, but apparently it was acceptable enough for me to return the following Sunday. The second Sunday was a duplication of the first, although I was less nervous. The lack of hospitality was disappointing, but I determined to try one more time the following week. This time a couple of people spoke to me briefly and I decided that integrating myself into this community was worth further effort. Gradually, week after week, I became more at ease and accepted.

I learned that there was an adult Bible study prior to the regular service each Sunday, so I began attending it. After several weeks of attending the study conducted by pastor Hill, I ventured a comment. As weeks turned into months I became more and more comfortable participating in the discussion and getting better acquainted with certain ones in the process. One brother whom I would grow to especially love was Leonard Lee. Leonard had a certain Lincolneze appearance: tall, thin and rough hewn. He had a poetic nature, loved music, had a sense of humor and possessed a strong faith. He had that unusual ability to say a great deal in a few words. One Sunday morning after our Bible study he approached and said, "I like the way you put words together." He and his wife, Inez were a few years older than myself and had grown children who also attended this church. I didn't know it at first, but he was suffering from a form of cancer that would eventually take his life. He faced that prospect with a faith that overcame the fear of death. Despite his illness he refused to allow anyone to feel sorry for him. He died in 2003. I felt richer from having known him.

What I didn't know at first was that this group of twenty to thirty people had only recently formed themselves into a congregation. They were drawn together by a mutual need for something different from what they had experienced in denominational churches. The catalyst in this regard appeared to be Marcus Hill, who had until recently been ministering in a local protestant church. Marcus was somewhat avant-garde in his approach to Christian ministry, and I found that refreshing. Because this fellowship fell outside the traditional mold of mainline Protestantism, two older couples began attending just to make sure their grown children were not getting involved in some kind of a cult. One of those couples were the Lees. The other couple was Herbert and JoAnn Erlandson. Herbert was a soft spoken man with a friendly demeanor and the first man to offer a friendly welcome to me. The fact that the fellowship had only recently begun to coalesce into a community was probably a good thing for me during this introductory phase, because they were more flexible and less formal than a long established church might be.

Even so, the religious ambiance and dialect spoken took a while to adjust to. The pastor didn't preach from a podium; he preached from a pulpit. The large meeting room was called the sanctuary. Each service was punctuated by the passing of the collection plate. The traditional pew—that odd looking piece of church furniture (not designed to bring comfort to the human frame), also took time to get accustomed to. The prominent display of the cross, stained glass windows and the hymnal with its traditional songs and archaic English were all foreign to me, and a little unsettling. Sometimes there would be a hymn containing lyrics I couldn't bring myself to sing. There were praise songs drawn from scripture that were intermixed with traditional hymns. I found them more pleasurable to sing. They were musical celebrations of faith and salvation that I found refreshing. Singing in the Kingdom Hall was limited and quite perfunctory. Here there was enthusiasm and joy.

Over time, it occurred to me that some of the things new to me, did not represent significant differences in substance. One example is the cross. Witnesses are taught that Jesus was hung on a single stake with no crossbar and view the traditional cross as a pagan misrepresentation. Some scholars argue that the crossbar on the Roman cross was actually situated on the top of the stake and looked like the capital T in English. I decided that whatever the shape of the cross was or how it is visualized today, it represented the life of Christ sacrificed for the sins of the world. Another example is the podium verses the pulpit. Both words identify the lectern the pastor stands behind when he speaks. As for pews as apposed to chairs, both provide a place for people to sit. And whether money is collected in a common collection box as in the Witness tradition, or by the passing of plates made little difference. Both are a means to an end—the collection of money.

Semantics also entered into the matter. If a Jehovah's Witness inquired about the standing of a particular person as a Christian, he would probably ask: "Is he or she *in the truth*?" Whereas these folks would more likely ask: "Has he or she *accepted Christ*?" Both questions mean essentially the same thing: is the person a true believer? Using the term sanctuary when speaking of the assembly room of the church is another example. Witnesses would never use that term, even though their assembly halls are set aside (sanctified) exclusively for religious use. The buildings Witnesses meet in are called Kingdom Halls while others usually refer to the building they meet in as the church. Again, it is a matter of semantics. People who refer to the building as the church understand that the people who meet in the building are the church—not the building. The titles for church offices such as pastor, elder and deacon are also to be distinguished from overseer, elder and ministerial servant, terms used by the Witnesses. Basically they describe functions that mean essentially the same thing. And while most pastors are identified as *ordained* ministers, the Witnesses speak of their overseers as *appointed*. Both terms identify those persons officially installed as leaders by their respective authorities.

The doctrinal premise of Aitkin Community Church was quite simple. To qualify for membership one need only affirm Jesus Christ as his or her personal Lord and Savior. The church constitution gave each member the right to interpret the Scriptures according to his or her conscience. The reason for this freedom sprang from a desire to break out of dogmatic theology so common in mainline denominations. This freedom of conscience extended to the pastor who was contracted to serve the congregation. That meant he was governed by his conscience as to what the Bible taught and to preach accordingly. While he preached *to* the congregation, he didn't necessarily speak *for* the congregation or take away their individual right to hold a different opinion on a particular matter. This wonderful freedom in Christ would later be challenged and lead to a destructive division in this body of believers. More about that later.

Some may wonder, especially former Jehovah's Witnesses, how I could be comfortable in a religious community where the pastor believed and taught some things I did not believe. That is a fair question. The answer rests on my understanding of the makeup of the earliest Christian assemblies and individual responsibility. In my reading of Scripture I saw considerable conflict in these matters present in the first century church. I failed to see *complete* agreement of belief and practice in the first century church even though that appears to be set forth as the ideal. The amalgamating of Jew and Gentile believer presented its own particular tensions and challenges. (cf. Acts 15) There is evidence that even the basic gospel was sometimes debated. There were some in the Corinthian church who questioned the resurrection hope. (1 Cor.15:12) There were also factions in this church. (1 Cor. 3: 1-4; 11: 17-19) There were disagreements about certain days being more holy than others, and the propriety of eating or abstaining form certain foods in the Roman assemblies of believers. (Rom. 14)

Some claim that those things mentioned in Romans 14 were nonessential things, but I question that assessment. Try telling a Seventh Day Adventist that worshiping on Saturday or Sunday is a non-essential thing and you will find yourself in serious debate. What is essential and what is non-essential is in the mind of the individual believer. What might be viewed as unimportant by one believer may be considered essential by another. It was in the context of such disputes that the apostle Paul said: "Who are you to pass judgment on the servant of another? It is before his own master that he stands or falls. And he will be upheld, for the Master is able to make him stand." (Rom. 14: 4 *RSV*) The important thing, in Paul's mind, was to avoid stumbling or hindering one another in such matters. (Rom. 14: 13)

And the apostle Paul, in a final warning to the elders from Ephesus, said: "I know that after I leave, savage wolves will come in among you and will not spare the flock. Even from your own number men will arise and distort the truth in order to draw away disciples after them." (Acts 20: 29,30 *NIV*) He also spoke of certain Christian brothers who stirred up trouble for him while he was in prison. (Phil. 1: 14-17) The apostle John reminds us that already in his day there were many false prophets and antichrists present. (1 John 4:1-3) So, from the very start there were serious disagreements and problems within the Christian community. Therefore, while I was sometimes discomforted by what I heard preached, I didn't feel personally contaminated by it. I decided that I was not responsible for what others believed and practiced. I was only responsible for what I believed and practiced. But more often than not, I found sound biblical principles advanced and worthy of acceptance.

Most importantly, Jesus anticipated this problem and addressed it in one of his parabolic illustrations. He likened the true sons of the kingdom to a planting of wheat in a field destined to be over-sown with weeds representing the sons of the evil one. The question was asked whether efforts should be made to separate one from the other. "'No,' he answered, 'because while you are pulling the weeds, you may root up the wheat with them. Let both grow together until the harvest. At that time I will tell the harvesters: First collect the weeds and tie them in bundles to be burned; then gather the wheat and bring it into my barn.'" (Matt. 13: 29,30 *NIV*) The harvest, Jesus explained, was the end of the present age and the harvesters would be his angels. At that time, and not before, the wheat-like believers would be separated from the weed-like ones. (Matt. 13: 37-43)

Human attempts to "purify" the Christian congregation by separating perceived "weeds" from perceived "wheat" have resulted in the creation of thousands of sectarian bodies. And it needs to be appreciated that the presence of "weeds" and "wheat" within a given community has paradoxical value. The apostle Paul wrote: "for there must be factions among you in order that those who are genuine among you may be recognized." (1 Cor. 11: 19 *RSV*) Apparently this tension provides the kind of testing that results in the refining of true Christians. An example of this can be seen in the seven churches in Asia Minor that our Lord examined. Nearly all of them contained people who were believing and practicing wrong things; at the same time there were faithful disciples of the Lord in their midst. (Rev. 1-3) The faithful servants of the Lord were not advised to separate themselves from those who were unfaithful in belief and practice. The unfaithful were urged to repent, and the faithful were urged to remain faithful. To the church or Thyatira, the Lord said:

> This is the message from the Son of God, whose eyes blaze like fire, whose feet shine like polished brass. I know what you do. I know your love, your faithfulness, your service, and your patience. I know you are doing more now than you did at first. But here is what I have against you: you tolerate the woman Jezebel, who calls herself a messenger of God. She teaches and misleads my servants into committing immorality and eating food that has been offered to idols. I have given her time to turn from her sins, but she does not wish to turn from her immorality, and so I will throw her on a bed where she and those who commit adultery with her will suffer terribly. I will do this now, unless they repent from the wicked things they did with her. I will also kill her followers, and then all the churches will know that I am he who knows men's thoughts and wishes. I will repay each one of you according to what you have done.

> But the rest of you in Thyatira have not followed this evil teaching: you have not learned what the others call " the deep secrets of Satan." I say to you that I will not put any other burden on you. But you must hold firmly to what you have until I come. (Rev. 2: 18-25 *TEV*)

The Lord's judgment was and remains an *individual* judgment. All we can do is endeavor to bring our personal beliefs and actions into harmony with revealed truth and seek out what is available in the way of Christian association and fellowship that allows us a measure of acceptance and freedom. To this can be added the fact that I was not being asked to preach from the house tops everything the pastor said. I didn't have to take printed copies of his sermons and go from door to door with them. This was another liberty I did not have as a Witness. Whatever was printed in official Watchtower publications was to be preached whether you agreed with all of it or not.

A short time after associating with the Aitkin Community Church, the men in the congregation went on a weekend retreat. Marcus Hill, asked me to give a sermon in his absence. He didn't offer a suggestion as to what I should preach about, he simply asked me to do it, and I did. In the years that followed I would preach a number of sermons in the absence of the current pastor. During my first year with the church, Marcus Hill, made the decision to return to college for a degree. He made a proposal to the church that would have enabled him to commute from school to church each Sunday, but the majority voted to reject it. As a result, Rick Perry, who until then had served as the music director, was elected as the new pastor. Rick's personality stood in sharp contrast to that of Marcus, who had a certain charisma and eloquent flow of speech; I observed that women were especially drawn to him. Rick was reticent in nature, less outgoing and intimate, and could minister without drawing undue attention to himself. I thought it was a good change for the congregation. As pastor, Rick continued to lead the music, which was his gift.

Not many months after this we were asked by the Adventist church to seek a different meeting place. Arrangements were made with St. John's Episcopal Church, to hold our Sunday service prior to theirs. Still later we met in the Aitkin High School band room. Finally, in 1995, an anonymous donor purchased an older church building in Aitkin that had until recently been used by the Moose Lodge. It had stood empty for some time. The donor also gave the congregation $10,000.00 to assist in refurbishing the tired structure. This move provided the congregation with a permanent location and is still being used by the few who have remained with it.

It was while we were meeting at St. John's that I was asked to conduct the Sunday adult Bible study class. At about the same time, I was approached by two young men, Tim Christianson and Dan Lee, who asked me to have a private Bible study with them. I agreed, and we began to meet at Tim's house each Wednesday evening. As the study became common knowledge, a few others joined us. So what began as a private study soon evolved into a congregational one and was announced as such in the weekly bulletin. This meant that I was now conducting both the Sunday and the mid-week adult studies. I continued these ministries for nearly ten years and found them most challenging and rewarding.

In my teaching I determined to adhere as much as possible to the language of Scripture. I felt this was the safest course for a teacher of the Word. I realized that those who are given that responsibility were subject to a stricter degree of judgment. James had written: "My brothers! Not many of you should become teachers, because you know that we teachers will be judged with greater strictness than others." (James 3: 1 *TEV*) For this reason I confined my studies to the Bible books themselves and used word studies and other scholarly materials to help my students grasp the sense of what we were reading. Often a topic raised in one Bible book was enlarged upon in other books and this enabled me to point out that the Bible was a unity and needed to be studied as a unity. The New Testament clarified much of the Old Testament and the Old Testament provided the necessary foundation for what was said in the New Testament. My familiarity with the Scriptures as a whole enabled me to expand on many things without going outside of the Bible. I don't recall one objection being raised in all of the years I directed these studies.

Even though I conducted adult Bible classes for years, I didn't become an official member of the church until 1998. My reluctance to "join" the church stemmed from the fact that I saw no evidence in Scripture to suggest the need for officially joining a local congregation. But after seven years I concluded that I might be able to help the congregation more if I applied for membership because there were service opportunities that were only open to members. I soothed my conscience by telling myself that there was no scriptural prohibition regarding such things. I had observed that binding oneself by becoming an official member had little effect on community loyalty. I saw a number of official members walk away without so much as a "fare thee well." The only church membership I placed any great value in was the one explained in Scripture: "Now you are the body of Christ and individually members of it." (1 Cor. 12: 27 *RSV*) Now that was a membership above all memberships! I felt that membership apart from church membership.

Pastor Perry recommended that I serve as president of the church's Leadership Council that helped formulate the direction of the church and its activities. I was voted into that office and served as president for two years (1999 and 2000). It was during the year 2000 that the Leadership Council drew up a more demanding schedule for the pastor, which was unanimously adopted and reviewed with pastor Perry. As the pastor's contract was negotiated one year at a time, it was necessary to present the contract to the church for approval. Rick had agreed to the terms of the new contract and the Leadership Council was in full agreement that he continue serving as pastor in 2001. However, the Saturday before the business meeting was scheduled to vote on the matter, Rick phoned and asked me to convene a meeting with the Leadership Council. At this meeting he announced to us that he had decided not to continue as pastor but would continue to serve until a suitable replacement could be found. We were quite surprised by his decision, but we respected it.

I, and several others were assigned to act as a search committee to locate a new pastor. Leonard Lee and I interviewed one candidate who provided us a résumé and also gave a sermon at the church, but we agreed that his style did not blend well with the personality of the congregation. The search committee then gave thought to a brother, Glenn Browning, who, together with his wife, Tamera had recently joined the church. Glenn had graduated from seminary and seemed qualified for the pastor position. He had his heart set on missionary work and was working to make that a reality. This was all the more remarkable in that they had four youthful children. However, when I approached him about the possibility of his serving as pastor, he said I could present his name for consideration. The Leadership Council had a couple of meetings with Glenn and Tamera, in which a contract was agreed upon. In April, 2001 Glenn was voted in as the third pastor to serve the church.

Chapter 23

Division
Decimates
Our Community

Of the three men who served as pastor of Aitkin Community Church, I grew the closest to Glenn Browning. Glenn was hard working, generous, a dedicated father and husband. He and his wife had their fifth child during his ministry with us. Leonard Lee and I regularly met with him each month during the first year of his ministry to discuss congregational needs and develop programs to reach out to the Aitkin community. Glenn and I shared a common interest in evangelizing and we did some of that in Aitkin. The Bible study held in the church each Wednesday evening was replaced by two smaller meetings held in homes. The idea was to invite people outside to these less formal gatherings as an introduction to the fellowship. The group he assigned me to initially met in the home of Larry and Heather Fontaine. Later, the group met in the home of Rich and Gina Courtemanche. Another sister, Nita Foster, was also assigned to this group. Nita, our music director, was the daughter of Leonard and Inez Lee, and had associated with the congregation from its inception. The Courtemanche and Fontaine families had more recently moved into Aitkin but had become very active in the church. This group experienced dramatic spiritual growth over a period of several years.

As previously explained, the congregation had been formed as a non-denominational church with the simple creed of personal belief in Jesus Christ as one's savior and the individual freedom to interpret the Bible. Glenn thought this creed was too simplistic, and he often mentioned that "people do not know what we believe." His desire was to bring the church's confession of belief more in line with traditional protestant doctrine. He believed such a change would strengthen the church spiritually. During his ministry the constitution was revisited and changes were made, but he felt that these did not go far enough. To make the kind of changes he had in mind would require major revisions of the constitution.

There was another factor that may have had an influence on his thinking. Glenn came to understand that I did not subscribe to the creedal definition of the relationship between the Father, the Son and the Holy Spirit. A short time after leaving Jehovah's Witnesses in 1981 a Baptist couple opened a Christian Book Store in a mall in Owatonna, Minnesota, and I was contracted to create their signage. In the course of the work they learned of my religious background and they recommended I read: *Was Christ God?,* a verse by verse commentary on the prologue of John's gospel, written by Spiros Zedhiates, a well known theologian and scholar. I prayerfully approached my reading of this book. I told myself that if God wanted me to believe in the equality of Father, Son and Holy Spirit, I was willing to accept that. I had already discarded major Watchtower teachings and I was willing to consider that here was yet another one that needed to be reexamined. The book failed, in my opinion, to prove that Jesus Christ was God in the *absolute sense* that his Father was God.

Now, in association with Aitkin Community Church, the relationship between the Father, Son and Holy Spirit come up from time to time in various sermons as well as in traditional hymns. On one occasion, Nita Foster's sister Ginny Lee asked me to explain the Trinity to the Sunday adult Bible class. I told her that the doctrine had been developed outside of the Bible in the centuries following the founding of the Christian church in the first century. I explained that as I was devoted to limiting myself to what the Scriptures specifically taught, I did not feel qualified to teach it. I made no other comment on the matter than that. She did not pursue it further.

However, I did decide to address the doctrine again and reread, *Was Christ God?.* I also purchased a recently published book on the topic which was titled: *God in Three Persons: A Contemporary Interpretation of the Trinity*, by Theologian, Millard J. Erickson. In 1997 I decided to research the matter more fully. After two years of work, I published my thesis in a 87-page book, titled: *The Father/Son Relationship*. While acknowledging the deity of Christ, I argued for the supremacy of the Father in that relationship. I made no attempt to circulate *The Father/Son Relationship* among members of the church, but I did give pastor Browning a copy. I was hoping that he would read it and that we could have some brotherly discussions on it. After waiting about six months and not hearing back from him, I approached him to find out if he had read it. I got the impression that it was not particularly his kind of reading material. He said the scholarly style of my writing reminded him of certain materials he had read in seminary which hadn't been of great interest to him. Whether he read a part of it and then set it aside, I do not know. I didn't get the impression at the time that he had been disturbed by what he read.

But as our conversations began to focus on the teaching more and more, it forced him to reevaluate his own understanding of the doctrine. It is my opinion that he gradually grew to see my understanding as a threat to what he believed to be traditional truth. This seemed to underscore the need for the church to be identified more closely with traditional protestant teachings. It was the beginning of a strained relationship between us. Up to that time, Glenn had expressed appreciation for the quality of my Bible study classes. He said that he and his wife had decided to join the church for two reasons: (1) they loved the music that Rick Perry provided and (2) the quality of the adult Bible study I conducted. In the praise portion of our service one Sunday, before he became our pastor, he said the congregation was blessed to have someone like me who was so knowledgeable of the Scriptures to teach the adult Bible class. But now he began to view me differently.

By the close of 2002, I was growing less and less comfortable with Glenn's preaching, and decided to resign from the church. Because I had developed a close bond with those meeting in the Courtemanche home, I continued to attend that fellowship. Sometime in 2003, I mentioned to the group that we had never done a study on the theme of the Bible. The idea that the Bible had a basic theme was a new thought to them and I was asked to create such a study. I did this and titled it *The Restoration of All Things by the Promised Seed*. This study opened up the Bible in a way the group had never looked at the Scriptures before. It drove home the sure conviction that the Bible was truly one book—a unity that clarified God's divine plan centered on Christ. (Eph. 1:5-10) This plan became clear as we worked our way through the various covenants and messianic prophecies which find their ultimate fulfillment in Christ.

The first three chapters of Genesis establish the ground for this theme of restoration, and the last three chapters of Revelation climax it with universal success. That study, which took about eight months to complete, laid the foundation for a stimulating approach to Bible study and discussion that continues to energize this fellowship today. Another study we went through was one I had created in 1994 and used in my Bible classes. This was a 11-part study on the prerogatives, offices and functions of the Lord Jesus Christ. I modified this latter study by adding a twelfth one which tied in with the elements presented in the *Restoration* studies.

A development that would prove fatal to the unity of the church was developing while our study group was enjoying the Bible studies mentioned above. The problem developed over efforts to change the church's constitution. About two years were spent going over the constitution and a number of changes were approved and ratified by the voting members of the congregation. Now, in 2004, Glenn pushed for yet another revision of the constitution. He felt that the changes had not gone far enough and The Leadership Council agreed to support him in this. To open the constitution up required a majority vote, and so the matter had to be presented once more to the congregation. At this time I would estimate that there were about forty or fifty persons attended the fellowship. Of these only about 30 were voting members. Prior to the actual vote there were some heated discussions about the matter. As it turned out, the voting members of the church were evenly divided: 15 for revision, 15 against. The failure to get a simple majority to agree to another revision was a disappointment to Glenn. I was not present when the vote was taken. My information came from those in our mid-week group who were part of the Leadership Counsel and voting members at the time the vote was taken.

It was on the heels of this disappointment that Glenn announced that he would no longer serve as pastor of Aitkin Community Church. The constitution stipulated that the pastor provide a thirty-day notice should he decide to resign. As I mentioned earlier, when Rick Perry resigned he stayed on for several months until we could find a replacement. Glenn had previously scheduled to be gone for the two weeks following his announcement and he calculated that those two weeks, plus two weeks of vacation time that he had coming, was sufficient as a thirty-day notice. The end result was that he never ministered to the congregation following his resignation announcement. This abrupt departure created a crisis that would seriously fracture the congregation. There were whose who shared Glenn's disappointment, and they also immediately resigned from the church. Others were less certain about what to do and remained with the fellowship for a period of weeks.

For a number of Sunday's discussions were had by those who remained in an attempt to figure out a way to save the fellowship. There was still a number who could have continued to associate with the church if they could work something out to continue regular services. To assist to this end, I wrote a letter to the remaining members of the Leadership Counsel, in which I offered to serve as an interim pastor until they could find a replacement. I offered to serve without salary through the six months remaining in 2004. That offer was rejected by the Leadership Counsel. I did preach a sermon one Sunday, and I believe another pastor was invited in as a guest speaker on another Sunday.

But, week after week, the number attending the Sunday service tapered off until there was little more than a handful attending the Sunday services. Those few of us who remained continued to meet in the church as well as continue the mid-week Bible study in the Courtemanche home. The division and the rancor created by the division seriously injured a number of innocent people. This injury was by far the most serious by-product of the division. Having previously experienced the acrimony and judgmental spirit that can destroy friendships and brotherly love, I was especially mindful of the need to withhold condemnatory judgment. Decisions made on both sides of the issue were made in good conscience. It is no one's prerogative to judge the servant of another. (Rom. 14: 4) If bad motives were held by certain ones, the Lord would deal with that in due course. In the meantime, the outstretched hand of brotherly love needs to be extended. Those few who continue to associate in the Aitkin Community Church continue to offer such a hand.

The events of June 2004 climaxed by Glenn Browning's resignation were not anticipated. The congregation had affection for him and was supportive of his ministry. He could have continued to preach from the pulpit those things he believed in strongly without a change in the constitution. There was no clique in the congregation seeking to undermine his ministry. Why he so abruptly ended his ministry I do not know. For whatever reason he chose to do so, his leaving as he did created a vacuum of leadership which forced us to move forward into a new paradigm of community worship.

The model established and flourishing in the Courtemanche home has been adjusted to fit the needs of the Sunday service. We have joyful music and a blessed community prayer service each week that allows for individual petition, praise, thanksgiving and a sharing of needs as well as blessings. The intimate nature of our meetings creates an atmosphere of openness, affection and mutual concern that encourages participation and fills one up in a spiritual way. We are strictly focused on listening to God through the inspired Scriptures. Each person is being assisted and encouraged to become a mature student of Scripture and learn how to live out their Christian discipleship. Each of us is given the freedom to take responsibility for what we ultimately believe. We do not sit in judgment of one another.

As far as I can see, we lack nothing. We have a leader: that leader is the Lord Jesus Christ. We are brothers and sisters living and working under his authority and direction. There is a celebration of faith that is palatable in our midst. That is not to suggest that there are not problems. Life, the human condition and the world are realities that will continue to bring difficulties large and small into our lives. This is an unavoidable reality no matter where we find Christian community and fellowship. The essential thing is that we meet all of these challenges with a mature faith, based on the sure hope of God's kingdom. Until that blessed kingdom becomes a worldwide reality we have a wonderful opportunity to be supportive and reassure one another in Christ's love. What the future holds for this little community of believers remains to be seen. I can only say that it is a source of great comfort and encouragement to me. Where the spirit of Christ is present, there is freedom. It is this precious spirit that ensures spiritual success and God's blessing.

Chapter 24

The
Quest
Continues

After reflecting on the human condition, the unpredictability of chance occurrence and the various pursuits he engaged in to make life fulfilling, Solomon summed matters up by saying: "This is the end of the matter: you have heard it all. Fear God and obey his commandments; this sums up the duty of mankind. For God will bring everything we do to judgement, every secret, whether good or bad." (Eccl. 12: 13 *REB*) Thousands of years later the apostle Paul would phrase the matter differently but come to essentially the same conclusion: "For all of us must appear before the judgment seat of Christ, so that each one may receive recompense for what has been done in the body, whether good or bad." (2 Cor. 5: 10 *NRSV*)

When I began my Christian quest, more than fifty-five years ago, I was focused primarily on the here and now. I viewed myself as being in the very center of God's will and had that special comfort of knowing I was safe within the walled city of his favor. The present world order was in its death throes with only a few years remaining before God's kingdom would bring it to a destructive end. The comfort and sense of security that world view brought me was later shattered by a series of events and discoveries which forced me to reevaluate my understanding of how God was working within the human realm and who and what I was as a Christian.

To have remained where I was and appear approving of a religious system I no longer believed was being used as Jehovah's exclusive earthly instrument, would have been grossly hypocritical. To simply go through the motions in a perfunctory way, following the line of least resistance by appearing to be what I was no longer able to be, would have sucked the very juices of faith and life out of me. I would have become little more than a lifeless shell.

I have never regretted my decision. In retrospect, I realize I could have handled matters more discretely and diplomatically, but the end result would have been the same. The reality is that no one can walk away from the Watchtower organization and retain any sense of honor or dignity in the minds of those who put their faith in it. In the end, however, this is a small price to pay in order to remain loyal to Christ. Jesus once said to a woman who inquired about true worship: "The hour is coming, and now is, when the true worshipers will worship the Father in spirit and truth, for such the Father seeks to worship him. God is spirit, and those who worship him must worship in spirit and truth." (John 4: 23,24 *RSV*) It should be every Christian's desire to be that kind of worshiper. Anything short of this will not win God's approval or the acceptance of his Son. (Matt. 7: 21-23)

The apostle Paul further counsels us: "Do not conform yourself to this age but be transformed by the renewal of your mind, that you may discern what is the will of God, what is good and pleasing and perfect." (Rom. 12: 2 *NAB*) I have come to appreciate, as Paul understood, that we are guided in our Christian quest by limited knowledge. "For we know only in part, and we prophesy only in part; but when the complete comes, the partial will come to an end. When I was a child, I spoke like a child, I thought like a child, I reasoned like a child; when I became an adult, I put an end to childish ways. For now we see in a mirror, dimly, but then we will see face to face. Now I know only in part; then I will know fully, even as I have been fully known." (1 Cor. 13: 9-12 *NRSV*)

This partial knowledge is sufficient for our salvation. Learning to live within the limitations of our understanding requires faith, patience and humility. With such knowledge we can understand the underlying causes for the present human condition and are provided a clear outline of God's will and purpose for his human creation. We can learn what he has done and will yet do to restore life and righteousness to his creation. This grand design unfolds under the authority and direction of his glorified Son, whom he has made heir of all things. "He has made known to us his secret purpose, in accordance with the plan which he determined beforehand in Christ, to be put into effect when the time was ripe; namely, that the universe, everything in heaven and on earth, might be brought into a unity in Christ." (Eph. 1: 9,10 *REB*)

It is in this protracted struggle that we experience the purifying process that the apostle Peter speaks about:

> "Blessed be the God and Father of our Lord Jesus Christ! By his great mercy we have been born anew to a living hope through the resurrection

of Jesus Christ from the dead, and to an inheritance which is imperishable, undefiled, and unfading, kept in heaven for you, who by God's power are guarded through faith for a salvation ready to be revealed in the last time. In this you rejoice, though now for a little while you may have to suffer various trials, so that the genuineness of your faith, more precious than gold which though perishable is tested by fire, may rebound to praise and glory and honor at the revelation of Jesus Christ." (1 Pet. 1: 3-7 *RSV*)

It is also within this process that we experience the reassuring evidence of God's love. Personally, I have gained a great deal in the refining process that the apostle Peter describes. To be tested as to where your heart is and to discover that it is focused on those things that God and Christ approve of, is a rewarding experience. To recall the man I once was and realize that I am no longer that man, is confirmation that God's Spirit is working in me and producing fruit to his honor. I am grateful to God for his patience. Experiencing his patience has made me more patient with others. I am so thankful to have the Lord Jesus as a mediator and advocate. It is for this reason that the dominant spirit I have from day to day is one of gratitude. This gratitude extends to those many people in my life who have shown me kindness, respect and affection. Now, with the onset of the winter of life I can say, I am where I want to be in relation to God and his Son, and doing what I can to continue to advance his cause in Christ Jesus and give support to the family of God. I regularly thank my God for those opportunities.

The fire of religious zeal that was kindled under the influence of the Watchtower system did not die out when I walked away from that system, because it was not the source of the fuel that fed that fire. When I first learned that there was an evil entity that reached into the heavenly realm itself, it settled my mind as to the presence of both good and evil coexisting in the world. To see the Almighty and Holy God vindicated and his name exalted in all the earth became a cause that captured my heart and mind. Up to that point in time there was nothing about me or my life that would suggest such a strong spiritual focus and consecration would ever dominate my life. But it did. That intensity has never waned. And, oh how important Christian fellowship has been these many years. The stimulating and energizing light of life that flows through a body of believers is essential for true spiritual growth. It is little wonder that we are advised not to neglect this association. "Let us hold fast the confession of our hope without wavering, for he who promised is faithful; and let us consider how to stir up one another to love and good works, not neglecting to meet together, as is the habit of some, but encouraging one another, and all the more as you see the Day drawing near." (Heb. 10: 23-25 *RSV*)

For those who are not presently associating in Christian community, I urge that they reach out for such community. It is through the interaction of one believer with another that we are able to build up and strengthen the bond of love that Jesus speaks of. (John 13: 34,35) If you have been severely wounded or betrayed by religious teachers you trusted, don't allow that experience to sour your spirit to the point where you can no longer commit yourself to a community of brothers and sisters in Christ. A bad marriage does not prove that the institution of marriage is bad; a bad religious community does not prove that the concept of religious community is bad. It is a matter of making a good faith effort to find the best available. To receive a blessing there needs to be something for God to bless. Some effort, some action must be taken before we can expect God to bless us. Praying for community must be accompanied by efforts to find community.

I strongly urge former Jehovah's Witnesses to seek Christian fellowship if they have not done so already. I know you long for such association but may be hesitant to take the risk of reaching out for it. You are not contaminated by brushing up against people who may believe things you think are untrue. While my association with Aitkin Community Church has had its problems, I am thankful that I found it. I found people who loved God as deeply as I did and I have had many opportunities to minister there. I would not have the present group to fellowship with had I not taken that original risk of reaching out. The main thing is to preserve your integrity, be sensitive and loving in all situations and maintain a good conscience.

If you make a good faith effort, you will be pleasantly surprised to find that there are others who love God and Christ as deeply as you do, have a deep thirst for the waters of truth, and want the same freedom of conscience that you seek. There is a movement in America away from the traditional format and doctrinal structure represented in mainline churches, so you should be able to find something in your area that allows for individual freedom while still adhering faithfully to biblical principles. Many find that the less formal atmosphere of a house church works best for them. Or, you may be able to take the initiative in this matter and find a way to create such a community. Remember that the size of the group is not important; when or where you meet is not important. What is important is that you are engaged in serious Bible study and discussion, sharing with one another and keeping in mind that where two or three are gathered in Jesus' name, he is there. (Matt. 18: 20)

Another matter that needs to be addressed in closing this memoir is my marriage. The reader understands that Mavis and I have had radically different perspectives and have had to struggle with those differences for many years. While our perspectives are dissimilar, we share many values and have gained a oneness that is quite remarkable. I am pleased to say that our relationship is healthier and more loving than it has ever been. While Mavis has never joined with me in my post-Witness ministry, she has grown supportive of it. Last year (December 20, 2005) we observed out sixtieth wedding anniversary, and were joined by people from as far away as Chicago and St. Louis, to celebrate with us. I am so thankful that we remained together despite our personality differences. Working through those differences and the unrealistic demands I placed upon her in the full time ministry, took years to resolve. We were helped in this regard by the ability to argue through our differences and seek resolution. That we are happy with one another and respect our differences is another blessing for which I am most grateful. I know it

means a great deal for Mavis to know that I truly love her and will be there for her as long as I live.

Mavis has a deep love for dogs and other animals. I have come to respect and admire her advocacy for animals—domestic and wild alike. Her heartfelt concern for them and the environment is a product of her love for God's creation. While she does not associate with me in community worship, she reads her Bible daily and is in constant prayer. She has grown in her unique way to be the person she is. She has an unquenchable curiosity about many things: health, nature and how things work. Knowledgeable about nutrition and natural remedies, she has helped us live healthier lives. She is like a mother to our four dogs and three cats. She is more disciplined than I am and has been much more productive in what she sets her mind to doing. She is a blessing to me and I thank God for her.

Writing this book has taken many years. There were times when I wasn't sure it would ever be completed. I have written it primarily for those who have pulled away from the Watchtower movement, in an attempt to encourage them to move forward in their walk of faith. But I believe there are elements in it that would be relevant to many others. There were parts of it that required a revealing of things about myself of which I am not proud. In writing about such things I relived them. There were times when I had to set the manuscript aside for weeks before I could continue. It is hoped that revealing some of my faults and weaknesses may encourage others who struggle with self. That God could take a very flawed piece of clay and mold it into something of value is most remarkable.

I conclude this record with a passage of Scripture that has become increasingly relevant to me. It is taken from the letter by the apostle Paul to the church in Philippi. While coming from a far different religious background than the apostle had as a Jewish Pharisee, I can relate to a religious life left behind in favor of something far superior. He wrote:

> I count everything sheer loss, because all is far outweighed by the gain of knowing Christ Jesus my Lord, for whose sake I did in fact lose everything. I count it so much garbage, for the sake of gaining Christ and finding myself incorporate in him, with no righteousness of my own, no legal rectitude, but the righteousness which comes from faith in Christ, given by God in response to faith. All I care for is to know Christ, to experience the power of his resurrection, and to share his sufferings, in growing conformity with his death, if only I may finally arrive at the resurrection from the dead. It is not to be thought that I have already achieved all this. I have not yet reached perfection, but I press on, hoping to take hold of that for which Christ once took hold of me. My friends, I do not reckon myself to have got hold of it yet. All I can say is this: forgetting what is behind me, and reaching out for that which lies ahead, I press towards the goal to win the prize which is God's call to the life above, in Christ Jesus." (Phil. 3: 8-14 *NEB*)

* * * *

Appendix A

The Faithful and Discreet Slave

This treatise was originally created in 1981. A few changes have been made to make the material more understandable for those not familiar with the history or theology of Jehovah's Witnesses. Other than that, the material is essentially as it was originally written. —*Ronald E. Frye, 2006.*

The Watch Tower Bible and Tract Society of New York, is one of the most authoritarian religious governing bodies on earth. The fierce loyalty that Jehovah's Witnesses worldwide have towards this Society is premised on the conviction that the Watchtower Society represents God's channel of communication to men on earth—His visible earthly organization. This means that Jehovah God speaks to men on earth only through this organization. Only it possesses God's Holy Spirit which communicates God's thoughts to men. Any person who has difficulty accepting everything this Society teaches, or doubts or questions something they teach or in any way shows a critical attitude towards anything they teach, is branded as wrong and lacking appreciation and gratitude for all the things God is providing for them through the Watchtower Society. Illustrating this point of view, the February 15, 1981 *Watchtower* article, "Do We Need Help to Understand The Bible?" said this on page 18:

> How shall we view the spiritual food provided by this "faithful and discreet slave"? Should it be viewed critically—"Oh, well, it might be true but then again it might not be and so we have to scrutinize it very critically"? Some apparently have felt that way about it. To support their way of thinking they have quoted Acts 17:11, which says of newly interested persons at Beroea: "Now the latter were more noble-minded than those in Thessalonica, for they received the word with the greatest eagerness of mind, carefully examining the Scriptures daily as to whether these things were so."

> But does this mean that those Beroeans were looking for flaws in the message they were hearing, or that their attitude was one of doubting? Does this set a precedent for regarding critically the publications brought forth by the "faithful and discreet slave," with a view of finding fault? Not at all.

The next several paragraphs go on to explain that the Beroeans were eager to believe what was being taught them—they wanted to believe it!

Then on page 19, under the subtitle: "Our View of The Slave," it added the following:

> We can benefit from this consideration. If we have once established what instrument God is using as his "slave" to dispense spiritual food to his people, surely Jehovah is not pleased if we receive that food as though it might contain something harmful. We should have confidence in the channel God is using. At the Brooklyn headquarters from which the Bible publications of Jehovah's Witnesses emanate there are more mature Christian elders, both of the "remnant" and of the "other sheep" than anywhere else upon earth.

> True, the brothers preparing these publications are not infallible. Their writings are not inspired as are those of Paul and the other Bible writers. (2 Tim. 3:16) And so, at times, it has been necessary, as understanding became clearer, to correct views. (Prov. 4:18) However, this has resulted in a continual refining of the body of Bible-based truth to which Jehovah's Witnesses subscribe. —*The Watchtower,* Feb. 15, 1981 page 19.

THE BEGINNING OF THE FAITHFUL AND DISCREET SLAVE: PENTECOST DAY 33 C.E.

The above style of presentation of scriptural matters can be very intimidating to those among Jehovah's Witnesses who begin to have serious doubts, reservations or questions regarding something the Society teaches. If they are in any way critical, they are viewed as having a bad attitude. The constant repetition that they are God's channel, his "faithful and discreet slave," is appealed to to give weight to every utterance of the Watchtower Society. Seeing that this is the case, it seems appropriate to examine the basis for the claim that they represent this so-called "faithful and discreet slave." The text that is appealed to as the basis for this claim is found at Matthew 24:45-47: "Who really is the faithful and discreet slave whom his master appointed over his domestics, to give them their food at the proper time? Happy is that slave if his master on arriving finds him doing so. Truly I say to you, He will appoint him over all his belongings." (*New World Translation*) The March 1, 1981 issue of *The Watchtower* on page 24, supplies the official interpretation of Jesus' words:

> Jehovah's Witnesses believe that this parable pertains to the one true congregation of Jesus Christ's anointed followers. Beginning with Pentecost, 33 C.E., and *continuing through the 19 centuries since then*, this slavelike congregation has been feeding its members spiritually, doing so faithfully and discreetly. Especially has the identity of this "slave" be-

come clear at the time of Christ's return or presence. The "slave" is identifiable by its watchfulness and by the fact that it is faithfully and discreetly providing spiritual food as needed by all in the Christian congregation. Indeed, this "slave," or spirit-anointed congregation, is *the one approved channel* representing God's kingdom on earth in the "time of the end." (Dan. 12:4) Witnesses of Jehovah understand that the "slave" is comprised of *all anointed Christians as a group* on earth at any given time *during the 19 centuries since Pentecost*. Accordingly, the "domestics" are these followers of Christ as individuals."—*The Watchtower*, March 1, 1981, page 24. (italics not in original).

According to this teaching then, this *composite "slave"* has had a *continuous, uninterrupted existence* from its beginning up to the present time. That there would be genuine Christians on earth from the beginning until the end of the world, is clearly shown in Jesus' illustration of the "wheat" and the "weeds" found in Matthew 13. The "wheat," representing the true sons of God, were sown in a "field," which is the world. The "weeds," or imitation Christians, were later sown in among the "wheat" by the evil one. Jesus explained that these two plantings were to *grow together* until the end of the world. Then, in the harvest period, the angels would go forth and separate the "weeds" from the "wheat." The "weeds" would be put in piles and burned; the "wheat" would be harvested and stored. Imitation Christians, or weeds, began to make their appearance soon after the Christian congregation came into being. These apostates, however, according to Watchtower teachings, would never get control of the "faithful and discreet slave" class—the "wheat," that is, the faithful Christian congregation or group on earth. Addressing this matter, the February 15, 1975 issue of *The Watchtower* had this to say on page 110:

> We note that Jesus did not say that the "faithful and discreet slave" would turn disloyal. But, as to the individual members of the "slave" class, Jesus merely indicated the possibility that not *all* would be loyal, just as one of the twelve, Judas, after a right start, had turned out bad. . . Christ would not let any such disloyal ones have domination over or *break up* his congregation and stop the work it is doing. —*The Watchtower*, February 15, 1975, page 110. (italics not in original)

Another *Watchtower* added:

> Though the "weeds" dominated the world's religious scene through the centuries, *some "wheat" was active* and spiritual food was provided for the "domestics." —*The Watchtower*, March 1, 1981, page 26. (italics not in original)

Bear in mind that the "wheat," according to Watchtower interpretation, means the on-going existence of the "faithful and discreet slave" as a group—the Christian congregation—all the faithful spirit-anointed Christians on earth at any one time, not representing the "wheat" scattered about in the world.

Another *Watchtower,* under an article titled: "How Are Christians Spiritually Fed?," said the following:

> Jesus had said: "Look! I am with you all the days until the conclusion of the system of things." (Matt. 28:20) Jesus Christ is the Head of the congregation, his slave, and his words show that he would strengthen them to feed his "domestics" *right down through the centuries*. Apparently, one generation of the "slave" class fed the succeeding generation thereof, as well as continuing to feed themselves.—*The Watchtower*, January 15, 1975, page 46. (italics not in original)

Again, it is clearly argued that these Christians were not fed as isolated, independent persons, but as a *collective body*: a congregation. Summing up the argument the same article said this on the following page:

> We see, then, that Jesus Christ himself called attention to this method of feeding his people: not as isolated, independent individuals, but as a close-knit body of Christians having real love and care for one another. —*Ibid.* page 47.

The claim presented above insists that there has been this *collective feeding program* in place from the beginning, and the "faithful and Discreet Slave" has had a continuous, uninterrupted existence from Pentecost A.D. 33 to the present moment. This claim is further argued for in another *Watchtower*:

> Down through the years the slavelike congregation has been feeding its true members faithfully and discreetly. From Pentecost, A.D. 33, up to this very present hour this has been lovingly and carefully performed. Yes, and these "domestics" have been fed on *progressive spiritual food* that keeps them abreast of the "bright light" that is getting lighter and lighter until the day is firmly established. (Prov. 4:18) —*The Watchtower*, July 1, 1960, page 435 (italics not in original).

According this last quotation, the "slave" has not only been continuously nourished by wholesome spiritual food, but it has also been nourished by *progressive spiritual food*, not regressing or remaining static, but always moving forward with the increasing light of truth. This, then, is the carefully laid premise regarding the Watchtower Bible and Tract Society's of the "faithful and discreet slave" illustration in Matthew 24. According to this premise, the "slave" came into existence on Pentecost

Day, C.E. 33 and was to have a continuous, unbroken history down through the centuries up to and including the end of the world. All during this time it would be feeding its members progressive spiritual food, thus becoming more and more enlightened as time went on. The question to be answered then is how does the history of the WBTS dovetail or square with this premise? If we enforce the consequences of the Society's interpretation of Matthew 24:45-47, what do we find? Remember that it must fit their history to be demonstrated as true. If their history does not square with their own premise, the premise is demonstrated as false. With these thoughts in mind, let us examine the Society's history as explained in their own publications.

THE BEGINNING OF THE WATCHTOWER RELIGION:
1870 C.E.

The Watch Tower Bible and Tract Society of Pennsylvania was founded in 1884 by Charles T. Russell, known for many years as "Pastor Russell." Russell was born in Allegheny, Pennsylvania in 1852. By the time he was sixteen he was already religiously disturbed. In a book *Jehovah's Witnesses in the Divine Purpose*, it makes these observations, reportedly in his own words:

> Brought up a Presbyterian, indoctrinated from the Catechism, and being naturally of an inquiring mind, I fell a ready prey to the logic of infidelity, as soon as I began to think for myself. But that which at first threatened to be the utter shipwreck of faith in God and the Bible was, under God's providence, overruled for good, and merely wrecked my confidence in human creeds and systems of Bible misinterpretations.

> During the next few months Russell continued to reflect over the subject of religion, unable to accept it, and yet unwilling to let go." Then Russell relates:

> Seemingly by accident, one evening I dropped into a dusty, dingy hall in Allegheny, Pa., where I had heard that religious services were held, to see if the handful who met there had anything more sensible to offer than the creeds of the great churches. There, for the first time, I heard something of the views of Second Adventism, by Jonas Wendell . . . Though his Scripture exposition was not entirely clear, and though it was very far from what we now rejoice in, it was sufficient, under God, to reestablish my wavering faith in the Divine inspiration of the Bible, and to show that the records of the Apostles and the Prophets are indissolubly linked.'"— *Jehovah's Witnesses in the Divine Purpose*, 1959, page 14.

An early associate of Mr. Russell was A. H. Macmillan, a Canadian, who spent many years serving at the Watch Tower headquarters, adds the following regarding the beginning of Russell's ministry in 1870 in his book, *FAITH ON THE MARCH:*

A renewed determination to continue his search for the truth opened a new chapter in this young man's life. Taking down his already well-worn Bible, he began a careful and systematic study of the Bible itself. As he read he thought, and the more he pondered the more convinced he became that the time was drawing near for the wise watching ones of the Lord's children to get a clear picture of God's purposes.

Fired now with real enthusiasm, he approached several young men with whom he had been associating, some in a business way and others socially. He told them of his rekindled interest, of his purpose to continue his direct study of the Bible without any consideration of established creeds. Immediately recognizing the possibilities, they said, 'Well, suppose we get together and study in a systematic way during certain hours each week.

So it started. This young man, who at eighteen years of age organized this little Bible class, was to become one of the best-known Bible students of his generation. He was to become one of the best-loved and the most hated—one of the most praised and most maligned men in modern religious history.

That was Charles Taze Russell, later globally known as Pastor Russell.— *Faith on the March*, by A. H. Macmillan, 1957, pages 19,20 (italics not in original).

According to the above record provided by Jehovah's Witness sources, Charles Taze Russell, in 1870, turned away from all existing Christian fellowships and on his own, just with the Bible, began a systematic study thereof. Commenting on the fruitage of that independent study of the Bible, the WBTS says:

He was not the founder of a new religion, and never made such a claim. He *revived the great truths taught by Jesus and the apostles*, and turned the light of the twentieth century upon these teachings. He made no claim of a special revelation from God, but held that it was *God's due time for the Bible to be understood;* and that, being fully consecrated to the Lord and to his service, *he was permitted to understand it.—Jehovah's Witnesses in the Divine Purpose*, page 17, see also *Studies in the Scriptures*, Vol. 1, "Biography," page 2, International Bible Students Association, 1927 edition. (italics not in original).

This, then, is the root-stock—the beginning of the Watch Tower Bible and Tract Society, as explained in their own words. It completely repudiates their carefully laid premise regarding the so-called "faithful and discreet slave" doctrine. By the year 1870, when young Russell began his *independent study* of the Bible, the so-called "faithful and discreet slave," would have been more than 1800-years old! The question has to be answered: Where was this "faithful and discreet slave?"

How could Russell "revive the great truths taught by Jesus and the apostles," independently of God's channel of communication—His earthly organization? If, as the WBTS insists, the "faithful slave" had been feeding itself progressively down through the centuries: "one generation feeding the succeeding generation thereof," why would the great teachings of Jesus and the apostles *need to be revived*? They would not if the premise regarding the "faithful and discreet slave" were true. Clearly, the history of Jehovah's Witnesses, flatly contradicts their basic premise regarding the "faithful and discreet slave."

It is clear that in order to justify their authoritarian system of today, they must argue that Jehovah is using an organization—an earthly channel that all must accept and submit to. But to insist upon it today, they must argue that this has been the case from the very beginning in 33 C.E. But the fact remains that Russell did not turn to any such earthly organization. He acted independently on his own. Today, more than a 100 years from Russell's start, Jehovah's Witnesses are outstandingly organization-minded. The organization always comes first. *The Watchtower* of March 1, 1979, in the article, "Faith in Jehovah's Victorious Organization," the expression "theocratic organization," appears no less than 15 times in just the first eleven paragraphs. This kind of mesmerizing repetition is constantly used to condition Jehovah's Witnesses to think that it is wrong for them to question anything the Society ever publishes as truth. In contradiction to this attitude towards organization, Russell and his associates were actually anti-organization. Consider the following from *The Watch Tower* of February 1884, in connection with Russell's view of earthly, religious organizations:

CHARLES T. RUSSELL'S VIEW OF ORGANIZATION

We belong to NO *earthly organization;* hence, if you should name the entire list of sects, we should answer, No, to each and to all. We adhere only to that *heavenly organization*—"whose names are written in heaven." (Heb. 12:23; Luke 10:20.) All the *saints* now living or that have lived during this age, belonged to OUR CHURCH ORGANIZATION: such are all ONE Church, and there is NO OTHER recognized by the Lord.

Hence any earthly organization which in the least interferes with this union of saints is contrary to the teachings of Scripture and opposed to the Lord's will—"that they may be ONE." (Jn. 17:11.) This quotation was reprinted in *The Watchtower*, March 1, 1979 on page 16. (Emphasis in original)

As the above shows, Russell believed in the *invisible church*. He did not believe in an ongoing, earthly church or organization. Now the antagonism Russell felt toward earthly organizations is understandable. He was, after all, a religious maverick. His small group of followers (in 1884) were without an organizational history. They sought to minimized that lack of history by arguing the God did not have on earth a continuous organization—a monolithic Christian congregation; that it was not God's way of doing things. In this way the Russellites could bring down, in their eyes, those religions that did have a history and explain away their lack of one. And in connection with the subject at hand, it is abundantly clear that Russell did not believe that Jehovah God had on earth an 1800-year-old "faithful and discreet slave" organization serving as God's exclusive channel of communication. He did not find it, and it did not find him! He and his associates had no fellowship with any existing religious organization, and were, in effect, disdainful of such organizations. They stoutly repudiated the idea that there was on earth since Pentecost A.D. 33 an earthly organization that one had to be identified with in order to serve almighty God.

Today, a hundred years later, those descendants of the Russellites who identify themselves with the WBTS argue the other way around: now it is necessary to be looking to a visible earthly organization, namely the Watchtower Society. But that was not the position in the beginning. As the situation changed, so their arguments changed. They argue for an earthly organization as strenuously as they once argued against one.

Just as their perception of organization was far different a hundred years ago from what it is today, so their view of Russell is far different from what it was in the beginning. Apart from brief references to him from time to time, Russell, for the most part, is unknown to modern-day Witnesses. His writings are not recommended reading nor are his books any longer published by the very publishing house he established and endowed with his own money. Yet, here was a man whom Jehovah's Witnesses still argue was used by God to "revive the great teachings of Jesus and the apostles." Why don't they study his books in the congregations of Jehovah's Witnesses if only from a historical standpoint? Because much of it, if not most of it, would be considered heretical today.

Russell was a prolific writer—a remarkable man in many ways. He drew up the charter of the WBTS; he was the principle writer and editor of the *Watch Tower* from its beginning in 1879 until his death in 1916. He composed many tracts, booklets and books and his sermons were printed in hundreds of newspapers across America. He authored six-volumes of *Studies in the Scriptures* (known originally as the *Millennial Dawn Series*). These volumes represented the definitive beliefs of the Russellites who preferred to be known as Bible students. These volumes constituted "the truth," by the Bible students. In this connection it is interesting to look at how the Bible students viewed his books in relation to Bible study. We get something of the flavor of this by what was published in 1910:

> If the six volumes of SCRIPTURE STUDIES are practically the Bible topically arranged, with the Bible proof-texts given, we might not improperly name the volumes—the Bible in an arranged form. That is to say, they are not merely comments on the Bible, but they are practically the Bible itself, since there is no desire to build any doctrine or thought on any individual preference or on any individual wisdom, but to present the entire matter on the lines of the Word of God. We therefore think it safe to follow this kind of reading, this kind of instruction, this kind of Bible study.
>
> Furthermore, not only do we find that people cannot see the Divine Plan in studying the Bible by itself, but we see, also, that if anyone lays the SCRIPTURE STUDIES aside, even after he has used them, after he has become familiar with them, after he has read them for ten years—if he then lays them aside and ignores them and goes to the Bible alone, though he has understood his Bible for ten years, our experience shows that within two years he goes into darkness. On the other hand, if he had merely read the SCRIPTURE STUDIES with their references, and had not read a page of the Bible, as such, he would be in the light at the end of the two years, because he would have the light of the Scriptures.—*The Watchtower*, September 15, 1910 page 298. (Emphasis in original)

Note the complete turnaround of matters now!. When Russell went to the Bible, although he wasn't inspired, he could understand it. But now, after the printing of the six volumes, no one could go to the Bible alone and learn the truth. Now the truth could only be found in the volumes which explained the Bible. They were the truth; and if you didn't agree with them, then you were in spiritual darkness. Today, of course, most of what was taught in those volumes is rejected by Jehovah's Witnesses. But at the time it was THE TRUTH, and you had to believe it— that's what the Russellites said, if you were to be in the truth!

So the authoritarian attitude displayed by the WBTS today is not new. I has been a characteristic from the beginning. Russell and the Bible students were no doubt sincere, God-fearing people who really did believe they were being enlightened by God and being used in a special way. But the facts show that this conviction was primarily based on self-delusion, and this self-delusion motivated them to speak in an authoritarian manner and condemn all whose who didn't agree with them. Assuming they were special, they unfortunately became most presumptuous in their presentation of Scriptural matters.

THE MAN RUSSELL WAS VIEWED AS THE FAITHFUL AND DISCREET SLAVE

Much, if not all of this religious presumptuousness, resulted from their attitude toward the man Russell and his writings. It is acknowledged by the Watchtower Society today that many Russellites were guilty of creature worship toward the man. This creature worship, I might add, was a natural consequence of what they had been taught about the man. He, individually, was identified as the special "servant" or "slave" of Matthew 24:45-47. In Macmillan's book, it say the following about this viewpoint:

> Often, when he was asked, Who is that faithful and wise servant? Russell would reply: "Some say I am; while others say the Society is." Both statements were true; Russell *was in fact the Society* (in a most absolute sense), in that he directed the policy and course of the Society. He sometimes sought advice of others connected with the Society, listened to their suggestions, and then decided according *to his best judgment* what he believed the Lord would have him do.—*Faith on the March*, pages 126,127 (italics not in original).

That Russell was so viewed is acknowledged in the book, *Jehovah's Witnesses in the Divine Purpose:*

> The view *generally held*, that Pastor Russell himself was the "faithful and wise servant" of Matthew 24:45-47, created considerable difficulty for some years. The insistence that Russell had been "that servant" led many to regard Russell in what amounted actually to creature worship. They believed that all the truth God had seen fit to reveal to his people had been revealed to Russell, and now nothing more could be brought forth because "that servant" was dead.—*Jehovah's Witnesses in the Divine Purpose*, 1959, page 69. (italics not in original)

It is important to note that this attitude toward Russell was not something privately arrived at by a few fanatics. It had been officially taught by the Watchtower Society as the following clearly states:

> There was some resistence from those who were not progressive and who did not have a vision of the work that lay ahead. Some insisted on living in the past, in the time of Pastor Russell, when the brothers in general had viewed him as the *sole channel* of Scriptural enlightenment. It was the *published and accepted thought* down til 1927 that he was "that servant" of Matthew 24:45.—*Jehovah's Witnesses in the Divine Purpose,* page 95. (italics not in original)

Note in the above statement that it was the *published thought* that Russell was "that servant" of Matthew 24:45 until 1927—eleven years after his death! But there is more. He was also identified with the man with the writer's inkhorn mentioned in Ezekiel, chapter nine, and the seventh messenger of Revelation. In Revelation, chapter one, the glorified son of man is pictured as holding seven stars in his right hand. Russell was viewed as being one of those stars. It was argued that the seven stars represented seven periods or epics during the Gospel age. In each epoch or age, God provided a special messenger for the earthly church. Russell was seen as the seventh and last such messenger. Concerning this *The Watchtower* of November 1,1917, published a year after Russell's death, contained an article titled: "A Tribute to the Seventh Messenger." In part, it said:

> The great drama of the Gospel Age opened with the apostle Paul as the chief messenger, or angel, to the Church. It closes with Pastor Russell as the seventh and last messenger to the Church militant. For the other five epochs of the Church, the Lord provided messengers in the order named; St. John, Arius, Waldo, Wycliffe and Luther. Each in his turn bore the message due to be understood during the epoch he represented. The two most prominent messengers, however, are the first and the last: St. Paul and Pastor Russell.[1]

Clearly, this cult-like view, this unscriptural view, of both the man and his writings, completely contradicts what was supposed to be the character of the so-called "faithful and discreet slave." This wrong view

---

1. The "seven messengers" concept is drawn from Revelation 1:20 which speaks of seven angels (messengers) sent to the seven churches addressed in the early chapters of Revelation. The Bible students taught that each "messenger" was a special person sent at certain times to the Christian church during the gospel age. The first of these seven messengers was said to be the apostle Paul and the seventh and last was Charles T. Russell.

was believed and taught for nearly 40 years. Repudiated by Jehovah's Witnesses today, but it was the "truth" then, and if you questioned it, you were in spiritual darkness. You didn't have the right attitude toward's God's Organization and his "channel." Yet people are asked to believe that God was behind all of this.

Following the death of Russell, the organization was in complete disarray. God's "wise and faithful servant" was dead. The seventh and last messenger to the church was dead. It must also be remembered that two years earlier, in 1914, the long looked-for end of the world failed to materialize. Many Bible students fell away from the organization as a result. Also, there was a power struggle within the headquarter's staff of the WBTS. Certain members of the board of directors opposed Rutherford as president. The tension came to a head in 1917, when on July 17, at the noon meal, Rutherford released to the Bethel family a "seventh volume" named: *The Finished Mystery.* A heated debate broke out which lasted five hours, wherein they argued over the propriety of the Society producing another volume to add to the existing six volumes written by the revered Pastor Russell. Rutherford had proceeded to produce this book without consulting the board of directors and they were livid. Ultimately, they and those who shared their views, left the organization.[2]

Today, Jehovah's Witnesses are told that those men opposing Rutherford were wicked, self-serving individuals and are painted with the broad brush of "evil slave." But at the time, they were acting out of a loyalty towards Russell—a loyalty that had been carefully cultivated and nourished in them by the WBTS for many years. How could they be faulted for reacting as they did to Rutherford's action which seemed extremely presumptuous to them? Their anger was generated by their loyalty to Jehovah's "faithful and wise servant," Charles T. Russell; a loyalty much like the loyalty that Jehovah's Witnesses display today—not to a man, but to a legal corporation, the WBTS. Those men were acting in a manner consistent with their convictions. To have acted differently would have been inconsistent with their basic understanding of how God had been using Pastor Russell as "that servant." To say, as the Witnesses now say, that such men were removed to "clean the organization" makes

---

2. Charles T. Russell had written six volumes of religious teaching during his life. These volumes came to be called *Studies in the Scriptures.* In 1917 Rutherford had a book published titled *The Finished Mystery* which he claimed was the posthumous work of Russell who died in 1916. The dissenters argued than nothing could be added to what the "seventh messenger" (Russell) had written during his life. *The Finished Mystery,* which was a commentary on the Bible books of Ezekiel and Revelation, identified Russell as the seventh and last messenger to the church during the gospel age.

no sense. Either Russell had been used as they had been taught that he had or he had not. He was either right or wrong. He was either true or he was a fraud. They believed that he was God's chosen servant.

These board members chose to leave Bethel rather than accept Rutherford's conciliatory offer to appoint them as traveling "Pilgrims," an office that corresponds roughly to that of their present day Circuit overseers. Through a legal technicality, Rutherford was able to dismiss these board members from the Pennsylvania corporation and replace them with men sympathetic to him. These events are discussed on pages 70,71 in the book, *Jehovah's Witnesses in the Divine Purpose.*

All of this internal strife was carried on against the backdrop of World War I which began in Europe in 1914. The period between 1914-1918 was a horrendous one organizationally for the Bible students. Their "wise and faithful servant" was dead. His prophecies regarding the end of the world in 1914 went unfulfilled. The organization was split into divisions over management. They were ridiculed publicly as false prophets. Some of their leaders were jailed over the war issue. Everything sort of ground to a halt at that time. But it was at this very time that something remarkable is said to have happened.

JESUS CHRIST'S (INVISIBLE) RETURN CHANGED
FROM 1874 C.E. TO 1914 C.E.

According to the present day perception of things, Jesus Christ returned *invisibly* in 1914 (thus moving the invisible return forty years forward from 1874) and after his coming was engaged in judging his earthly servants. This was in fulfillment, they say, of Matthew's words: "Happy is that slave if his master on arriving finds him doing so. Truly I say to you, he will appoint him over all his belongings." (Matthew 24:46,47 *NWT*) Of all the world's religious organizations only the Bible students received his approval . Accordingly, in the spring of 1919 the Bible students were entrusted with *all* of the earthly interests of God's newly established heavenly kingdom. Speaking of this remarkable appointment during the very time their organization was in shambles, they say:

THE WITNESSES DESCRIBE THEMSELVES AS
REJECTED BY GOD IN 1914 C.E.

In the year 1914 C.E., at the close of the "appointed times of the nations," [earlier referred to as the "times of the Gentiles"] the Lord Jesus Christ was installed in the heavenly Messianic kingdom. Thereafter he undertook an inspection of the "slave" or "steward" class on earth. (Matt.

25:14-30; Luke 19:11-27) He did find dedicated, baptized, anointed disciples on earth who, in spite of World War I and persecution and other difficulties, were striving to serve the interests of Jehovah's Messianic kingdom. They were endeavoring to feed in a spiritual way the faithful "domestics" or "body of attendants" of the now reigning Lord and Master, Jesus Christ.

The facts of modern history show that in the year 1919 he revived these much afflicted disciples and gathered them together in a united body. Then he appointed them as his "slave" class "over all his belongings," this is, over all his royal interests on the earth. (Rev. 11:7-12) It was this active body of dedicated, anointed Christians who, in the summer of 1931, embraced a name to distinguish them from Christendom's sects, namely, Jehovah's witnesses.—*The Watchtower*. December 1, 1971, page 750.

Did you notice in the above that Jesus was said to have "*revived* these much afflicted disciples*" in 1919? The reason for their putting the proposition that way is because they say they were in religious bondage during the war years of 1914-1918. Then, miraculously, in 1919 they were *revived* to carry forth their new exalted place as the Lord's sole channel of communication to men on earth. They explained this further in another magazine:

In the year 1919 God's people experienced a complete release from the politico-religious bondage that had been imposed on them during World War I.—*The Watchtower*, January 1, 1977, page 14.

How is it that the 1800-year-old "faithful and discreet slave"should be spoken of as being in "politico-religious bondage" in 1914-1918? It seems contradictory to what they have said about this "slave," namely, that it would always remain faithful and continue down through the centuries feeding itself on progressive, wholesome spiritual food. Clearly, something is amiss here. The reason for putting matters as they do is because of their own evaluation of themselves during the period between the years 1914-1918. This is what they have to say about their spiritual condition at that time:

Like the Israelites of Isaiah's day, the spiritual Israelites sold themselves because of wrong practices and came into bondage to the world empire of false religion, that is to say, to Babylon the Great, and to her earthly paramours. (2Ki. 17:17; 1 Ki. 21:20,25) An outstanding instance of this occurred during World War I of 1914-1918.—*The Watchtower*, November 15, 1980, pages 26, 27.

Another *Watchtower* had put the matter as follows:

> But the Scriptures describe them as having *unclean garments* because of their long association with Christian apostasy. (Zech. 3:3,4) They had many practices, characteristics and beliefs similar to the weed-like sects of Christendom. So from 1914 to 1918 a period of fiery testing came upon them, not unlike the ancient period of Babylonish captivity of the Jews back in 607-537 B.C.
>
> . . . All this came to pass in connection with transgression on their part in having the fear of man, not conducting themselves in a strictly neutral way during the war years and being *tainted with many religiously unclean practices*. Jehovah and Jesus Christ permitted these witnesses to be reproached, persecuted, banned and their officers imprisoned by the nations of the world. By the summer of 1918 the strong organized voice of the Watch Tower witnesses had been silenced, killed collectively as prophesied in Revelation 11:7,8. Notice, however, that this watchman's voice was not stilled until they had completed their *pre-1914 phenomenal work of warning the peoples of the nations*. —*The Watchtower*, July 15, 1960, pages 435,436. (italics not in original)

FACT: ALL WORLD KINGDOMS TO END IN 1914

Note how they described themselves in the above references: having unclean garments, being contaminated by Christian apostasy, wrong practices, characteristics that were weed-like, having fear of man, violating their neutrality in connection with the war effort and selling themselves because of wrong practices. I think you will agree that you couldn't get much worse than that! They even compared their experience as corresponding to Israel's captivity in Babylon. Now the ancient Israelites were apostate when they were deported to Babylon. So, in effect, they are saying that they, too, were at this time apostate! And, as regards the so-called "phenomenal work of warning the peoples of the nations," prior to 1914, it must be remembered that they preached a false alarm for nearly forty years when they argued that Christ had become invisibly present in 1874 and marked the beginning of the 40-year "harvest period," which would end in 1914 with the complete overthrow of all of earth's rulers and kingdoms. Concerning this Russell had proclaimed in 1889:

> We consider it an established fact that the final end of the kingdoms of this world and the full establishment of the Kingdom of God will be accomplished by the end of A.D. 1914.—*Jehovah's Witnesses in the Divine Purpose*, page 55.

The failure of 1914 to see the end of the present world as predicted was catastrophic for the Watchtower movement. It completely destroyed any confidence in them as true prophets. Russell had long argued that the climactic events of 1914 would vindicate his complex calendar of end time events. When that failed to happened, it undermined his entire chronological prognostications.

As significant as those failures were, they were not included in the catalog of sins Jehovah's Witnesses charge themselves with in the 1914-1918 period. Why? Surely, the whole structure of the "end times" chronology was destroyed by that failure. They had misrepresented God and Christ and had misled tens of thousands of trusting believers with false expectations. Yet they fail to mention this when cataloging their sins during that period. Instead, they define that false prophesying as a "phenomenal work." The only forthright admission of their failed prophecies that I could find was published in 1930:

> All of the Lord's people looked forward to 1914 with joyful expectation. When that time came and passed there was much disappointment, chagrin and mourning, and the Lord's people were greatly in reproach. They were ridiculed by the clergy and their allies in particular, and pointed to with scorn, because they had said so much about 1914, and what would come to pass, and their "prophecies" had not been fulfilled. — *Light*, 1930. Book one of a two- book set written by Rutherford, page 194.

How can it be argued during that period they had been acting as a "faithful and discreet slave?" By their own measure they described themselves as unfaithful, disapproved by God, so much so they had to be abandoned by God as ancient, unfaithful Israel had been abandoned by God. In what way had they been "discreet" in preaching the false alarm regarding 1914? There is simply no evidence to distinguish them as a "faithful and discreet slave," dispensing wholesome spiritual food. at this time.

It is appropriate to acknowledge that the Bible students under Russell did teach a few Bible truths. But they were also preaching many scriptural aberrations: the date-setting, the false teaching about Christ's return (invisibly) in 1874, the false teaching about the end of the world occurring in 1914, their idolatrous attitude towards Russell and his writings, their judgmental and condemnatory attitude toward all those who would not accept their presumptuousness. These things overshadowed and contaminated the few Bible truths they did have. Just like today; Jehovah's Witnesses have a few teachings that are correct, but like their predecessors—the Bible students, they overshadow these things with their arbitrary private interpretations that go far beyond sound biblical exegesis and spoil what they do have right.

A MIRACULOUS RECOVERY IN 1919

Getting back to the 1914-1918 period and their being approved by Jesus Christ for enlarged kingdom privileges, they have this to say:

> A faithful remnant of some thousands of the "domestics" of the "faithful and discreet slave" class survived this time of testing. From the spring of 1919 forward they began to rise from the dust of inactivity to their new lofty service as watchmen to the world. (Dan. 12:2; Rev. 11:11,12) The Scriptures also describe them as being clothed with new garments of clean identification to represent Jehovah's interests in the earth."—*The Watchtower*, July 15, 1960, page 436.

This evaluation of their new importance is truly incredible!. They admit to having prophesied falsely for nearly forty years regarding the last days and the end of the world; they admit to being unclean and so apostate that God had to abandon them to what they call "Babylon the Great" (the world empire of false religion), and then they expect people to believe that in just a few months from all of this they are suddenly glorified and exalted with new, lofty privileges of services—overseeing all of the enlarged kingdom interests of the master, Jesus Christ! That is just incredible.

Now that's like going to a businessman who, through his own foolishness, got himself into financial difficulty and lost a good deal of your money and he had to declare bankruptcy, and then saying to this man: "Well done! You lost a small fortune of mine so now I am going to entrust my whole fortune into your hands!" Now that's just ridiculous. If you can accept that—the explanation of things that the Society sets forth in relation to its history, I'm afraid you can be conditioned to believe anything they say. But as incredible as that explanation is, it is at least equaled by another one. The Bible students can trace their history back no further than 1870 A. D.—the year the teenager, Russell, began his little Bible class. So by the year 1919, their organizational existence was less than fifty years. Yet this is how they describe themselves in relation to their appointment in 1919:

> Now that the long expected Kingdom had become an established reality in heaven, surely its growing interests in the earth after 1919 would not be left in the hands of a novice organization of spiritual babes. And that proved to be true. It was the 1900-year-old "faithful and discreet slave," the old Christian congregation, that was entrusted with this pre-

cious Kingdom service. Rich in its loyalty and integrity, long in its patient suffering of persecution, strong in its ancient faith in Jehovah's precious promises, confident in the leadership of its invisible Lord, Jesus Christ, obedient in its centuries-old commission to be witnesses in the earth, finally cleansed by a fiery test by 1918, the matured "slave" as represented by a remnant now stood ready for new assignments of service.—*The Watchtower*, July 15, 1960, page 436.

And on page 438 of the same magazine they added:

Yes, beyond doubt the old but awake "faithful and discreet slave" stands today as a wonder watchman to the peoples of the nations. Just as their Master, Jesus Christ, stood for the rise and fall of many in Israel in the first century of the Christian Era, so now before the whole world the anointed witnesses stand as a guide to survival for a minority of mankind but prove to be an occasion of stumbling into Armageddon destruction for the rest. (Luke 2:34).

Really! To argue that this novice religious organization, less than fifty years old, was the 1900-year-old "faithful and discreet slave," rich in its loyalty and obedient to its centuries old commission, is simply ludicrous. And yet this is what the Watchtower Society would have you believe. In fact, from the Witness point of view, you *must* believe it if you are to be put right with Jehovah God. To question the Society's exalted position in this matter is anathema in their eyes.

THE QUALITY OF THE "FOOD" SERVED AFTER 1919

Did the shattering disappointment experienced by the WBTS in 1914, teach it to avoid privately interpreting the Scriptures regarding date-setting time features? No, it did not! Immediately after the 1914 disappointment they got themselves trapped in the same thing again. In 1920, a year after their so-called new lofty service appointment, the WBTS published a book titled *Millions Now Living Will Never Die*. Newspaper advertisements were used to herald the lecture services that accompanied this book. This campaign lasted until 1925. This book, together with Russell's six volumes known as *Studies in the Scriptures* and *The Finished Mystery* published in 1917, constituted the *truth* being preached. Russell was still viewed as the "wise and faithful servant" and his time feature prophecies were still being advanced, taught, including Jesus' invisible return in 1874.

What was the message contained in the *Millions Now Living Will Never Die* book? It deals with the work of reconstruction on the earth to be accomplished by the kingdom of God. Restoration of natural Israel to

God's favor was argued for, just as Russell had argued for it. An elaborate system of time period calculations are employed to prove that God's favor began to return to the Jews in 1878. Additional calculations regarding the Jubilee system of Israel was used to establish that 1925 would be a marked year. Concerning this, the book said:

> A simple calculation of these jubilees of fifty years each would be a total of 3500 years. That period of time beginning 1575 before A.D. 1 of necessity would end in the fall of the year 1925, at which time the type ends and the great antitype must begin. What, then, should we expect to take place? In the type there must be a full restoration; therefore the great antitype must mark the beginning of restoration of all things. The chief thing to be restored is the human race to life; and since other scriptures definitely fix the fact that there will be a resurrection of Abraham, Isaac, Jacob and other faithful ones of old, and that these will have the first favor, we may expect 1925 to witness the return of these faithful men of Israel from the condition of death, being resurrected and fully restored to perfect humanity and made the visible, legal representatives of the new order of things on earth. —*Millions Now Living Will Never Die*, page 88.

> As we have heretofore stated, the great jubilee cycle is due to begin in 1925. At that time the earthly phase of the kingdom shall be realized. The Apostle Paul in the eleventh chapter of Hebrews names a long list of faithful men who died before the crucifixion of the Lord and before the beginning of the selection of the church. These can never be a part of the heavenly class; they had no heavenly hopes; but God has in store something good for them. They are to be resurrected as perfect men and constitute the princes or rulers in the earth, according to his promise. (Psalm 45:16; Isaiah 32:1; Matthew 8:11) Therefore we may confidently expect that 1925 will mark the return of Abraham, Isaac, Jacob and the faithful prophets of old, particularly those named by the Apostle in Hebrews chapter eleven, to the condition of human perfection. —*Millions Now Living Will Never Die*, pages 89,90.

Finally, on page 97 it concludes its dogmatic prediction regarding 1925:

> Based upon the argument heretofore set forth, then, that the old order of things, the old world, is ending and is therefore passing away, and that the new order is coming in, and that 1925 shall mark the resurrection, it is reasonable to conclude that millions of people now on earth will be still on the earth in 1925. Then, based upon the promises set forth in the divine Word, *we must reach the positive and indisputable conclusion* that millions now living will never die.—*Ibid*. pag 97. (Italics not in original)

This, then, was the grand message that the Bible students associated with the WBTS started off with following 1919, the year they supposedly were exalted to become God's exclusive channel of communication to the people of earth in the "last days." This book, distributed worldwide in many languages was said to be done under the auspices of the Lord Jesus Christ. If you did not accept them and their message you were not showing appreciation for the Lord's "faithful and discreet slave" organization—that is the premise crafted by the Society's second president, Joseph F. Rutherford.

History, of course, gave the lie to this prophesy, and as ludicrous as it now sounds, it was the *truth* at that time! This *truth* was being served up as timely spiritual food for those associated with the WBTS. They were expected to believe it and *teach it*; otherwise you would be in spiritual darkness. At this time, in 1920, Russell was still viewed as the "faithful and discreet slave" of Matthew 24:45-47, and his calculation of the "last days" as beginning in 1799. The last forty years of that period was said to have begun in 1874, when Christ returned *invisibly* and would conclude with the end of all earthly kingdoms in 1914.

The book, *Jehovah's Witnesses in the Divine Purpose*, makes much of the success of the "millions campaign" as they called it. This "campaign was the advertising done in connection with the book. This official historical overview of that campaign says absolutely nothing of *the contents* of the book. There had been a slowdown in the growth of the movement following the disappointment of 1925 but this slowdown was attributed to those who did not "wait" or endure. Discussing these matters they said:

> From 1922 though 1925 Jehovah God helped his people to wait or endure, carrying on his kingdom preaching on a widening scale. This resulted in bringing into the sanctuary many more to be members of this remnant consecrated by Jehovah. This was evident from the increasing attendance at the annual celebration of the Lord's evening meal, 32,661 participating in 1922; 42,000 in 1923; 62,696 in 1924; and 90,434 in 1925.

> Evidently, however, there were some who did not "wait" with the Lord's faithful remnant. In 1926 there was a reported decrease in the attendance on March 27 at the Lord's evening meal to 89,278. The year 1925 especially proved to be a year of great trial to many Jehovah's people. *Some stopped waiting and went with the world. —Jehovah's Witnesses in the Divine Purpose*, (1957) page 110. (Italics not in original)

No mention is made in the book as to *why* the year 1925 was such a trial for many of Jehovah's people. In this way, by uttering half-truths they color their history to suit their own delusional perception of things. They are always editorially exonerated, always right even when they are wrong. And anyone who is religiously stumbled by their miscalculations and false predictions is labeled as wicked; failing to "wait" on Jehovah, as though God would test his people with lies. Yet they argue that what they were preaching was under the direction of the Lord Jesus Christ! It appears to me that those who could survive these disappointments with their confidence in the WBTS still unshaken, were more credulous than they were faithful.[3]

THE CLAIM THAT WHAT THEY PREACH HAS BEEN REVEALED TO THEM BY JEHOVAH GOD

The Watchtower Society doesn't claim to be inspired but it speaks with the same degree of certainty as though it is. And they demand that they be taken at face value as though inspired—not permitting Jehovah's Witnesses to question or express doubts or reservations about anything they teach. Then they beg off from responsibility when something previously preached as truth is set aside or a prophecy goes unfillfilled. Then they say, "we never claimed to be inspired in the first place." But note how strongly they present their *uninspired* views to Jehovah's Witnesses:

> As Jehovah *revealed* his truths by means of the first-century Christian congregation so he does today by means of the present-day Christian congregation. Through this agency he is having carried out prophesying on an intensified and unparalleled scale. All this activity is not an accident. *Jehovah is the one behind all of it.* The abundance of spiritual food and the amazing details of Jehovah's purposes that have been *revealed* to Jehovah's anointed witnesses are clear evidence that they are the ones mentioned by Jesus when he foretold a "faithful and discreet slave" class that would be used to dispense God's *progressive revelations* in the last days. Of this class Jesus said: "Truly I say to you, He will appoint him over all his belongings."—*The Watchtower,* June 15, 1964, page 365. (Italics not in original)

When you argue that, "As Jehovah revealed his truths by means of the first- century Christian congregation so he does today," and that "Jehovah is behind all of it," and they are being used in "dispensing God's progressive revelations," they are in fact, claiming divine inspiration.

---

3. Those Bible students who stayed with the WBTS through the disappointment of 1914, probably felt that this latest disappointment in 1925 was the last straw, and could not find reasonable justification for looking to the organization for spiritual direction any further.

According to the dictionary, to reveal means "to communicate or make known by supernatural means or agency; to disclose or make manifest through divine inspiration." (Webster's Third New International Dictionary) In other words, something revealed is not something learned through ordinary means. Divine or supernatural inspiration is the only remaining avenue for revelation. The same dictionary defines inspiration or inspired as "moved by or as if by a divine or supernatural influence, effected by divine inspiration." The dictionary's definition of inspiration is very similar to revelation. Both involve a supernatural influence which qualifies men to receive divine truth and that is the essence of the Watchtower Society's claim. So the use of the word revealed and revelation as opposed to inspired or inspiration, is really a matter of semantics—a distinction that represents no difference and is only called upon to explain away changes, contradictions and disappointments.

If the WBTS is merely a group of religious men, sincere but not especially divinely guided, then its experiences make sense because it illustrates the human factor which has resulted in miscalculations and cultishness. But if Jehovah is behind all of this, as they claim, then it does not make sense. The confusing, contradictory message, false prophesying, the cultic view of Russell and now towards the WBTS, does not reflect the divine mind. Almighty God has demonstrated over and over again through his word, that he can take an imperfect person and have this man speak a clear, accurate message if it is his will to have such a message preached. That message does not have to be updated, changed, reargued or explained away. The prophets of God were never, never wrong! Why would anyone acquainted with the Society's prophetic history take them seriously when it comes to uttering prophecy?

Since 1975 the organization has undergone another disappointment regarding a date. While they like to avoid talking about it and you can be sure that any future history they write will gloss over it, yet the fact remains that they did speculate seriously about 1975 as seeing the end of the world. There is no question that many Jehovah's Witnesses fully expected that to happen and when it didn't happen, some were stumbled. While it is true that the Society did not dogmatically say the world would end in 1975, it laid the groundwork for that speculation and printed articles that argued for its accuracy. Of course, when that year came and passed without anything happening, there was a great deal of upset among Jehovah's Witnesses. Addressing that upset they said the following the year following 1975:

It may be that some who have been serving God have planned their lives according to a mistaken view of just what was to happen on a certain date or in a certain year. They may have, for this reason, put off or neglected things that they otherwise would have cared for. But they have missed the point of the Bible 's warnings concerning the end of this system of things, thinking the Bible chronology reveals the specific date. — *The Watchtower*, July 15, 1976 page 440.

On the following page they added:

But it is not advisable for us to set our sights on a certain date, neglecting everyday things we would ordinarily care for as Christians, such as things that we and our families really need. We may be forgetting that, when the "day" comes, it will not change the principle that Christians must at all times take care of all their responsibilities. If anyone has been disappointed through not following this line of thought, he should now concentrate on adjusting his viewpoint, seeing that it was not the word of God that failed or deceived him and brought disappointment, but his own understanding was based on wrong premises.—*Ibid.* page 441.

Nowhere in this discussion, which was titled "A Solid Basis for Confidence," did the publishers acknowledge any responsibility for *planting* those wrong expectations. Yet, the truth was that for nearly a decade they had fed the very attitude they were now rebuking. However, the bad effects of the disappointment of 1975 continued to hinder organizational unity. Finally, in 1980, they did come around to accepting some responsibility in an effort to heal the bad spirit that persisted:

With the appearance of the book, *Life Everlasting–In Freedom of the Sons of God* [1966], and its comments as to how appropriate it would be for the millennial reign of Christ to parallel the seventh millennium of man's existence, *considerable expectation was aroused* regarding the year 1975. There were statements made then, and thereafter, stressing that this was *only a possibility*. Unfortunately, however, there were other *statements published* that implied that such realization of hopes by that year was *more of a probability than a mere possibility*. It is to be regretted that these latter statements apparently overshadowed the cautionary ones and *contributed* to the buildup of the expectation already initiated.

In its issue of July 15, 1976, *The Watchtower*, commenting on the inadvisability to setting our sights on a certain date, stated: "If anyone has been disappointed through not following this line of thought, he should now concentrate on adjusting his viewpoint, seeing that it was not the word of God that failed or deceived him and brought disappointment, but that his own understanding was based on wrong premises." In saying "anyone," the Watchtower included all disappointed ones of Jehovah's Witnesses, hence including *persons having to do with the publication of the information that contributed to the buildup of hopes centered on that date.—The Watchtower*, March 15, 1980 page 17. (Italics not in original)

The above admission of culpability in the disappointment regarding 1975, shows that they not only misled and disappointed their readers, they deceived and disappointed themselves as well. They have taken themselves so seriously as the repository of all divine enlightenment that they are even bold enough to preach their speculations worldwide, which they did between 1966 and 1975! The WBTS claims that it has never been guilty of acting as a false prophet, but the fact remains that it has prophesied falsely many times. It prophesied falsely for nearly forty years prior to and including 1914; it falsely between 1914 and 1918 in the book *The Finished Mystery*; it continued to prophesy falsely from 1920 to 1925 regarding what was to happen in 1925; and the organization has acknowledged that they planted the seeds and nourished the speculative plant that led to the hopes centered around 1975. Despite its denial that it has never acted as a false prophet, its history belies that denial. The Bible is explicit in describing the difference between a prophet of God and a false prophet.

However, the prophet who presumes to speak in my name a word that I have not commanded him to speak or who speaks in the name of other gods, that prophet must die. And in case you should say in your heart: "How shall we know the word that Jehovah has not spoken?" When the prophet speaks in the name of Jehovah and the word does not occur or come true, that is the word that Jehovah did not speak. With presumptuousness the prophet spoke it. You must not get frightened at him. — Deuteronomy 18:20-22 *NWT*.

The Scriptural definition presented above is the only valid definition that can be applied in determining who is and who is not a true prophet. Men may dance around that definition and offer specious arguments as to why their false prophecies do not come under that definition, but that is nothing more than self-justification and self-delusion. At the same time they were critical of those who had been looking to 1975 as the probable beginning of God's kingdom rule, they used the occasion to reinforce their insistence that the generation that witnessed the events of 1914 would not die off until all of the "end times" prophecies were fulfilled:

Just as surely as the generation living and hearing Jesus' warning in the first century was the generation that experience a fulfillment of his words, *just as surely* will this generation—the generation seeing the major ful-

fillment of his "sign" identifying the last days of this system of things—
be the generation to experience the global tribulation due to come.—*The
Watchtower*, July 15, 1976 page 435

In putting matters that way, saying: "Just as surely" as Jesus' inspired prophecy regarding what was to befall his generation, will also
befall the 1914 generation, they imply that their word is just as valid as
the Lord's word. At the same time, they beg off from failed predictions
by saying "we never claimed to be inspired." The quotation below illustrates this.

> The "slave" is not divinely inspired but continues to search the Scrip-
> tures and carefully scrutinize world events, as well as the situation of
> God's people, so as to understand the ongoing fulfillment of Bible proph-
> ecy. Because of human limitations, at times there may be an incomplete
> or incorrect understanding of some matter that may require correction
> later. But this does not mean that the "slave" should avoid publishing a
> possible explanation until the final, complete understanding is available.
> —*The Watchtower*, March 1, 1981, page 29.

The above reasoning is just a smoke screen to becloud the fact that
they preach dogmatism that often proves untrue. They have never couched
their words in a cautionary way, saying, "Well this is our present understanding," or "We are not certain about this, but this is our opinion." No,
they speak with certainty, just as Pastor Russell did—just as Rutherford
did, and they insist that Jehovah's Witnesses take them just as seriously
as they would Jesus Christ himself! Then, when they are proven wrong,
they excuse themselves from any serious responsibility by saying, "we
don't claim to be inspired." In other words, they would have people think
that they are empowered by God to preach whatever they *think* is the
truth and you are obliged, by God, to accept what they *think* and teach it
to others. The mindset is that even if something is later proved to have
been wrong that is of no serious consequence. This means that Jehovah's
Witnesses can preach from the housetops everything that is printed in
The Watchtower, because even if it is wrong it will not harm you or those
you preach to. That rationale is nonsense. No prophet of God ever
preached error. God's spokesmen were pure in their inspired statements.
Truth and error do not flow to us in God's revealed word.

The Lord Jesus Christ is our heavenly Father's exclusive channel of
communication to people on earth. And by means of God's Holy Spirit,
operating through the Bible and in the hearts and minds of individual
believers, he makes known his will. We are given *complete knowledge*
when it comes to how we are put right with God and what he expects

from us in return. We have *partial knowledge* in many other areas, including Christ's return. The apostle Paul wrote: "For at present we see in hazy outline by means of a metal mirror, but then it will be face to face. At present I know partially, but then I shall know accurately even as I am accurately known." (1 Cor. 13: 12 *NWT*) When certain ones were offended by what the Lord said about eating his flesh and drinking his blood and walked away from Jesus, he asked his immediate disciples, "You do not want to go also, do you? Simon Peter answered him: 'Lord, whom shall we go away to? You have sayings of everlasting life; and we have come to know that you are the Holy One of God.'" (John 6: 67-69 *NWT*)

Oftentimes, when one leaves the organization of Jehovah's Witnesses they are asked, "Where are you going to go? What religious organization are you going away to?" The apostle Peter gave the answer to that question: we can only go to the Lord Jesus himself. It is not "where" we go but to "whom" we go that determines the success of our Christian quest. Peter's conclusion is consistent with everything we read in the New Testament. Constantly we are directed to the person of Christ, not an organization. He promised that he would remain with them during all ages to come. "And, look!," he said, "I am with you all the days until the conclusion of the system of things." (Matthew 28: 20 *NWT*)

The WBTS has created the concept of organization authority and has used Matthew 24: 45-47 to give support to their creation. But in doing so they have read their concept *into* the Bible, not *out* of it. Jesus' illustration of the faithful servant mentioned in Matthew, chapter 24, was but one of several parables regarding Christian responsibility and the need to be diligent in the discharging of those responsibilities. Certain ones were given more responsibility than others in the matter of providing for the household of faith. The apostle Paul identifies such ones when he said, "And he gave some as apostles, some as prophets, some as evangelists, some as shepherds and teachers, with a view of the training of the holy ones for ministerial work, for the building up of the body of Christ, until we all attain to the oneness in the faith and in the accurate knowledge of the Son of God, to a full-grown man, to the measure of growth that belongs to the fulness of the Christ." (Eph. 4: 11-13 *NWT*) Only by being faithful in the discharging of those responsibilities would they gain the Master's approval and be rewarded when he returned in glory with his angels. That promised return is still future. There is nothing in Matthew or the other synoptic Gospels to suggest the interpretation the WBTS applies to his words. It has merely been plucked out of its context and twisted to mean what it was never intended to mean.

We are told in Scripture that the world is like a field in which has been planted with both true and false believers. According to Jesus' word, they were destined to grow together until the end of the present age. There was to be no attempt by men to try and separate such ones. Attempts to gather the true believers together in one church or organization down through the centuries has only led to thousands of conflicting and quarreling denominations and sects. Because this matter is central to the issue before us, Jesus' words take on special importance.

> Another illustration he set before them, saying, "The kingdom of the heavens has become like a man that sowed fine seed in his field. While men were sleeping, his enemy came and oversowed weeds in among the wheat and left. When the blade sprouted and produced fruit, then the weeds appeared also. So the slaves of the householder came up and said to him, 'Master, did you not sow fine seed in your field? How, then, does it come to have weeds?' He said to them, 'An enemy, a man did this.' They said to him, 'Do you want us, then, to go out and collect them?' He said, 'No; that by no chance, while collecting the weeds, you uproot the wheat with them. Let both grow together until the harvest; and in the harvest season I will tell the reapers, first collect the weeds and bind them in bundles to burn them up, then go to gathering the wheat into my storehouse.'"

> . . . "Explain to us the illustration of the weeds in the field." In response he said: "The sower of the fine seed is the Son of man; the field is the world; as for the fine seed, these are the sons of the kingdom; but the weeds are the sons of the evil one, and the enemy that sowed them is the Devil. The harvest is a conclusion of a system of things, and the reapers are angels. Therefore, just as the weeds are collected and burned with fire, so it will be in the conclusion of the system of things. The Son of man will send forth his angels, and they will collect out from his kingdom all things that cause stumbling and persons who are doing lawlessness, and they will pitch them into the fiery furnace. There is where their weeping and the gnashing of their teeth will be. At that time the righteous ones will shine as brightly as the sun in the kingdom of their Father. Let him who has ears listen." (Matt. 13: 24-30; 36-43 *NWT*)

The idea that Russell and his associates were delivering the final message from God to the world proved false. Those Bible students who survived that failure and continued their association with the WBTS were immediately given confidence by president Rutherford that the end of the present world was only a few years away. That speculation and prediction also fell to the ground unfulfilled. Jehovah's Witnesses, for decades, were assured that the generation of 1914 would live to see the establishment of God's kingdom on earth. That, too, proved false. Jesus was said to have returned *invisibly* in 1874, and when that time frame became untenable, they moved the date forty years ahead to 1914. The plain truth is that the Watchtower Witnesses have *never* been where they thought they were in relation to the outworking of God's purposes. Therefore, they have *never* been delivering to the world God's special message of the hour. While identifying itself as the nineteen-hundred-year-old "faithful and discreet slave," their brief history, and especially their deceptive gopsel, belies such a claim.

No doubt the Bible students wanted to believe that Charles T. Russell was that special "servant" of Matthew 24: 45-47. They wanted to believe his eschatological timetable which predicted the world's end in 1914. No doubt those who remained with the Watchtower organization wanted to believe that Joseph F. Rutherford was Jehovah's spokesman and put faith in his date-setting predictions set forth in *Millions Now Living Will Never Die*. And Jehovah's Witnesses believed that the generation of 1914 would not pass away before the end of the present world. Those same Witnesses wanted to believe that 1975 would prove to be the year Christ's millennium would begin. But in every instance they were wrong. Their wanting it to be right did not make it right. Their eagerness to believe it true did not make it true.

As the Witnesses have long argued, it is not wrong to test what men say by what God says in his own word, the Bible. According to that word, we are encouraged, even commanded, to "Make sure of all things; hold fast to what is fine. (1 Thess. 5: 21 *NWT*) Moreover, Christians are told to use their individual thinking ability to make judgments as to what is right and wrong. The apostle Paul wrote, "But solid food belongs to mature people, to those who through use have their perceptive powers trained to distinguish both right and wrong." (Heb. 5: 14 *NWT*) According to Young's Analytical Concordance, the Greek word translated to "distinguish" (Gr. *diakrisis*), means *to thoroughly judge* a matter. It is not disloyal or presumptuous to carefully examine whatever we are taught to believe; it is a matter of doing what mature Christians are supposed to do.

Accepting those associated with the governing body of the WBTS as the Lord's exclusive channel of communication as necessary for salvation, is a basic tenet of Jehovah's Witnesses. Apart from them no relationship with God is possible. I once believed this doctrine and it motivated me to convert people to our religion. But once I discovered serious errors in our history and a concerted effort to conceal or misrepresent those errors, I was forced to reexamine the foundation of my faith—not in God—but in men. I did so in the hope that my faith in the organization would be restored. But the more I compared the word of God to the teachings of the Society, and listened to their explanations of their history, the more I realized their claim was without historical or scriptural support. In the end I was forced to dismiss their claim that their organizations represented the "faithful and discreet slave" of Matthew 24: 45-47. I concluded that they were just another human organization that had, unfortunately, taken themselves too seriously. This attitude led to the sin of presumptuousness. It also created the spirit of judgment and contempt for all other Christian associations and churches.

It was not easy to pull away. It was difficult emotionally as well as intellectually. But it was something that needed to be done in order for me to move forward spiritually. My wife and I were Jehovah's Witnesses for more than 30 years. Much of that time was spent in full time service. But the more we studied the word of God and accepted what it said as opposed to what someone said it said, the more we were learning the truth that sets one free. (John 8: 32) While much has been lost due to being disfellowshiped in 1981 for apostasy—our family and nearly all of our former friends will not speak to us, we have gained much. We are developing a closer and more accurate understanding of our relationship with God through his Son our Lord Jesus who died for us all. This is the greatest gain of all. We have learned that our experience is not unique; others have also undergone similar experience and have come to essentially the same conclusion as we have. By sharing our experiences we are able to encourage one another and not despair or become discouraged, but move ahead spiritually.

Appendix B

Jehovah: The Covenant God

When speaking of God's dealings with mankind, the Witnesses usually define that in terms of "organization." One of the most common terms in their vocabulary is the phrase, "Jehovah's organization." Although the very *topic* of "Organization" is not to be found in their Bible dictionary, *Insight on the Scriptures*, organization is the breath of life to the Witnesses. Without it the Society could not exercise the strong control it does. Speaking of God as "A God of Organization," is intended to validate and justify their human organizational control. Examples of how they work the theory of organization into scriptural history are shown below:

> As the canon of books of God's Word was expanded and the Christian Greek Scriptures were added to complete the Bible, each book was written directly to the Christian congregation *as an organization* in its behalf. Thus *the Bible is an organizational book* and belongs to the Christian congregation *as an organization*, not to individuals, regardless of how sincerely they may believe that they can interpret the Bible. For this reason the Bible cannot be properly understood without Jehovah's *visible organization* in mind.—*The Watchtower,* October 1, 1967, page 587. (italics not in original).

> But what about the human realm? Well, the Deluge of Noah's day brought an end to all antediluvian organizations that might have existed on earth—except one. Noah and the seven other flood survivors emerged from the ark as *a family organization*. . .The Descendants of Abraham were richly favored by Jehovah, and nobody can reasonably deny that they eventually became *a national organization.*—*The Watchtower*, July 15, 1984, page 11. (italics not in original).

> Any person who wants to survive into God's righteous new order urgently needs to come into a right relationship with Jehovah and His earthly organization *now.*—*The Watchtower*, November 15, 1981 pages 16,17 (italics in original)

The world view presented above reflects the concept that there are but two organizations in existence today: (1) Jehovah's organization and (2) Satan's organization. If you are not in Jehovah's organization you are, by default, in Satan's organization. To be in Jehovah's organization means to be working under the direction and control of the Watchtower Society. That is the only way one can come into a right relationship with Jehovah and the only way one can correctly understand the Bible, according to this world view. But do the Scriptures really present matters that way? We should all desire to have a right relationship with God in order to secure a place in his kingdom by Christ Jesus. Since the rebellion in the garden of Eden, the need and hope of something better has lived in the hearts of all people. The question has always been, how do we prepare for that future? Men cannot be trusted to teach you how a healthy relationship with God is made possible, when those men have their own agenda woven into their teaching.

The apostle Paul, speaking about what is today called the Old Testament, said: "All Scripture is God-breathed and is useful for teaching, rebuking, correcting and training in righteousness, so that the man of God may be thoroughly equipped for every good work." (2 Tim. 3: 16,17 *NIV*) Those inspired writings were enlarged upon during the first century of the present era to include what most people speak of as the New Testament and what the Witnesses call the Christian Greek Scriptures. Together, they form one unified record of God's progressive dealings with the human family and reveal how he has determined to crown his earthly creation with success and life. Through those Scriptures the curtain of secrecy has gradually been pulled back by God to reveal his eternal purpose of redemption and renewal in the Lord Jesus.

> Blessed be the God and Father of our Lord Jesus Christ, who has conferred on us in Christ every spiritual blessing in the heavenly realms. Before the foundation of the world he chose us in Christ to be his people, to be without blemish in his sight, to be full of love; and he predestined us to be adopted as his children through Jesus Christ. This was his will and pleasure in order that the glory of his gracious gift, so graciously conferred on us in his Beloved, might redound to his praise. In Christ our release is secured and our sins forgiven through the shedding of his blood. In the richness of his grace God has lavished on us all wisdom and insight. He has made known to us his secret purpose, in accordance with the plan which he determined beforehand in Christ, to be put into effect when the time was ripe: namely, that the universe, everything in heaven and on earth, might be brought into a unity in Christ. (Eph. 1: 3-10 *REB*)

The blessed promises given in the above are secured for believers by means of covenant. A brief review of the covenant arrangement proves helpful in understanding God's means of revealing his will through various covenants. He has formed covenants with individuals as well as bodies of people, through which he has revealed certain features of his ultimate purpose. There is, as a result of the covenant process, a unity in Scripture that binds it all together into a single unit. The Hebrew word from which we get the English word covenant is *berit.*. While there remains some uncertainty regarding its etymology, the way in which it is used in Scripture enables us to know that it identifies a special bond or contract between men or between God and men. Concerning this we read:

> Whatever the etymology, the OT term *berit* came to mean that which bound two parties together. It was used, however, for many different types of "bond," both between man and man and between man and God. It has a common use where both parties were men, and a distinctively religious use where the covenant was between God and man. The religious use was really a metaphor based on the common use but with a deeper connotation.— *The International Standard Bible Encyclopedia,* Vol. 1, page 790.

The concept of covenant was common in the ancient world to identify solemn agreements made between individuals as well as between God and men. Sometimes, but not always, sacrifices were used to ratify such covenants. In modern usage we often hear the word used in relation to marriage. In this case two parties bind themselves together with a solemn pledge of fidelity to uphold their corresponding roles in the marriage covenant. The marriage covenant takes on an even greater significance when God is called as witness to the covenant. What we learn in the Bible is that God has chosen to bond himself to various ones down through history by the covenant arrangement.

The first time the word is used in the Bible is in relation to God's dealings with Noah. God had determined to bring the ancient world to a destructive end because of its gross wickedness. He revealed that determination to Noah, said to be a righteous man who walked with God. (Gen. 6: 9,10) To Noah, God said: "I am going to bring floodwaters on the earth to destroy all life under the heavens, every creature that has the breath of life in it. Everything on earth will perish. But I will establish my covenant with you, and you will enter the ark—you and your sons and your wife and your sons' wives with you." (Gen. 6: 17,18 *NIV*) In this particular covenant some action was demanded of both parties. God would execute his judgment against that ancient world and cause the waters of the flood to engulf the earth, but he would protect Noah and his family if they followed his commands and constructed the ark according to his specifications. Noah also had to oversee the collection of basic specimens of animals and birds to be taken into the ark together with sufficient provisions to preserve their lives for the duration of the flood and its aftermath.

After the flood, God continued his covenant relationship with Noah. To him and his sons God said, "I now establish my covenant with you and with your descendants after you and with every living creature that was with you—the birds, the livestock and all the wild animals, all those that came out of the ark with you—every living creature on earth. I establish my covenant with you: Never again will all life be cut off by the waters of a flood; never again will there be a flood to destroy the earth." (Gen. 9: 9-11 *NIV*) God established the rainbow as a perpetual sign of this covenant. (Gen. 9: 12-16) This post-flood covenant with the earth was a unilateral one: God simply declared that he had bound himself to never again destroy all things by the waters of a flood as he had done. That covenant remains in force to this day.

The next covenant to appear in Scripture is the covenant that God made with Abraham, the son of Terah, a descendant of Noah's son, Shem. Called by God to leave his residence in Ur, a cultured city believed to have had between 300,000-400,000 inhabitants, situated on the Euphrates River in what is now Iraq. Abraham and his extended family obediently journeyed westward to an unknown destination that God said he would show him. (Gen.12: 1) God made a sevenfold promise to Abraham: (1) He would make him into a great nation; (2) He would bless him; (3) He would make his name great; (4) He would be a blessing to others; (5) those blessing him would be blessed; (6) those cursing him would be cursed; (7) and all the people of earth would be blessed through him. (Gen. 12: 2,3) Abraham moved about in this new country as a sojourner, never owning any parcel of land in it. (Acts 7: 4,5) It was in this land that God made a covenant with him that consisted of promises regarding his becoming a great nation and one day inheriting the land as his possession. (Gen. 15:1-7)

This covenant was accompanied by sacrifices. Abraham was ordered to take three animals: a young cow, a goat and a ram, cut them in half and lay the halves opposite each other. He was also told to take two birds: a dove and a pigeon, and lay them opposite one another. After dark, while Abraham fell into a deep sleep, God caused a flaming torch to pass through those pieces, which confirmed the covenant by sacrifice. (Gen. 15: 9-17) "On that day Jehovah concluded a covenant with Abram a covenant, saying: 'To your seed I will give this land, from the river of Egypt to the great river, the river Euphrates.'" (Gen. 15: 18,19 *NWT*)

The Abrahamic covenant, with its promised blessings to the human family, was to have an everlasting affect. Understanding the ramifications of this covenant is essential for a Christian believer to determine his or her relationship with God. This covenant bond was passed on through Abraham's son, Isaac, and through Isaac to his son Jacob, and to Jacob's (Israel) descendants as a nation. Those descendants eventually, under God's providence, came into bondage to Egypt and were subjected to slavery for hundreds of years. (Gen. 15: 13) Finally, the time came for God to fulfill his promise that Abraham's descendants would be delivered from slavery and receive the land their forefather had wandered in centuries earlier.

The Israelites, now the size of a small nation, were delivered from Egyptian slavery under Moses, their divinely appointed leader. They made their way through the Red Sea and into the wilderness of Sinai. These dramatic events are recorded in Exodus, chapters 12-14. In the third month after that miraculous escape, the Israelites found themselves in the peninsula of Sinai near the foot of a mountain. It was here that God would enter into a national covenant relationship with Abraham's descendants. A unique feature of that covenant was its priesthood, together with an elaborate system of sacrifices. There were over 600 laws embodied in the Mosaic law covenant by God. The preamble to that covenant, the ten commandments, set forth the basic principles embedded in that agreement between God and the nation. The body of law that followed those commandments made it clear how their God wanted them to fulfill their part of that covenant bond. The success of this covenant relationship rested on the participants faithfulness to the terms of the covenant. (Exodus 19: 5-8)

This covenant relationship did not run smoothly. Time and again the people fell into idolatry and rebellion. In his covenant faithfulness, God blessed them when they were obedient but punished them when they were not. The various prophets that God raised up at various times served as covenant enforcers, so to speak. It wasn't that these prophets were bringing forth new laws but rather drawing attention to the fact that the nation was acting in violation to their covenant with God and what God was going to do about it if they failed to repent and change their ways.

Israel's experience demonstrates that being in covenant relationship with God is no guarantee of his approval and blessing. Faithfulness to the terms of the covenant is the essential thing. From the beginning,

God's approval and blessing has always been conditioned on faithfulness. Some Israelites were convinced that God would never allow the temple that bore his name to be destroyed. The temple was sacred and the priesthood that functioned in relation to it was sacred. But the time came when the name of God and his temple would be of no protection to them. Jeremiah, the prophet who served at the very time the temple in Jerusalem was destroyed, was used by God to warn his covenant people and move them to repentance:

> The word that occurred to Jeremiah from Jehovah, saying: "Stand in the gate of the house of Jehovah, and you must proclaim there this word, and you must say, 'Hear the word of Jehovah, all you of Judah, who are entering into these gates to bow down to Jehovah. This is what Jehovah of armies, the God of Israel, has said: "Make your ways and your dealings good, and I will keep you people residing in this place. Do not put your trust in fallacious words, saying, 'The temple of Jehovah, the temple of Jehovah, the temple of Jehovah they are!' For if you will positively carry out justice between a man and his companion, if no alien resident, no fatherless boy and no widow you will oppress, and innocent blood you will not shed in this place, and after other gods you will not walk for calamity to yourselves, I, in turn, shall certainly keep you residing in this place, in the land that I gave to your forefathers, from time indefinite even to time indefinite." (Jer. 7: 1-7 NWT)

The Israelites put too much confidence in the fact that they were a chosen people—a covenant people. They were lulled into a false sense of security because they had the very temple of God in their midst and their priests regularly offered sacrifices in that temple. The divine name, Jehovah or Yahweh, was also viewed as a protection. Did not the proverb say, "The name of Jehovah is a strong tower. Into it the righteous runs and is given protection." (Prov. 18: 10 NWT) However, there was no magic in the mere use of the divine name. Attaching that name to practices that Jehovah condemned only served to make such practices more reprehensible.

The nation repeatedly fell into sin and idolatry which led to their ultimate rejection as a nation. They had poured out upon them the many curses Moses had intoned hundreds of years earlier. (Deuteronomy, chapters 27,28) We are helped by what we read in the New Testament to better understand the basic flaw that existed in the law covenant arrangement. There was, from the beginning, a conflict between the statute law and the people's ability to perfectly keep that law. In his letter to the church in Rome, the apostle Paul explains the difficulty created by law received by a people weakened by sin. Using himself as an example, he says:

> My experience of the Law is that when I want to do good, only evil is within my reach. For I am in hearty agreement with God's Law so far as my inner self is concerned. But then I find another law in my bodily members , which is in continual conflict with the Law my mind approves, and makes me a prisoner to the law of sin which is inherent in my mortal body. For left to myself, I serve the Law of God with my mind, but in my unspiritual nature I serve the law of sin. It is an agonizing situation, and who can set me free from the prison of this mortal body? I thank God there is a way out through Jesus Christ our Lord. (Romans 7: 21-25 *PMET*)

The apostle identified two conflicting laws at work in his natural self: (1) the law of his mind and (2) the law of sin in his body. His mind approved all that was holy and good, but his flesh was under the control of the law of sin. To be sure, as it is put in the above translation, "it is an agonizing situation," in the mind and heart of one who desires above all else to live a godly life. The law given to the Israelites was completely holy but the condition of the people, held prisoners by inherent sin, were incapable of keeping that law perfectly. And while there were appropriate sacrifices mandated under the law for specific failures and sins, those sacrifices did not correct the fundamental problem of sin. Nor did they provide the one offering the sacrifice a clean conscience. The sacrifices offered under the aw provided a ceremonial cleansing, but did nothing to remove the problem of inherent sin. (Hebrews 10: 11)

The covenant nation of Israel knew who the true God was; they knew and used his divine name; they had his temple and the Levitical priesthood and they had God's law. But all of those things together could not save them from sin. They were well organized in a systematic way ordained by God, but that systemized worship could not save them. In using the nation as he did, God demonstrated that something better than what the law of Moses provided was needed. Paul identified that something better when he said, "I thank God there is a way out through Jesus Christ our Lord." That way out is presented to us in the Scriptures as the new covenant. At the very time Jeremiah was forecasting doom for Jerusalem and its Temple of Yahweh, he spoke of a future restoration and hope:

> Look, the days are coming, Yahweh declares, when I shall make a new covenant with the House of Israel (and the House of Judah), but not like the covenant I made with their ancestors the day I took them by the hand to bring them out of Egypt, a covenant which they broke, even though I was their Master, Yahweh declares. No, this is the covenant I shall make

with the House of Israel when those days have come, Yahweh declares. Within them I shall plant my Law, writing it on their hearts. Then I shall be their God and they will be my people. There will be no further need for everyone to teach neighbour or brother, saying, "Learn to know Yahweh!" No, they will all know me, from the least to the greatest, Yahweh declares, since I will forgive their guilt and never more call their sin to mind.—Jeremiah 31: 31-34 *NJB*.

The new covenant went into force on Pentecost Day when the assembled disciples received the baptism of the Holy Spirit. (Acts, chapter 2) This baptism with the Holy Spirit was the seal of God's approval and a token of the life to come. In this way the new covenant was inaugurated and set in motion. The basis for that new relationship was made possible by the holy sacrifice of Jesus Christ, who would serve as the perpetual high priest in the new covenant. From that day forward, all those who would come into a holy relationship with God would do so by means of this covenant. It would be through the new covenant that the promises given to Abraham as the father of many nations would be fulfilled.

The Bible is clear in explaining how the covenant made with Abraham and the new covenant work together for the salvation of the world. The New Testament book that thoroughly discusses the new covenant is the book of Hebrews. The superiority of the new covenant over the law covenant is demonstrated in three areas: its promises, its priesthood and its sacrifice. As for its promises, God said he would write his law on the hearts and minds of his people and remember their sins no more. (Hebrews, chapter 8) The priesthood is superior because it is exercised perpetually by the glorified Son of God. (Hebrews, chapter 7) The sacrifice is greater because its one sacrificial offering provides the complete expiation of sin. (Hebrews, chapters 9 and 10)

A few years after the Pentecost experience, the apostle Peter was directed to the home of a man named Cornelius, a Roman centurion. This gentile was the first of Bible mention to be brought into the new covenant, which up to that time was made up primarily of believing Israelites. In this way, God demonstrated that the time had come to extend the benefits of the new covenant to non-Israelite believers. (Acts, chapter 10) In this way the obstruction—the dividing wall—separating Jew and Gentile was removed.

So then, remember that at one time you Gentiles by birth, called "the uncircumcision" by those who are called "the circumcision"—a physical circumcision made in the flesh by human hands—remember that you were at that time without Christ, being aliens from the commonwealth of Israel, and strangers to the covenants of promise, having no hope and without God in the world. But now in Christ Jesus you who once were far off have been brought near by the blood of Christ. For he is our peace; in his flesh he has made both groups into one and has broken down the dividing wall, that is, the hostility between us. He has abolished the law with its commandments and ordinances, that he might create in himself one new humanity in place of two, thus making peace, and might reconcile both groups to God in one body through the cross, thus putting to death that hostility through it. So he came and proclaimed peace to you who were far off and peace to those who were near; for through him both of us have access in one Spirit to the Father. So then you are not longer strangers and aliens, but you are citizens with the saints and also members of the household of God, built upon the foundation of the apostles and prophets, with Christ himself as the cornerstone. In him the whole structure is joined together and grows into a holy temple in the Lord; in whom you also are built together spiritually into a dwelling for God. --Ephesians 2: 11-22 *NRSV*.

We have in the above a description of the Christian congregation as it exists in the new covenant. The covenant promises made to Abraham come into play within the new covenant arrangement. Jesus Christ is identified as the promised seed (offspring) of Abraham, through whom all families of earth were to be blessed. The apostle Paul, in his letter to the Roman church, makes plain that Abraham's justification by means of faith, was not for Abraham alone, but for all those who would have the faith of Abraham. "Now the words, 'it was reckoned to him,' were written not for his sake alone, but for ours also. It will be reckoned to us who believe in him who raised Jesus our Lord from the dead, who was handed over to death for our trespasses and was raised for our justification." (Romans 4: 23-25 *NRSV*) In this way, by means of faith, both Jew and Gentile become heirs to the promises given to Abraham, whom the apostle calls "the father of us all." (Romans 4: 16)

The apostle Paul provides a powerful argument to gentile believers in the territory of Galatia, regarding the role that Jesus Christ plays in their being benefitted by the promises given to Abraham. He establishes the fact that the glorified Son of God is the promised seed. Jesus alone, he argues, is the one through whom blessing would flow to people of all nations on earth. "Now the promises were spoken to Abraham and to his seed. It says not: 'And to seeds,' as in the case of many such, but as in the case of one: 'And to your seed,' who is Christ." (Gal. 3: 16 *NWT*) The apostle rules out any thought or suggestion that anyone other than Jesus

Christ is the seed of promise. It is through this "seed," and this seed alone, that blessings are received. Their faith in the seed resulted in their being forgiven their sins and reconciliation with God. Those once far off from the covenant God were now his children.

> For in Christ Jesus you are all children of God through faith. As many of you as were baptized into Christ have clothed yourselves with Christ. There is no longer Jew or Greek, there is no longer slave or free, there is no longer male and female, for all of you are one in Christ Jesus. And if you belong to Christ, then you are Abraham's offspring (seed), heirs according to the promise. (Gal. 3: 26-29 *NRSV*)

In saying that these gentile converts were Abraham's seed, Paul was not contradicting what he had said earlier about Jesus Christ alone being the promised seed. They had the faith of Abraham, and it was for that reason that they could be spoken of as his seed or children. "Surely you know that those who adhere to faith are the ones who are sons of Abraham." (Gal. 3: 7 *NWT*) They were receiving the blessing promised:

> Now the Scripture, seeing in advance that God would declare people of the nations righteous due to faith, declared the good news beforehand to Abraham, namely, "By means of you all the nations will be blessed." Consequently, those who adhere to faith are being blessed together with faithful Abraham. (Gal. 3: 8,9 *NWT*)

These gentile believers were not being told that through *them* blessings would flow to others; they were *recieving* the blessing promised as a result of their faith in the promised seed, Jesus Christ. The apostle Paul was driving home the point that what they had in Christ Jesus was not available under the law covenant, and it would be destructive to their faith in Jesus Christ to try and live under the commands of the law. The law covenant had been an unbearable burden to the nation which received it, and these gentiles were endangering themselves by seeking God's approval through an observance of it. The apostle makes plain that the most important covenant of the past was not the law covenant, but the covenant God made with Abraham. "My point is this: the law, which came four hundred thirty years later, does not annul the promise. For if the inheritance come from the law, it no longer comes from the promise; but God granted it to Abraham through the promise. (Gal. 3: 17,18 *NRSV*) To Abraham, God had said: "in you all the families of earth shall be blessed." (Gen. 12: 3b *NRSV*)

The first family of earth to be blessed was Israel. In this nation of natural descendants of Abraham, there proved to be many who had the faith of Abraham, and responded to the gospel of reconciliation through Jesus Christ. The blessing received by means of faith was being justified or declared righteous. This justification resulted in peace with God and the hope of glory. "Therefore, now that we have been declared righteous as a result of faith, let us enjoy peace with God through our Lord Jesus Christ, through whom also we have gained our approach by faith into this undeserved kindness in which we now stand; and let us exult, base on hope of the glory of God." (Rom. 5: 1,2 *NWT*) Because Israel had been in covenant relationship with God they were spoken of as those who were "near" in relation to him. Gentiles, who had never been in covenant relationship with God were said to be "far off" in relation to God. Now, under the covenant that offered complete redemption and forgiveness of sins, both those who were near and who were far off were brought close to God in Christ. Now that the long promised seed of Abraham had come, saving faith in that seed (Jesus Christ), was possible for both Jew and Gentile. Those once alienated from God now became his sons. As sons of God, they also had become heirs of Abraham—his children—his seed. They, both Jews and Gentiles, were experiencing in their life of faith, the promised blessing due to come to the nations by means of faith. This is the good news that was destined to be preached until the end of the age. There is no other.

In the age to come, under the kingdom rule of the glorified Son of Man and his bride, life-giving blessings will flow to those who make up the groaning creation that the apostle Paul alludes to in Romans, chapter 8. For now the only means of reconciliation with God is through faith in Jesus Christ, the mediator of the new covenant. The glorified Lord also serves as high priest after the order of Melchizedek in the new covenant. He does not function as high priest for anyone outside of the new covenant anymore than the Aaronic priesthood functioned for people outside of the law covenant. Those outside of the new covenant have neither a mediator or a high priest in Jesus Christ.

Jehovah God, the covenant God, invites us to become reconciled to him through faith in Christ. When we do this we become sons of God and joint heirs with Christ. We also become sons of Abraham and heirs to the blessings that flow from his promised seed, Jesus Christ. This is the blessed gospel or good news to be proclaimed in "this day of salvation." (2 Cor. 6: 1,2) This "day" will end when the Lord returns to claim his own and execute judgment on the nations. Now, therefore, is the time to lay claim to the inheritance God and Christ extends to us all.